A PILOT'S TALE

Terror, Luck, Africa, and Angels

Andy Walker

Printed in the United States of America
Alta Press Publishing

Cover design by Emma F. Mayo

ISBN: 978-0-578-29276-2 (paperback)

This book is dedicated to my son, Jan Michael "JM" Walker, flight medic extraordinaire, who saves lives confined in the back of a speeding helicopter. With his Christ-like ability to forgive, he absolved me of my failures when the chips were down, a gift I'll cherish forever.

To Piney,

Finest ski patrol leader Alta ever had! Thank you for all you've done for the mountain I so cherish, and for your unwavering friendship to me and my family for all these decades. I hope to make a few more turns with you before the game's up!

Cheers!

Andy

"Once you have tasted flight, you will forever walk the earth with your eyes turned skyward, for there you have been, and there you will always long to return."
— Leonardo da Vinci

"If you can walk away from a landing, it's a good landing. If you can use the aircraft the next day, it's an outstanding landing."
— Chuck Yeager

PART 1
ALASKA

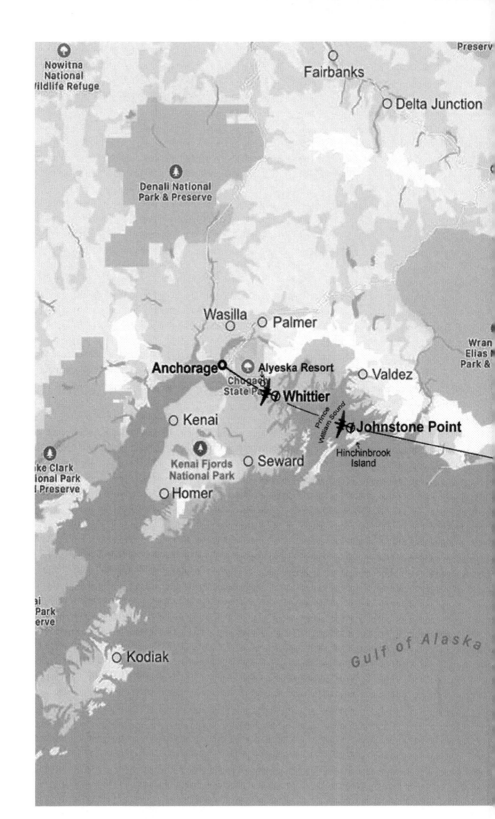

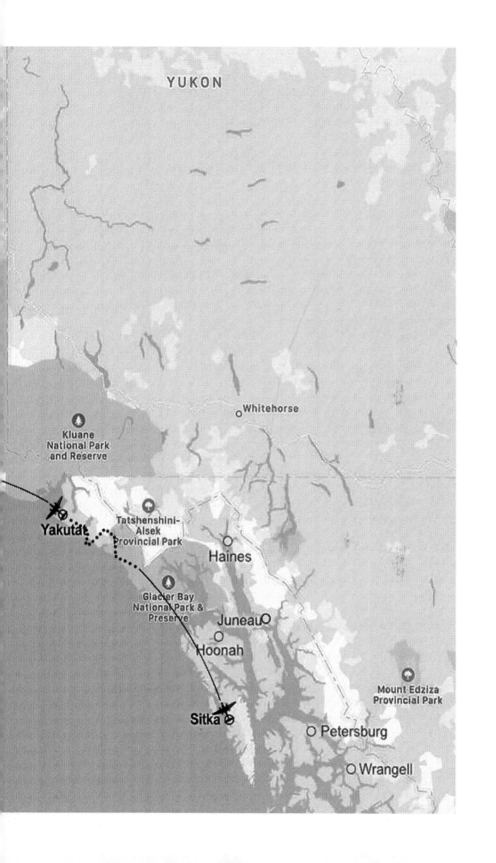

CHAPTER 1

250 MILES NORTHWEST OF SITKA, ALASKA SEPTEMBER 1994

I'm terrified I'm about to kill my parents and leave my son father-less. The line between survival and death is razor-thin, and I am balanced on its edge right now.

Stalagmite-shaped rime ice casts the leading edges of my wings, painting them ghost white, while growing horizontally forward into the onrushing air. Slowly, steadily, as if telling mere fibs instead of Pinocchio's lies, they elongate. The freezing air is saturated with liquid droplets cooled well below freezing in a precarious state known as supercooled. These drops immediately transmute into a tenacious layer of ice upon impact with a wing or any object that happens into their path.

I'm approaching the edge of a black hole from which there's no escape in aviation physics. Stated as axiom it says simply: "Never run out of airspeed, altitude, and ideas all at the same time." This trifecta is one nobody wants, paying only in extinction.

By waging a chance into this storm, whose hazards were forecast in much narrower bands, I'm now confronted with an airplane that's dying for my risk-taking.

The first sign of trouble came a few minutes ago when a red warning flag popped into view in one of my instruments. It tells me my compass has failed. There are backups, but they're poor substitutes. The information I'm supposed to glean from this defunct instrument doesn't just disappear. An index at the top of the gauge still hovers above a number on a floating compass card, and my job is to keep that number under that pointer. The disk crawls imperceptibly below the index, and I can't fight off my ingrained habit of steering to keep them aligned. Inside a cloud, there's nothing but gray scaling between angelic white and cave black. Up, down, and sideways are meaningless concepts except for what can be read on instruments in the cockpit. I can't detect I'm turning. It's too slow, like trying to watch a minute hand move across a clock face. When I can pry enough consciousness free to crosscheck with my B team cues, I see I've drifted way off course and, flustered, make a big turn back to fix it.

I do not yet suspect the demon that's killing us. I think I've simply lost a single electrically powered instrument.

An endless tapestry of wet, gray goulash palls and blinds us. My autopilot will ease my burden tremendously right now, so I push a button to engage it. It won't engage. I remember I've lost the compass that's hooked to the autopilot. The same voltage that motivated that warning flag putters a few more inches in the matrix of wires behind the instrument panel and tells my autopilot not to engage. Critical information is missing.

An aircraft compass is also called a DG, short for Directional Gyro. I have two. The spinning gyroscope in the main one is driven by an electric motor. It's directly in my field of view. There's another in the copilot's instrument cluster whose gyro is spun by air that whistles past a tiny paddlewheel in its instrument case. That air comes from a pump that's driven by some gearing on the right engine. Right engine quits, copilot's DG quits.

The electricity for my DG can come from any of three sources—alternators installed on each of the two engines and the battery. Naturally, engineers chose the DG with the most backup to connect to the autopilot. In accordance with Murphy's Law, my DG—the one with all the backups—failed, sticking me with hand flying the airplane.

I check my circuit breaker panel. No breakers are popped. Well, I guess it just failed. This isn't beyond my flying skills, but it's troublesome, and I have an inner voice whose volume is growing too loud to ignore.

It's rare in aviation that any single failure becomes catastrophic; there's too much redundancy built into systems and operating procedures to thwart us with a single, easy strike. Most pilots use baseball's vernacular to track the gravity of a situation. It's rare an airplane is lost with less than three strikes, but we learn early to sit up straight and watch out even when just a single one befalls us. I'm pushing well into three-strike territory with ice building on my wings, a gyro failure, and being forced to hand fly the airplane.

Now another red-warning-flag alert stating "OFF" appears in my Course Deviation Indicator. The loss of this instrument eliminates radio-directed steering commands, so I can no longer navigate precisely. Ground-based navigation aids, known as VORs, are no longer readable by my radio equipment. Maybe we're just out of range. I remember Air Traffic Control telling us to expect a frequency change in twenty minutes. That was about twelve minutes ago. Getting that kind of advanced notice on an upcoming frequency change is a good indication our position is teetering on the limits of the line-of-sight positioning necessary for VOR navigation or voice communication. I believe we'll be back in range momentarily.

I look out the side window and clearly see the ice forming on our wings is getting worse. This airplane is not certified to fly in icing conditions. If it were, it would have rubber "boots" affixed to the leading edges of the wings that I could inflate with a switch in the cockpit, breaking up the ice to wash away in the slipstream. My propellers would either have electric heaters or alcohol spray directed on their leading edges to whisk away the ice, and my windscreen—at least a small portion of it right in front of my eyes—would be heated. I have none of these features and never intended to get into icing conditions. There are a lot of dead pilots that could've made that same claim.

I notice it's 12:41, close to the time I wanted to attempt contact with ATC on the new frequency. I click the mic button. No tell-tale clicks or static—nothing. Silence. Suddenly I know there's nothing random about the warning flags I'm seeing. I shoot a glance at a small auxiliary panel just above my left knee, terrified to verify my hunch, but it can't be avoided. Both ammeters, gauges that show the condition of my alternators, display tiny, sewing-needle sized pointers that seem the size of redwood trees right now, pegged on zero. I've lost both alternators. My mouth dries up, and I reach with a trembling hand for my water bottle. I can barely swallow through my fear-clenched throat.

We're in grave danger. My inner voice has lost count of strikes. Probably enough to kill two airplanes. My father sits in the copilot's seat casting glances at me that I sense peripherally. He knows we're in trouble. He has no idea the details pouring through my consciousness, but there is palpable fear in this cockpit, and he knows it. My mother, seated directly behind me, is less aware of our plight, and I don't intend to broadcast our state just yet. For one thing, I'm too busy, and for another, I see no purpose in adding another person's anxiety to the stream of tension gripping me. My job is to escape this confluence of horrors that I've flown us into.

I don't know how long ago my alternators failed, but I know the reservoir of electrical energy in my battery is draining away. With no river of current flowing to recharge it, there's a finite amount of power it has to offer. It can't last much longer as evidenced by my electrical components dying one by one.

While this airplane is not designed or certified to fly into icing conditions, engineers did incorporate a smattering of ice protection into some critical components to allow a pilot enough time to escape inadvertent icing. Pitot tubes facilitate the magic to calculate my speed. I have two, both electrically heated. The fuel tanks must vent as fuel is consumed. Otherwise, a vacuum will develop in the tanks and starve the flow of fuel to my engines. These vents are also electrically heated. If my battery becomes fully exhausted, these components will ice over. Then I won't know how fast I'm flying. Vacuums in the fuel tanks will suck the life out of my engines, and I'll lose my air powered gyroscopes. This will positively be the end of us. When in a cloud, if there are no gyroscopic instruments to reference, ninety seconds is about the most one can expect before the airplane slips and slides into an uncontrollable death spiral. Our certain plunge into the freezing Gulf of Alaska below will have us swallowed and obliterated in less than two minutes.

I have to get out of this ice. Often, just a couple of degrees colder will cause supercooled water to become solid. I can stand solid ice particles, except their big brother—hail—all day as they bounce harmlessly off the hull. Hail, on the other hand, redesigns the sleek shape of an airplane, tending to ruin its aerodynamic properties. I avoid hail at all costs.

The forecast called for icing between 6,000 and 12,000 feet above sea level. We're cruising at 14,000, but we can only stay this high for thirty minutes without supplemental oxygen. It looks like I'll have to fudge the rules a little to get over the ice, but I'm confident my physical conditioning will allow it with little risk. I elect to climb. I enrich the fuel mixture to each engine with red knobby-handled levers pushed forward, then advance the fluted black handles of the propeller controls all the way forward to maximum RPM, and finally, push the smooth black throttle handles to the firewall, milking out every ounce of power available from my engines.

Smoothly, imperceptibly, I pull back pressure on the yoke to raise the nose into a shallow climb. In icing conditions, the steeper my wing's angle relative to the impacting airflow, the farther back the ice will form under them compounding the aerodynamic degradation already tearing at my wing's clean design. At 15,000 feet the ice is getting worse. Something about the darkest part being just before the dawn encourages me to try higher. I have to choose which poison I think less deadly. Altitude wins. I have hundreds of flights in gliders up to 18,000 feet never feeling the effects of hypoxia, and I don't believe we'll need to be so high for long. A process known as ablation will melt the ice from my wings if I can just get out of the ice.

Now I notice it's freezing in the cabin. "Oh crap," I say aloud. "We've lost our heater." It runs on the same gas that powers our engines, but it needs electricity to control it. Safety features shut it down as soon as electrical current falls below limits. Our breaths now come in streams of fog, adding an eerie visual effect to our confines. It's ten degrees below zero outside, and we don't have much insulation to protect us without the heat offered by our now-dead furnace.

My parents bundle up in whatever coats and coverings they can dig from their carry-on bags. I'm so engaged in the unfolding nightmare, I'm barely aware of my own physical discomfort.

As we approach 16,000 feet, my gamble for frozen precipitation isn't paying off. I can no longer discern anything but darkest hues of gray through the ice encrusted windshield. Stalagmite-shaped wedges on my wings are now growing like the snoots of pants-on-fire lying wooden puppets, and we're down to 110 miles per hour with all our 580-horsepower straining to limits. We're no longer climbing.

A clean Shrike Commander stalls at 68 miles per hour. With this heavy layer of ice enveloping us, I have no idea what speed is adequate to generate enough lift to counter gravity. Not only is our lift degraded by huge margins by the deformation imparted by the ice, but we also weigh a good deal more than we would without it. I wonder if I can expect the tell-tale signs of shaking and buffeting before a stall fully develops, or will we fall through the stormy sky all of a sudden, like Galileo's lead balls from the leaning tower of Pisa.

My mother leans forward and asks if we're having some kind of emergency. I pull a whopper of a lie from my rattled mind and say, "Well, yes, but just a minor one. Hang on and I'll have it all fixed in a minute."

The truth is, I'm feeling so much fear my hands are shaking, not from the cold. I'm facing too many unknowns, and impending panic nudges against the threshold of my wit, threatening certain catastrophe. My situational awareness is narrowing to pencil beams, making the simplest thought exercise eclipse any other mental task no matter how menial. All at once, I realize we have only a single viable option left. I have to pull the plug. There seems no escape out the top of this icy demon, and my airplane is down to a tiny fraction of its performance capabilities. I suspect we'll stall any second, and I'm not sure I can recover from a stall in an airplane so crippled by ice. I know my transponder stopped sending ATC any radar signals long ago, so they don't know where I am. It would be an awfully big stretch of probability for another airplane to be out here flailing around, miles off the coast of Alaska, in this big icy storm, so I feel confident we run little risk of hitting someone below us in an emergency descent. I turn the airplane thirty degrees left, well out to sea, wanting to ensure there's nothing but ocean below us once we break out the bottom of this cloud whose base altitude is unknown.

I reach for the throttles and ease them back to idle. Slowly, slowly, slowly, to protect our engines from thermal shock induced by sustained full power that has all twelve cylinder heads of our two engines glowing red. I must baby them, or they'll be overwhelmed by the freezing air outside. Too radical a reduction of combustion within them could easily crack steel and aluminum and turn our mighty engines into inert blocks of heavy metal. I lower the nose rapidly enough to accelerate quickly and even extend the landing gear into the slipstream as soon as my speed reaches 150 mph. I continue lowering the nose until we're indicating 180 mph, which is the maximum speed we can safely fly with the landing gear extended. At this speed, hurricane strength air blasts against the bony structure of my landing gear. It sounds like one more mile per hour will rip the wheeled protrusions right off the airplane. The wings offer little lift as they deform more and more into aggressive impediments to the wind. The cruel wail of our defiant, misshapen ship shrieks at my ears, frazzling what little faculty I have left.

We're now descending at 4,000 feet per minute. This plunge will be over in less than four minutes, and we'll either see the ocean before we smack into it, or we won't. The die is cast and now we wait, and hope, and pray to whatever gods soldiers find in their battle-weary foxholes.

Dear God, how did I get here?

CHAPTER 2
WIESBADEN, GERMANY
1955 TO 1958

F our Wright R-3350 engines spin gigantic propellers to pull our Lockheed Super Constellation in a lazy drone, 23,000 feet above the Atlantic Ocean. With my mother and two older siblings I, one year from the womb, am en route to Wiesbaden, Germany, to reunite family to father. With two-bar Captain's insignia on his shoulders, he's teaching weapons telemetry, one of the specialties he studied preparing him for the now-frozen Korean War.

The rumbling pulse of 13,000 horsepower cascades through wings and fuselage into the cells of my tiny body, casting spoor trails into my young life.

Wiesbaden is home to the US Army's 7405th Support Squadron. It's the height of the Cold War, and the army's airbase here serves a large part of the spying eyes the West casts on Russians in transit flights to West Berlin. Huge cargo planes are fitted with the most advanced aerial cameras in the world, giving Americans tremendous insight into Soviet malfeasance on the ground in East Germany.

Taking these behemoths into the air from the 7,000-foot runway less than half a mile from our front door rattles the glass in our three-story apartment building.

As a toddler riding my apple-red Murray tricycle around the grounds near our home, I sometimes dive into bushes or under parked cars, terrified as a deafening roar leads an ominous shadow directly over my head. My adrenaline commands "flight" even while my youthful curiosity begs against survival instincts to look up at this frightening spectacle. I fight daily for the courage to watch instead of cower, and finally, in time, win the internal battle to gape wide-eyed at the glorious monsters.

These breathtaking childhood episodes, interspersed with the Blue Angels aerobatic team flying their Grumman Tigers from our airbase, drives my development in a singular, irrevocable direction. When I am four, we leave Germany to return home to Salt Lake City, Utah. My guts stir with dreams of aluminum airplanes driven by ear-splitting engines, and peace may not be had until I myself am in command of such a craft.

CHAPTER 3

DIVERSIONS, REVELATIONS, AND PRINCE

My single-mindedness erodes in the years leading from adolescence to young adulthood. My family has ventured into the ski business, and from early elementary school onward, I'm thrust into a life married to skis and snow-covered mountains. My skills develop, and passion for sport overwhelms my aviation ambitions. The Vietnam War has just ended, leaving vastly more pilots in the military than are needed. That avenue to pilot training presents a dead end for the foreseeable future.

My parents jump at a once-in-a-lifetime opportunity to acquire a restaurant 9,400 feet above sea level at Alta Ski Resort. The building is circa 1950, the year, 1965. Trade work in carpentry, plumbing, electrical, and maintenance are necessary skills needed to keep the structure and its appliances serviceable. I find fascination and natural ability in all of them.

With 2,200 acres of pristine ski resort high in the Wasatch Mountains to exploit, I'm thrust into an alpine version of life on the Mississippi leaving no envy for Tom and Huck. I literally live on the mountain in my family's lodge. Snow skiing becomes the language I speak most fluently.

Childhood offers the miracle of limitless possibilities without the kind of self-doubt that normally hamstrings grown-ups. I see skiers coming down steep runs high on the mountain and imagine not only being able to do that, but do it better than anyone. Ski seasons pile up with ever more daring escapades as my brothers and I goad each other in crazy, limit-busting gains. Fearlessness and the rubber bodies of youth seem to allow us a degree of immortality. We fall with spectacular, limb-twisting, head-bashing tumbles but never seem to sustain serious injury. Advances, available only to the young and reckless, build my confidence, and in time, I nurture visions of grandeur into extraordinary craft. I build a tremendous degree of confidence that registers somewhere deep in my bones. As I age, that confidence empowers uncommon progress in other areas of my life. None of it comes without John McEnroe-like temper tantrums. I'm brutally hard on myself but usually manage to push through my impatience.

At twenty, so young my parents need to sign waivers for me, I'm competing professionally in Freestyle Skiing. Until two years ago, this brand-new genre of skiing was called "Hot Dogging." The audacious, crash-inducing, injury-certain spectacle draws huge crowds anxious to see insanity in motion. Soon, however, serious injuries become too common as athletes compete to be the most flamboyant maniac on the mountain for huge cash prizes and superstar glory. Sponsors are forced to find ways to rein in the antics lest they face devastating legal liability. They develop new rules that make it a game of skill instead of sheer daredevil madness. The name is changed to Freestyle Skiing, and any contact with the snow with other than skis and poles, as well as losing any equipment during the competitor's run, becomes disqualifying. This is my life. *ABC's Wide World of Sports* stages cameras all over the hill among thousands of cheering spectators. Events typically open with paragliders zigzagging the sky with colored smoke trailing from their skis after launching from peaks high above. Heart's "Crazy On You" and The Doobie Brothers' "Long Train Running" mix with dozens of rock 'n roll hits rending the air from gigantic speakers dimmed occasionally for emcee comments. For a year, I'm consumed with mogul bashing, swinging short ballet skis gracefully across mountainscapes, and flying through the air performing acrobatic tricks for the pleasure of giant crowds anxious for thrilling crashes. Two thousand years ago, these are the people that would be in the Colosseum watching gladiators slay one another.

Spring turns ski runs brown and swells the Little Cottonwood stream to its banks. Rainbow, Brook, and Cutthroat trout fight to reclaim homes in whitewater pools, and the ski season fades into memory.

Stark reality intrudes on my fantasy of fame and glory on the covers of Wheaties boxes and feature clips on *Wide World of Sports*. I don't possess the self-discipline and dedication to forgo the party life enmeshed in this free-spirited enterprise, and a hard look in the mirror leads to an unavoidable conclusion. It's time to move on.

I enroll at the University of Utah in the fall of 1975, ambling through general education studies with a declared major of Mechanical Engineering. After the crazed antics of last year, surprisingly, I find the challenge of student life fulfilling and enjoy this new academic lifestyle immensely. In fact, so much that my "all or nothing" disposition thrusts me into new tunnel-vision that sees only cranking through classes as servant to my aspirations. I attend classes non-stop through summer quarter and barrel right into my second fall quarter.

My primary form of recreation remains mated to Alta's ski slopes, and I'm still skiing 'til my quads fail during quarter breaks. Fall course work ends, and I'm eager to return to my winter cavorting.

"The Child," in Spanish, is "El Niño," and refers to the Christ child whose birth is in December. Atmospheric scientists adopted the Spanish name to describe weather phenomena, normally beginning in December, unique to a sloshing Pacific Ocean. When its warmer water, normally piled up near Australia, "sloshes" across the earth eastbound toward the western shores of South America, we get unusual weather patterns in North America. The El Niño of 1976 brings drought conditions to Utah through what is normally the beginning of winter. Wildflowers still populate the slopes of my winter playground, forestalling my typical winter pastime.

Frustrating as it feels in the moment, this life-altering circumstance can justly be precipitated only by something named for the divine.

Knowing I wasn't irretrievably affixed to the ski hill, my best friend's father, nicknamed Prince from childhood, calls me early during the fall quarter break. He knows I've developed a sizable stable of skills in the building trades and wants to know if I'll take a trip with him to a property he owns in Pocatello, Idaho. My assignment is to help him decide whether to develop or sell it.

Somehow it slipped my awareness all these years that Prince is an aircraft salesman. He has an office on the east side of the Salt Lake International Airport on the second floor of Thompson Flying Services' aging domicile. Thompson's, the largest and oldest flying service in Salt Lake, engages in flight training, charters, and aircraft maintenance. Its roots date back to "Tailspin Tommy" Thompson circa 1925, when the airport was still known as Woodward Field.

Prince asks me to meet him at the General Aviation side of the airport, giving specific directions to assure our 6:00 a.m. rendezvous.

I feel giddy driving to the airport under crystal-clear, star-canopied skies. I'm going to get to fly in a light airplane, and I can hardly contain my excitement. Prince waits outside the hangar, frost already reforming on his windshield though I'm fifteen minutes early.

We open the old hangar doors to a chorus of creaks and groans, fighting the frozen hinges and unbending wooden structure. Prince finds a light switch which seems to release only a trickle of energy to a bulb offering an anemic glow in the hangar. The confines are barely spacious enough to contain this single airplane. It's a 1970 Beechcraft V-tailed Bonanza, gleaming white with light-blue accents. Prince attaches a pull-bar to the nose wheel, and we strain to tug the 2500-pound six-seater into the chilly morning air.

After carefully inspecting the aircraft's exterior with a flashlight, Prince determines it's airworthy and climbs into the cockpit's primary piloting seat, on the left side, through the only entry door, on the right side of the fuselage. I manage something closer to clambering aboard, acutely aware of Prince's amused glances at my clumsy footing and lack of familiarity with airplanes. Upon completion of my inelegant entry, Prince instructs me how to close and latch the door, adjust my seat, and harness myself securely to this leather-covered throne.

This gruff, no-nonsense fifty-ish year old man is a lot more affable than first impressions reveal. While I hope to make an impact of fearlessness, Prince knows I'm unnerved. This is a new and unfamiliar world to me, and it completely uncorks my long dormant desire to fly. I'm too awestruck to realize I'm uncomfortably cold. Every neuron strains to forge indelible memories of preflight tactics. When Prince inclines the red rocker master switch to ON, gyroscopic instruments begin to whirl to speed, issuing quiet, low frequency whines that spin up in ascending pitch. Cockpit lighting is set intentionally low to preserve our night vision. It feels like an insulated cocoon lighted by what appear as a hundred fireflies that landed in random, geometric patterns on the instrument panel. A hint of electrical ozone taps my olfactory, issuing, I suspect, from heating radios and instruments. Prince tunes in a frequency on one of two communications radios, and an automated weather report fills the cockpit. To immature ears, it's mostly unintelligible gibberish. The instruction ends with a call to "advise you have information tango."

"Hey, Prince, I understood about three words of that. What's tango?" I ask.

"They update the weather report whenever anything changes. Ever since some investigator said a pilot's outdated altimeter setting contributed to an accident, controllers are adamant that everyone under their watch have the most current report. They won't let you budge 'til you acknowledge the latest one. Every time it changes, there's a new letter assigned like alpha, bravo, Charlie. You know, right on through the alphabet. Then they start over," he explains more thoughtfully than I expect.

Prince switches to another frequency to get a clearance to depart the airport area, advising that he has Tango.

We get our clearance, and Prince sets numbers into boxes embedded in the instrument panel. He opens a tiny window next to his left shoulder and shouts "CLEAR" into the brightening sky. He pushes a button, and the propeller begins a strained rotation, wrestling cold oil and frozen metal against frozen metal not yet lubricated. A fuel pump pressurizes tiny pipes injecting a strong, atomized fuel spray into all six cylinders. Sparks from two independent sparkplugs installed in each cylinder head ignite the volatile mixture of air and gas, and the engine roars to life. Prince points at gauges showing rising oil pressure and cylinder head temperatures. Hand signals are easier and more meaningful than words as the engine, even at idle, is surprisingly loud. He sets in yet another frequency and requests a clearance to taxi. We're instructed, in Latin it seems to me, to taxi to Runway 34 Right. That's code, I soon learn, for a runway that's aligned to 340 degrees on a magnetic compass. In this part of the country, there's a difference of 16 degrees between true and magnetic north, so when we line up pointing 340 degrees on our magnetic compass, we're precisely aligned to Brigham Young's grid layout of Salt Lake City where streets point directly north, south, east, and west. "Right" tells us there are two runways here that align to 340 degrees, and we're instructed to proceed to the one on the right.

Prince carefully taxis our Bonanza along assigned taxiways to the runway's threshold. There we stop to do some final checks, making sure our engine and all systems are working properly. Minutes later Prince calls the tower, and we get our takeoff clearance. He lines up on the runway, tiny white lights embedded in its centerline every fifty feet, and eases the throttle to the firewall. The burst of power is much louder than I expect as our 300-horsepower Continental engine slingshots us down the runway. Rudder pedals expertly massaged maintain our alignment as speed increases rapidly. I find myself hanging on as if I might be ejected if I don't squeeze the armrests with all my might. This is known as "white-knuckle" flying and is universally experienced by those unfamiliar with breaking earth's gravitational bonds. At eighty miles per hour, Prince eases back on the steering wheel, gently pitching the nose up, and we're airborne, the earth quickly shrinking away beneath us.

More radio chatter precipitates another frequency change that renders further ATC communications sparse. We turn slightly left in the vacant sky and proceed visually toward Bountiful, ten miles north of Salt Lake City.

On the eastern horizon, the colors of dawn begin to ignite. The stars are erased quickly from view as our climb accelerates sunrise, and muted pastels of red, yellow, and orange quickly intensify to heated tones, blending along nature's perfect, iridescent complexion. Prince continually increases the cockpit lighting as the sky turns from dark night through degrees to sunrise, finally revealing the fiery orb that finds us anew every twenty-four hours. Prince reduces power from takeoff to climb setting and just now I notice heat, harvested from the hot cylinders immediately ahead, bathing us in dry warmth.

My thrill is a fun spectacle for Prince to enjoy. He's not much of a small talker, but more of a strictly business, Joe Friday kind of guy. Even so, I regularly catch him grinning at me. My titillation is obviously contagious. We reach our altitude of 9,500 feet above sea level, and Prince backs off the power to cruise, quieting the engine to something closer to purr than roar. We're cleared to leave air traffic control and switch to some other frequency. To learn this dance, I can see immense fields of knowledge I'll have to cultivate, but my resolve to become a pilot is reignited in a blazing inferno.

Settling into a comfortable flight with navigation radios set to steer our way, Prince begins discussing the project ahead of us for which this grand adventure is merely preface. I've completely forgotten the purpose of our trip, and it takes me a minute to grapple with the mission on which we're embarked. I can barely tear my eyes from the magnificent views out every window. The Great Salt Lake flooding the valley floor as far north and west as I can see, the Wasatch mountains' jagged peaks and ridgelines extending northward forever on our right, and Matchbox scale neighborhoods, cars, and trucks on ribbons of highways dizzyingly far below.

Distracted as I am, we make plans for after landing, and Prince then leaves me to my euphoria. The mundane project ahead flees from my consciousness the moment my pilot's lips stop moving. I'm enthralled and simultaneously scared. I love this emprise even more than I'd anticipated, especially after too many of my young life's desires have proved unattainable. I worry I can't make this my bride, a spouse for which I can't imagine competition. Maybe, somehow, someday, I'll find a way to make this miraculous province mine.

The engine's power dims as Prince smoothly pulls the throttle to low power for descent, and I'm vaulted back into the moment. We glide down slowly in a beeline for the city ahead, our aerial path unrestricted by the mountainous terrain below that make the same journey for automobiles quite circuitous. Wheat-brown sagebrush-covered hills mold gradually into Pocatello's 4500-foot valley floor, and we clearly see the airport northwest of the city.

Prince selects a new frequency in COMM 1, and I can hear the Latin-ish exchange between pilot and tower controller. Gratefully, they seem to understand one another clearly, though I've corralled only a few words. Soon we're lined up to land on runway 21. He extends the flaps allowing slower flight and drops the landing gear. A mechanical latch releases the wheels to freefall, then they lock down hydraulically. The unlocking is startlingly loud and I'm shocked, wondering if some critical piece of the airplane hasn't just broken off. Prince, amused by my terror, continues descending to a soft touchdown on the runway centerline. We taxi to a parking area, shut down, exit, and tether the airplane. Most of me is still 9500 feet in the air.

Prince has an old, weathered 1967 Lincoln Continental he keeps here in free public parking. The door-lock pins pop up with enough vitality to give confidence there's still charge in the battery. Entering its cavernous sanctuary, dry leather crackles under our weight, absent from this large bench seat for months. Too impatient to allow the engine to become accustomed to warming fluids, we drive southeast away from the airport to attend our business. It's warm here for December, low fifties, and I'm soon coatless and comfortable in morning's full sun. We arrive at the subject home and walk through and around it, Prince dutifully taking no-nonsense notes. By the end of an hour, I've convinced him this project will almost surely cost more than he'll ever recoup and suggest he sell it. There appears to be much more than cosmetic work to be done, and the housing market here is not demanding. My ignorance of aviation and airplanes doesn't translate to real estate ventures, and my position on the home is easily made. Prince concurs. Mission accomplished, we drive back to the airport. It isn't even lunch time yet, so we walk straight to the gleaming Bonanza and repeat the now slightly more familiar steps choreographed for me just prior to daybreak today.

The late morning air is still calm, harboring no turbulence to trouble us. Level at 8,500 feet with the complex takeoff and climb phases behind us, Prince is willing to entertain questions, multitudes of which well from my guileless heart.

"If a wing falls off, will it still fly?"

"Sure, but just from here to the ground"—pointing—"right down there."

"Can it fly if the engine quits?"

"Let's see."

He pulls the power to idle and smiles. He glides in easy "S" turns. I'm sufficiently scared to amuse my mischievous, not entirely Joe Friday-like friend, and find myself again squeezing innocent leather-covered armrests into submission.

Prince returns the airplane to steady state flight and we continue in an increasingly serious conversation about growing up, pursuing dreams, and achieving success. I never realized his rags to riches story and am deeply moved by his direct sharing. He managed to catch the prettiest girl in school and, in addition to her, made his career dreams lifelong companions. I wonder if such brash confidence can be learned. A short internal dialogue says it can, and Prince listens as I relate my dreams of aviation but lack of direction to get pointed the right way. Thoughtful silence lies stark and a little unnerving against the soft hum of our propeller screwing its way through the air at 2100 RPM.

The universe opens a portal to a new world I'd only imagined when Prince offers me a deal that will change the rest of my life.

CHAPTER 4
BUILD IT AND YOU SHALL FLY
DECEMBER 1976

The CEO of Thompson's has recently passed away. Since his passing is unexpected, there's no one groomed to take his place. Because Prince has been associated with this outfit for such a long time and is known and trusted as a competent business leader, he's asked to fill in as temporary CEO until the Board of Directors can find a permanent replacement.

I'm flying with the CEO of Thompson's Flying Service and have just made a favorable impression on him regarding my building judgment and skills.

The board recently made a decision about expanding the organization. The "Aircraft Parts" retail business is evolving into a profitable enterprise in Salt Lake City as the number of airplane owners calling SLC their domicile is growing steadily.

Like all specialized professions, the aviation community has a highly esoteric language and seems, to a degree well past overboard, to have invented acronyms for everything. All airports have a three-letter code. While the post office and lay population believe SLC means Salt Lake City, it's not so in aviation speak. To the entire aviation community, it means Salt Lake City International Airport and has a unique and precise latitude and longitude in any aviation associated database. Similarly, while ANC means Anchorage to the postal service, it means Ted Stevens Anchorage International Airport throughout the world of aviation. I find the nomenclature interesting but a little frustrating. SLC, ANC, SEA, DEN, all seem obvious. So why, I wonder, is Nashville BNA, Hartford BDL, or Maui OGG? Lots of cultivating ahead.

Thirty minutes from landing, after a pep talk concluding with the weathered adage that I can do anything I want if I want it bad enough, Prince has an idea. He looks me in the eyes and says, "Andy, I'm going to prove to you right here that what I've said about having anything you want is true." He explains what the board is up to and that he's currently the boss of the company. He says, "I'll make you a deal. You build this parts department, work your tail off and get it done as fast as possible, and charge me no overtime, and I'll buy your flight training through solo."

I'm gobsmacked! I feel lightheaded. Did I just get offered free flight training? I'm going to learn to fly—FREE? It takes me a minute to come to my senses, but when I do, I heartily agree to the deal.

With the Bonanza safely tucked away back in its hangar, Prince tells me to follow him. In a two-car caravan we cross North Temple and, 200 feet later, turn right into a big parking lot. Thompson's engine overhaul shop stands at the west end of the lot, directly beneath the final approach path to SLC's runway 34R. Prince takes me inside and introduces me to the shop manager, Vince. He tells Vince he's just hired me to build the parts department and wants to do a little brainstorming to conjure up some details.

Two of Thompson's buildings are on this side of North Temple, just south of the airport proper. One is an old parts storage building. Light shows between many of the boards that side this old barn-like building with abundant buntings of cobwebs. Between them and the dust and dirt covering everything, it seems more like a Hollywood set for a spooky movie complete with warped squeaky floorboards. Filth aside, there's a fortune in aircraft parts in thousands of bins within.

Right next to this ancient relic stands the modern steel structure in which I'm now standing. It occupies a seventy-by-two-hundred-foot footprint with a concrete apron extending out a huge garage door on its north side. This is for engine testing after overhauls are completed. It's hoped that the physical space for the new "parts" business can be inside this building.

After looking over the shop floor, I suggest partitioning off a space twenty feet wide and eighty feet deep giving me just over ten percent of the floor.

I drift back eleven years to the Watson Shelter, the ski lodge my folks acquired at Alta. I can smell the wildflowers in the rarefied air over the actual scents of toluene and other industrial solvents infusing this shop. I remember my youthful exuberance at helping my father with the rigors of tearing up old, four-inch-thick tarred roofing, then framing, and paneling walls, installing electrical circuits and plumbing runs, and fixing trim to make it look professional. I learned then exactly the skills I'll use now to launch myself toward this elemental longing.

I assure them I can make it two stories netting 3200 square feet instead of 1600. Vince has no office per se, unless you call a three by eight-foot folding table with two folding chairs an office. We sit at the table, Prince remains standing, and I draw a rough plan. Prince looks over my shoulder. "Good enough. Do it!"

It's December 13 and I tell them I'll start tomorrow. I go home and draw up detailed plans and a materials list. I'm back at the shop in the morning and meet the rest of the mechanics. They all seem like nice guys who like drinking coffee, smoking cigarettes, and listening to Paul Harvey on the radio. They're not too keen on me remodeling the shop floor and making a bunch of dust for the next year, but by the time I get well under way, we've all become such good friends that no one minds.

I'm given my own key and start showing up an hour before everyone else at seven a.m. I rarely stop before seven in the evening. It's December. It's dark and cold when I walk in, and just as dark and cold when I drag out twelve hours later.

When classes resume in January, I slow to part-time but still typically manage six to eight hours a day. The plan matures as the construction progresses, and Vince gets a big office complete with bookshelves and a proper desk at the west end of the structure.

By March, the framing is complete. I still have wiring, drywall and mud, trim, and painting ahead of me but it's clear that the plan is coming together. Prince drops by every few weeks and seems pleased with my progress. He stops by at lunch on Friday, March 11th to tell me it's time to start my flying lessons. I'm to report to the flight training department the following Tuesday. They'll be expecting me at noon.

The manager of the flight training department, Joe, shakes my hand warmly when I find him in his office. We talk for a couple of minutes and then he hands me some keys attached to a red plastic identification tag with N2241J written in black magic marker on both sides. He tells me to go out and find the plane—a red-and-white Cessna 150 tied down just around the corner of the building—and start snooping around it.

Just getting to glide my fingers along its smooth aluminum skin and the leading edges of the propeller has me giddy. I don't dare caress its cool, smooth surfaces too passionately for fear I'll awaken and the whole image will pop like a soap bubble. I feel almost desperate to keep this moment real. It's been coursing the byways of my soul and the deepest vaults of my being from infancy.

Joe approaches and walks me through a complete preflight inspection, then puts me in the left-hand cockpit seat, and that sunny, warm March afternoon marks the truth of Prince's promise and the beginning of the rest of my life. I'm still awake.

Flight training through solo turns out to have less value than I'd imagined when Prince offered it. Thomson's coughed up $650 for my training through solo. Had I been getting overtime pay, I'd be ahead by about $1100 now. I still have four more months ahead to finish the project.

That's why they made Prince CEO. He's shrewd and gets things done.

Just before I finish the project in July, Vince pulls me aside and offers me a job as a mechanic once I complete the job. I tell him I know nothing about mechanicing.

"We'll train you."

Thompson's becomes my school away from school, not only for flying but for mechanicing on airplanes and engines.

In the next two years, with money borrowed from my parents, I acquire all the pilot's licenses and ratings I need to launch into my flying career, but I still need a whole lot more hours in the air. Another year invested gets me a rare certificate for a pilot—an Airframe and Powerplant Mechanic's license. Untold hours studying bone-dry texts to pass the written exams for this ticket seemed like a colossal waste of time and energy. But a gifted friend, and my primary mentor from that era, was both an extraordinary pilot and mechanic, and he continuously egged me on to stay with it. Looking back, the wisdom in his pestering was visionary. I'm awed at the doors it opened along my path.

It all started with a flight to Pocatello one winter's day when snow refused to fall.

CHAPTER 5

ANCHORAGE AND RAM AIR
SEPTEMBER 1994

Seventeen years into a tumultuous flying career, grace smiles my way when I stumble into a venerable flying job supplemental to my present airline pilot job. I'm wildly happy with my new home. Anchorage, Alaska is bordered on the east by the breathtaking Chugach Mountain range. The 250-mile-long massif is densely populated with stunning glaciers and fragmented peaks ascending thousands of feet above the coastal plane. Grizzly bears, mountain goats, moose, elk, and reindeer roam the chain in large numbers. The south border of Anchorage is etched by a huge sea channel called the Turnagain Arm. It branches off the Cook Inlet stretching all the way from the Gulf of Alaska, 180 miles to the south. Turnagain is named for Captain Cook's canny course reversal triggered shortly after entering the arm, when his sailor's sense presaged a debacle in the narrowing channel.

The sea washes into and out of the Turnagain Arm twice daily with so much volume that high and low tides are separated vertically by thirty feet. When the tide is out, dangerous mudflats, capable of swallowing people whole, are exposed along much of its length. In the winter, ice floats free on the water at high tide, but crushes together like giant talus fields, house-sized ice blocks cocked askew by the constrained acreage available at low tide. This turquoise, usually white-capped, water body plays out its dance immediately adjacent to the Seward Highway along its 40-mile length. Skiers are treated to breathtaking views from the high elevations on Alyeska Resort's ski slopes, situated at the extreme eastern end of the artery.

Near the summit of Alyeska Ski resort with the Turnagain Arm of the Cook Inlet in the background. The author is third from the left.

With Japan Airlines training behind us, the new pilot contingency shows up in Anchorage a few at a time, buying homes, enrolling kids in school, and learning the lay of the land. We feel like prisoners of war released from a harsh and difficult life with nothing but beauty and abundance decorating the horizon in all directions. Parties gin up weekly, each with a unique theme. In the dead of cold, dark winter, one such party is Hawaiian themed with surf boards leveraged as martini bars, and straw hats, beach balls, and towels scattered generously about Sam and Kate's cul-de-sac home.

I meet a next-door neighbor who is friends with our hosts. He too is a pilot but owns his own company. With a small fleet of twin engine, fire-spotting airplanes, Doug, owner of Ram Air, is in search of a relief pilot to spell his full-time pilots from time to time. A few minutes of discourse, over beer and martinis on a freezing winter night at a surfing party, reveals the job is a perfect fit for me.

A few weeks of training sandwiched between my international flight schedule qualifies me with The Department of the Interior's Office of Aviation Services or OAS. One of the most difficult training programs I've ever undertaken is complete on April 30, 1994. While the FAA does prescribe minimum standards and recency of experience for pilots to fly airplanes, their rules, exercised at the bottom limits, are barely enough to keep an aviator's number of landings equal to his number of takeoffs. The second you plop another human being into the airplane, the rules get a lot more arduous. You can kill yourself but not if somebody else is riding with you. If the person or persons sharing your aircraft are paying for the privilege, it's an entirely different set of regulations, and compliance is challenging with proficiency standards strictly enforced. The OAS takes this another step, demanding elite flying skills that are frequently evaluated. Ram Air and its cadre of pilots fall under this scrutiny. Since Doug's airplanes are so complex, the FAA and OAS consider them too difficult to fly safely in clouds with only a single pilot at the controls. With technologically advanced autopilots capable of precision flying and navigation, it isn't unusual to get a waiver if your single pilot demonstrates he can manage the automation of the aircraft to a degree that the flight operation is considered as safe as having two pilots in the cockpit. Doug has advanced autopilots installed in his airplanes, and with extensive training, I gain enough proficiency in their use to earn that coveted single pilot authorization.

The airplanes used for these missions are Rockwell Aero Commanders. Doug owns three of them, all identical model AC-50 Shrike Commanders. They're reputed to be so dependable and safe that they served as the first Air Force One, flying President

Eisenhower on short haul trips around the US mainland during his presidency.

I can hold 156 gallons of fuel in the two wing-mounted fuel tanks in my Commander and, at the most economical cruise speed, can eke out just over six hours of flying. That's fully loaded with one pilot and six passengers and their baggage.

The Boeing 747s I fly for Japan Airlines, by comparison, consume 156 gallons of fuel, at takeoff thrust, in about 28 seconds.

Doug's stable of Shrike Commanders are not certified to fly in icing conditions. Their primary use is visual fire spotting. They're certified to fly in instrument conditions but not when ice is known or forecast to be present in the clouds. In summer season when fires are burning, it's not terribly difficult to avoid icing conditions. When winter approaches and temperatures drop, icing becomes harder to avoid. If it's unavoidable at altitude, the choices are either to fly below the clouds or scrub the mission. Sometimes flying below clouds is too dangerous in mountainous areas. Alaska is essentially all mountainous.

Wildfires are spawned almost exclusively by lightning. As summer drags on and vegetation dries out, thunderstorms can set multiple wildfires in minutes. A fleet of US government satellites are tasked with tracking and recording lightning strikes. Fire-spotting pilots normally assemble in a sophisticated auditorium complete with an IMAX type screen. To say we gather for a "pre-dawn" briefing is not quite accurate in most of Alaska in the summer months. Pre-dawn starts about midnight, just after sunset. The next solar event of consequence is sunrise, and that's complete by 4 a.m. We normally gather at 5 a.m. to learn where lightning strikes most likely ignited fires the night before. Pilots are assigned to patrol specific sectors to look for smoke. Smoke often precedes fire in lightning-struck trees and might smolder for hours before erupting into full-blown flame. If a fire-spotting pilot can observe a smoking tree, he or she can call in exact coordinates to dispatchers, and a helicopter can be on the site a short time later. A single firefighter can douse the cinders in minutes, saving what could have turned into a ten-thousand-acre inferno in a few hours. The cost of the fire-spotting operation is expensive only when looked at through narrow vision. It saves countless millions of dollars, real estate, and lives each year.

Fire season ends early in Alaska as rain and cooler temperatures blanket the state, usually by early August. That's right in the height of fire season in the lower 48. Doug usually finds an attractive contract available somewhere in the western US, allowing him to profit from his business for another month or two. This year, 1994, he secures two—one in Wenatchee, Washington, and another in McCall, Idaho.

CHAPTER 6
ALASKA'S INSIDE PASSAGE

All aircraft need careful maintenance to safely defy gravity, but aircraft awarded OAS contracts must demonstrate the very highest standards of care. Most complex aircraft are on what is known as a progressive maintenance schedule. That breaks up the required inspections into bite-sized pieces often referred to as A, B, or C checks. There's typically one big one called the D check which is much more involved. The airplane must be hoisted on jacks, landing gear retracted and extended, engine cowling completely removed, engine diagnostic exams meticulously completed, and all inspection panels removed so cables and wires can be carefully examined.

One of our airplanes, N999GB, has just completed its D check at our home base hangar on Lake Hood, adjoining Anchorage's Ted Stevens International Airport, ANC. The airplane presently flying the contract in McCall, N17DL, is approaching hours of service that mandate its D check.

Doug asks if my schedule will accommodate bringing the newly inspected airplane to McCall and taking 17DL back to Anchorage. My JAL schedule fits the mission perfectly with a few days to spare.

At 5:21 a.m. on September 13th, I lift the nose of N999GB from runway 07L at ANC, into perfectly still air destined for McCall. I packed a thermos of coffee, some peanut butter sandwiches, raw

carrot sticks, a bag of mixed nuts and, most importantly, my restroom, an empty Folgers Coffee can complete with lid.

The sun hugs the horizon directly ahead. I've taken off to the
east and make a slight right turn to overfly the Turnagain Arm,
doing my best to be a good neighbor to those below not inclined
to be up at the crack of dawn. The 590 HP at my fingertips makes a
calamitous roar as I tear upward, away from earth at two thousand
feet per minute. It's early enough that I'm completely alone in
the sky, and with the fall equinox near, the horizon ahead offers a
prolonged show of blazing dawn colors. I feel fully alive, brimming
with passion in the warm embrace of an airplane I dearly love flying and over geography that leaves me breathless.

Looking east, I can see all the way to the end of the Turnagain
Arm and practically over the short mountain stretch to Whittier,
just twenty miles beyond. In addition to military operations, now
all but extinct, Whittier serves as a major launch point for cruise
ships sailing the inner passage to Vancouver and Seattle. I haven't
felt this kind of ardor about flying since that first flight with Prince
nearly eighteen years ago. It's tranquil and, simultaneously, terribly exciting to be off on such a long journey down the coast of
southern Alaska.

Drinking in the splendor surrounding me in all directions
brings a smorgasbord of bliss to every sense. Blinding white glaciers cover much of the high terrain to the east, descending, then
terminating in accelerating retreat. Spilling from their calving
mouths, tongues of water tumble, cutting the tundra and forests
in endless folds and forks like so many lightning bolts. Fjords as
numerous and dizzying as Norway's snake the coastline. It's stunning. My engines sing quietly in unerring drones, RPMs perfectly
synchronized. I feel like a glorious speck in a perfect universe, and
consciously give thanks for all the miracles this life brings.

I'll need to stop twice for gas. Four hours and thirty-one minutes after lifting off from ANC, I approach Ketchikan, the south-
ernmost town on the Alexander Archipelago, on a nearly windless
day. It's 9:52 a.m., Alaskan Standard time, as I maneuver around

mountains painted in multiple hues of green and blue, finally descending over water to a point where I can turn to line up on runway 11. Cleared to land, I ease the Commander down to sea level and flare onto the threshold, braking gently to taxiing speed. I follow the directions of Ground Control and find an aviation orange-vested woman flagging me to a parking spot. She crosses her red-tipped flashlights, signaling my stop. I shut down my engines and run a parking checklist.

My back side is form fit to the seat, and each leg resists intentions to move. But creaking muscles and tendons surrender, and I abandon the cockpit to stand on the tarmac. Once outside, I'm invigorated by the cool morning sea breeze that brings scents of wet marine province mixed with a little aviation fuel. There are some low white summer-time clouds hugging the higher mountain elevations nearby, but mainly, the sky is a deep sapphire blue. Seagulls pepper the sky over the adjacent water and squawk their welcoming accolades.

Coffee can toted along for dumping and rinsing, I ask the marshaling lady to top off my fuel tanks with 100 octane low-lead fuel, and head for the terminal and restroom. Walking feels good, and I pick up my stride as muscles and tendons become reacquainted with full quotas of oxygenated blood.

I take care of business in the restroom and find cold water from a washroom tap revitalizing when I splash handfuls on my face. I pace around the terminal, realizing this is the only exercise I'll get for several more hours. There's beautiful local artwork decorating the walls and huge glass windows showcasing sensational views in all directions. I find the weather office and get an updated briefing for the next leg of my trip—all good. Break time's over and a long day lies ahead, so I find the cashier, pay for my gas, and return to the Commander. A quick preflight assures me the ship is in good condition, and I climb aboard. Following normal procedures, I fire up both engines and receive a clearance to taxi. Moments later, I'm cleared for takeoff, and my twin Lycoming engines scream to life. Together, plane and pilot buoyantly divorce gravity's tenacious pull, and we turn, with a figure skater's grace, southeast to braid the islands below. Established on course in a stabilized climb, I say farewell for now to this beautiful region and revel in the maritime scene below, riddled with sun-glittered waterways flowing in large and small arteries into the coastal waters.

Eight minutes after takeoff, I enter Canadian airspace and check in with the local controlling agency. They clear me along my planned route and update my weather noting clear skies all the way to Bellingham, Washington.

I spot Mount Baker's glacier-covered slopes from a hundred miles away, giving me an easy navigation solution to get to Bellingham. Cruising two hundred miles per hour along the inside passage leaves me reminiscing about how I got my first flying job. I smile—and wince.

My mechanic friend, Terry—everyone called him "T"—had taken me under his wing teaching me both flying and mechanicing skills. He seemed to know just about everyone in Utah's aviation circles and was generous with introductions. He also had a 1947 Luscombe, a tiny tailwheel type 2-seater airplane powered by an 85 HP engine. T had rebuilt both engine and airplane and put an eye popping red-and-yellow-sunburst paint job on the finished product. He taught me to fly his Luscombe knowing the "taildragger" experience would be great for my flying skills. I'd logged seventy hours of taildragger time by February that year.

I was working full-time for Thompson's as an apprentice mechanic while T worked for the State of Utah, a thousand feet down the tarmac. He was one of those guys that couldn't sit still and always had side jobs going. In the winter of 1978-79, he was rebuilding a Super Cub for the guy who had the Powerline Patrol contract with Utah Power and Light. Larry, the owner of Heber Valley Flying Service, had the only set of two 180 HP Super Cubs in Utah, and that was UP&L's minimum requirement to bid the patrol contract. Larry maintained a tight hold on that lucrative pact for years.

T thought it would be great experience for me to help with the rebuild in Heber, so I joined him on weekends working long days. It was unimaginable to friends and family that I was spending weekends working on an airplane instead of skiing. But my infatuation with aviation had me ensnared, and I found intense fulfillment putting in the hours that might eventually lead to an airline pilot's career. During the course of this project, I became close to Larry.

One day in early February, Larry and his patrol pilot nearly came to blows. The pilot walked out in a rage swearing he was never coming back. He didn't. Larry needed a new patrol pilot and fast. He asked me how close I was to getting my Commercial Pilot's license. I replied that if I hunkered down I could have it in a couple of weeks. He said, "Do it and you'll be the new powerline patrol pilot."

On February 24th, Larry put me in the back of his operative Super Cub, N7145 Zulu, the one we weren't in the middle of rebuilding, and flew me down to SLC, to my scheduled Commercial Pilot's license check ride. On the ramp in front of TransWest Aviation, I jumped from the Cub into a Piper Arrow with an FAA designated examiner, and two hours later, I woke Larry who waited for me in the pilot's lounge. The ink on my Commercial Pilot's license was literally still wet when Larry put me in the front seat of the Cub and gave me a powerline patrol checkout on a 138 KV, 138,000-volt line that ran up Parley's Canyon. After landing in Heber, Larry climbed out and told me to take the plane around the pattern and do as many touch and gos as I needed to feel comfortable in the airplane. After a couple of hours, I was exhausted and felt good with the Cub. Larry showed me the trick he used to keep the plane ready for winter flying. We pushed it into a hangar and drained the oil into a big can. He kept the lights on inside to raise the temperature and brought the oil into the main office, heated all night, to keep it warm. He instructed me to arrive at seven the next morning and pull the Cub out onto the ramp. I was then to set the parking brake, a novel system with which I was quite unfamiliar, pour in the warm oil, and fire up the engine. The next step in this careful choreography was to go inside and make a pot of coffee.

It's unheard of, and surely illegal under "careless and reckless" regulations, to leave an unchained airplane running unattended. But that's the way things had always been done in Heber, and who was I to argue. I dutifully followed instructions, excited to get out on my first day of patrol. My observer was Larry's daughter, Susan. Larry arrived, delighted to see I'd complied with all his instructions. Susan showed up about 7:45, her partner parking their big Chevy Monte Carlo right next to the Cub. They got out, and we were all enjoying a cup of bad coffee when we heard a muffled *bam bam bam bam bam* in decreasing frequency. Everyone ran for the ramp and there sat the Cub, ninety degrees to how I'd left it, engine stopped. The right brake had released because I set it poorly, and the plane pivoted on the left wheel into the Monte Carlo, cutting a long line through the left rear quarter panel and up into the trunk, managing to hit a spare can of motor oil inside. Oil was everywhere, making us initially think there was serious engine damage. Soon we discovered the errant can in the Chevy's trunk, ripped to shreds, and realized the only damage to the Cub was to the propeller. Its tips were curled, and a couple of half inch square chunks of aluminum had broken off.

Larry had a spare prop in the hangar, and we went about exchanging the bad prop for the good. Larry bid us farewell on our maiden patrol trip and said he'd fix the car. He was a heck of a good welder.

After we were gone, Larry called T and told him what had happened, seeking advice on an appropriate punishment. Together they decided I should buy the wrecked prop. $600 at $50 per paycheck. Seemed fair enough to me. I packed that old bent prop around for a long time as a reminder of what foolishness can get you. I finally gave it to a fellow Japan Airlines pilot when I was moving from Oahu to Kauai, sixteen years later. I watched that relic drive off down Kuailima Rd in Lanikai, one tip on the passenger's floor, the other poking into the air resting against the leather seat-back of a silver, 1992 Porsche Cabriolet.

I touch down three hours and thirty-six minutes after takeoff from Ketchikan, and my rigor mortis continues to gain ground on my mobility. After refueling and checking the airplane and weather for the rest of the journey, I depart Bellingham's runway 16. I'm now in Pacific Standard time, cheated out of one hour from this day. I leave the earth's surface behind at 4:00 p.m.

Ground-bound vehicles will traverse five hundred and fifty-two miles in an average of nine hours and forty minutes getting from Bellingham to McCall. My Shrike cuts the mileage to four hundred and six and her two hundred miles per hour gait makes this breathtaking flight run quickly. Most of the Pacific Northwest's towering volcanos are behind me, but I can still make out a few. I skirt around the south face of the visual reference I'd used to get to Bellingham. Views of Mt. Baker's 10,781-foot eminence and her namesake ski resort present a majestic spectacle. The large resort center sits well below the permanent glaciers covering higher elevations. Ski trails cut through thickly wooded slopes look like an upside-down tree with trunk at the top and branches fanning out at the base.

I cross the Cascade Mountain range which drops away to the Columbia Basin. I sight the Wenatchee River and watch it ally with the Columbia. Just south I spot Wenatchee's seven-thousand-foot runway where I flew another fire-spotting contract only a month ago. The Columbia River runs mostly east to west at this latitude providing unprofaned visual feasting. Bordering on sacred, the views add sustenance for my depleting energy.

Statuesque mountain ranges rise from the basin floor in dark pine and indigo shades along consecutive ridges in deepening shadows. I cross the Snake River whose prodigious waters make possible the endless potato supply for which Idaho is famous. Ten minutes later, I'm banking left to line up on McCall's runway 34. I land at 7:28 having lost another hour when I transited into the Mountain time zone, beating sunset by exactly thirty minutes. The flight from Bellingham took two hours and twenty-eight minutes. From takeoff in Anchorage, I've logged ten hours and thirty-six minutes in the air. That's a far sight longer than the eight-hour maximum allowed for a flight crew of two to fly under airline transportation regulations. My foggy brain concurs; it's a good rule.

My parents live nearby in Victor, Montana, and I haven't seen them in twenty-five months. We prearranged a rendezvous here in McCall, and delightfully, they're here to meet me. Doug has graciously acquired quarters for us in a rustic, two-bedroom home situated well off a quiet road. "Fir Lane" fronts our cottage and is lined with mature western larch and lodgepole pine. I'm up at 5:30 every day, Christmas-morning excited to step outside into a wall of pine-scented enchantment. Light upslope winds chase rising air high on east-flanking mountaintops, amplifying my morning chill. Sleep-induced lethargy flees in the alpine splendor with concerts provided by hermit thrush and pine grosbeak finch, percussion added by noisy, red-napped sapsuckers. I'm not sure if they're singing or making fun, but their voices thrill me all the same. My folks enjoy sleeping in, given whole days to explore while I fly. For four days during free afternoons, our reunion blazes with fun and conversation. There's so much to cover since we last met in August 1992. They've moved from southern Utah to the Bitterroot Valley in Montana, and I've settled into my new home and employment in Alaska.

We enjoy dinners out every night and take long walks in unseasonably mild evenings. McCall is a mountainous town just over five thousand feet above sea level, densely treed with a wide variety of conifers including spruce, Douglas fir, and ponderosa, plus other pine species colonizing our road. It's a close-knit community that offers hero's welcomes to firefighters that come to save their beloved mountain paradise. A homier, more tranquil setting for our reunion is unimaginable.

Two uniformed forest rangers accompany me during my search missions which normally turn up a lot of wildlife but little smoke. So far, we've chased moose, elk, and mountain goats—antics the rangers encourage. These are dedicated professionals with meticulously mapped routing for us to search. The views of the Payette National Forest from our treetop plus fifty-foot vantage are exhilarating. Every ranger I fly with knows the terrain, flora, and fauna from years, usually decades of hiking, rescuing, trail maintenance, and camping on the folded glades below. This is their backyard, and sharing it with them in this comfortable flying workhorse is a gripping adventure.

CHAPTER 7

GLIDERS
1981

Shortly before graduating from Utah State University in 1981, I meet a woman named Fawn, and in reckless haste, we decide to wed in late summer. Meanwhile, I've been invited to return to Driggs, Idaho, for another season giving scenic glider rides around the Tetons. The income for a glider pilot is minuscule. I do this job not for money, but because it's thrilling. Even though I'm also qualified to tow gliders and do the routine maintenance on all the aircraft, my daily income could never buy a steak dinner with a glass of wine.

My boss, Fred, is a Vietnam veteran with a cavernous heart and bright, almost clown-like rosy-red cheeks. They fit his cheery nature to a tee. I'm reluctant to accept his job offer this summer having joined lives with Fawn, my fiancée, and her eight-year-old daughter, Gretchen.

"I'll follow you anywhere," Fawn quips in her first cliché of the day, "but it's gotta be fun for all three of us!"

This seems an easy promise to make and keep if we can just figure out housing. My betrothed fights to keep her smile subdued, wanting a full accounting of serious attention to this first *team* decision. Gretchen's already not very on board. We'll be stealing her from her friends, maybe forever. But when she learns she can take her best buddy, a boy cat named Lily, who's nipping at the edge of less rigid sexual identities, she softens considerably. Fawn is quite excited to flee the Cache Valley and engage this grand dare, but motherhood comes first, ensuring Gretchen's well-being.

Fred assures me he'll find us suitable housing. We worked well together the previous summer, and he really wants me back and seems amply sympathetic to our domestic needs.

Last summer I was happy to sleep on a Naugahyde couch in the back of the hangar. That won't work this year. Being a lifelong resident, Fred knows almost everyone in the community. A friend offers him the use of a two-story, two-bedroom cabin that overhangs the Teton Creek in Alta, Wyoming. When Fred calls with the news, the deal is sealed. We all dance and jump for joy. Lily flees the house.

Normally, the Teton Creek flows in mild currents if at all. But in the spring, it can roar like the Colorado. The noise from its breaking waters is a lullaby to us every night 'til midsummer when it begins to tire. We have scored a summer vacation home far beyond our means. Fawn, Gretchen, and Lily hang out on the well-varnished Douglas fir deck for an hour or two each morning, taking full advantage of our prize. I normally drive ten minutes to the airport early each day to prep the airplanes and gliders. Fawn's an early riser and takes pleasure in making me breakfast. Later, she comes to the airport with Gretchen and brings a big sack lunch of bologna-and-cheese or tuna-fish sandwiches.

With her dark auburn pageboy haircut framing her slender face inset with jewel-blue eyes, she works the front desk booking glider tours while Gretchen, slight with a full allowance of her mom's genes, but lighter, longer, and playfully curly hair, endears hearts. This probably nets more bookings than might otherwise sign. Gretchen's recompense—enough coloring books and crayons, children's books, and acres of safe outdoor haven, to fill a dreamy summer.

Days pass with endless delight as little can match the thrill of "coring" a six-thousand-foot-per-minute thermal in a glider making good a climb from eight to eighteen thousand feet in a couple of minutes. If I'm unable to find a good thermal after dropping off the two-hundred-foot rope affixed to the Bellanca Scout tow plane, I aim for our "house thermal." At the base of Grand Targhee ski resort is a large, black asphalt parking lot that absorbs sunshine with insatiable thirst. That massive, heated surface can be counted on to generate balloons of rising air—thermals—whose upward locomotion flourishes in unstable air that portends great soaring. By the time that bubble reaches ten thousand feet, its dynamic power lifts gliders as effortlessly as I throw a paper airplane. Free rides to eighteen thousand feet happen all afternoon once the cycle begins. Approaching the core of a thermal, I pull in one notch of flaps to configure for slower, higher lift flying, and bank to sixty degrees, riding the tiger with intoxicating glee. The two g's of force that angle-of-bank imparts on bodies coupled with frenzy-fast pirouetting has brought many a passenger to nausea, requiring well-coordinated use of the sick-sack or a major cleanup effort once back on the ground. In three summers of giving glider rides, I never have a single guest sorry for the thrill. I get to circle the Grand Teton hundreds of times this summer, with Fawn and Gretchen on board on two occasions. The ship's rental plus the cost of the tow up to altitude cost as much as I made all summer. Their delicious screams of delight and thrill are worth far more. In late August when it's time to go, my net earnings are preceded by a minus sign. The price feels fair for this summer's reckless lifestyle, something soon to vanish forever as youth leaks away.

Driving home to our cottage on the Teton Creek late one afternoon, I'm reveling in this waning summer's fun with memories that drill to my nucleus. The August afternoon sun plays lengthening shadows across the road, and burbled wind smacks my face and musses my short hair through the open window. I'm struck with an immensity of rapture so grand that without awareness, I find "The Sound of Music" gaining a footing in my mind infilling with details and full orchestration. I encourage them.

Then suddenly, embarrassingly, a coal black cloud of anguish overtakes me. A knife of pain stabs at my thoughts as memories of a recent, nearly disastrous flight take center stage. The von Trapps, Austria, and Rodgers and Hammerstein retreat like puffs of smoke.

On August 1ˢᵗ, not a full month ago, I'm assigned a charter flight from Driggs to Boulder, Colorado. A middle-aged woman is my only passenger. It's a last-minute assignment as my passenger, Ruth, just happens into the office early in the afternoon wondering if she can charter a plane to Boulder then and there. Fred pulls me from the afternoon's schedule of scenic glider rides and assigns me the trip. Only yesterday I had an FAA check ride in the Cessna turbo 206 to be used, so it's clear I'm proficient and up to speed in this airplane.

I rush through preparations and call the weather service for a briefing and to file my flight plan. I top off the fuel tanks and gather Ruth and her baggage, and we're airborne at 3:35 p.m. Some high mountains make a perfectly straight-line flight impossible without supplemental oxygen, but I can do it almost straight. The route should be no more than four hundred and thirty miles. At one hundred and eighty-five miles per hour, I figure I can have Ruth at the Brungard Aviation terminal in Boulder in two hours and thirty minutes.

I decide on a fuel management technique I learned in more elementary flying days. I'll fly exactly one hour on the left tank, then switch to the right tank and repeat. Discounting for climbing fuel consumption, an irresponsible mistake, this technique will tell me when I can expect to run out of fuel. I'm flying Ruth under commercial flying rules that mandate more care than my return flight, which will be solo. We land at 6:08, two hours and thirty-three minutes after takeoff. I've run one hour out of the left tank, one out of the right, plus thirty-three more minutes out of the left. I know getting back to Driggs without fueling up will be tight, but I elect to try it thinking my plane's performance and endurance should be better than book because I've been so light both directions. I also don't have money or a credit card for gas and hadn't talked to Fred about this in my haste to depart.

I crank up my engine and depart Boulder at 6:35. I'm burning fuel from the left tank. I decide to fly 'til I run out of gas in that tank. A little math after that will give me a good idea of how much time I have left in the right tank. I trust this method more than the fat needles of the fuel gauges which are painting a worrisome picture, but I persevere. I figure if I can get a full hour before this tank runs dry, I'll probably make it. This kind of planning is worthy of license revocation it's so foolhardy. "Probably make it" is not how flight operations are done, and I'm showing immaturity I wouldn't expect from a student pilot with twenty hours. I've got over two thousand. At 7:28 my engine sputters. My left fuel tank is dry. I made it fifty-three minutes. That one hour was only barely enough fuel to get me to Driggs. In a perfect world, if I made it exactly one hour out from Boulder, I could expect to run out of gas taxiing in at Driggs. There wasn't a drop of reserve in the calculation.

I switch to the right tank, and my engine zings back to life. I'm in a fix growing rapidly graver as I consider my situation. My mind is battling to do math that I repeated over and over. No matter how I cut it, I only had one hour and twenty-six minutes of fuel left when my engine lost power. I needed an hour and thirty with no reserves. Sunset is one hour away, so not only am I positively going to run out of gas, it's going to happen after dark in high mountainous terrain near the Tetons.

Admitting this kind of mistake can cost a pilot his license. Any kind of infraction in my record will torpedo my airline aspirations. I own up to this or die. My life or my dreams. My mouth is so dry my tongue feels swollen. I run the calculations again. It's certain, I have only these two choices.

I frantically study my aeronautical chart but can't pinpoint my location. I can't find any airports near where I think I am. I'm beginning to panic. I see no towns, no roads, just a massive expanse of sameness over this high-plains desert in the middle of

Wyoming. My life now depends on radio communications, and I'm in such a remote area, I don't know if there will be anyone in range to hear me.

I make a best guess at an air traffic control frequency from my chart. With a trembling hand, I bring the mic to my mouth and push the button. "Casper Radio, Cessna 756 Xray November on 122.2, Over."

"Cessna 756 Xray November, Casper Radio, go ahead." I can hardly believe it. They answered! Oh my God!

I tell them my predicament. They assign me a discrete "squawk code" so they can positively radar identify me. I dial it into my transponder, and in seconds, I'm radar identified. They want to know how much fuel I'm certain I have remaining. With my struggle to pull the trigger and ask for help, and finally realizing I'm unlikely to find my location on the map, I've eaten up most of what I had and am only certain of fifteen more minutes. The controller, never expressing anything but professional courtesy and clear instructions, turns me right to a new course and explains to me there's an airport twenty miles ahead, right on my nose on my new heading. It's in Jeffrey City, Wyoming. He wants me to acknowledge when I get it in sight. He tells me it's 6442 feet above sea level. I immediately begin descending from 10,500'. He gives me a frequency for pilot-controlled lighting at the airport. I tune it in on my second Comm radio and switch to that transmitter and click the mic button four times. The runway lights bloom brightly, bringing it clearly into sight. I report it's five miles ahead and that my landing is assured. He releases me to the local traffic frequency and wishes me luck.

I've had my wits scared out of me but still manage a decent landing. I taxi to a parking ramp, half expecting the engine to quit any moment, but it doesn't. I park, chain my plane down, and walk off to find a payphone. It's quickly getting dark. Before reaching a phone, I hear sirens approaching in the distance. I realize the controller alerted the fire department, and they're rushing this way, probably expecting to find a smoking hole in the ground off the end of their runway. Instead, they find my airplane, chained securely to their ramp. I hustle toward them, embarrassed enough to match their red spinning lights with my Santa cheeks. We shake hands all around, and after some paperwork, a policeman gives me a ride to the local motel where they put me up for the night at no charge. They even bring me dinner. People can be so kind, even to careless idiots.

The next and hardest call I ever make is to Fred back in Driggs. I tell him the story, and I can hear the disappointment in his voice. Of course he's happy the airplane and I are in one piece, but I've shown judgment far below what he ever imagines seeing from me. He jumps in our tow plane at 5 a.m. the next day with two five-gallon jerrycans of avgas and flies them down to Jeffrey City, arriving about 6:00. I don't sleep much that night, get up early, and walk to the airport to wait for Fred. There isn't much talk. A lot of consternation and disappointment on Fred's face is about all I get. He returns to the Scout to fly back to Driggs, assuring himself plenty of time to prepare for the day's business. He instructs me to fly the Cessna to Lander and fill it up, hands me a credit card, and is gone. He doesn't fire me, though he has every right. I suspect my contrition and the friendship we've developed in the two summers I've worked for him sway the deal in my favor. The FAA never does an investigation, and no black marks ever land on my record. I realize I should learn to be as generous with "Mulligans" as the universe.

I invite Rodgers and Hammerstein back, but they seem reluctant. Soon, however, I begin pushing and shoving this dark memory back into that special chamber inside me where guilt, regret, and my "do over" wish list reside. My heart begins beating again. "The hills are alive…"

CHAPTER 8
SEPTEMBER 17, 1994
ALASKA BOUND

Since part of my mission is to take N17DL back to Anchorage, I've arranged it so my folks can join me on the flight. Not only will this significantly extend our meeting, but it also gives them the dramatic experience of seeing the "inside passage" along the west coast of Canada and Alaska. Altitudes flown in unpressurized piston airplanes provide infinitely better sight-seeing platforms than the tiny windows in jetliners that cruise six or seven miles above the ground. One of the key advantages of the Aero Commander for a spotting airplane is its high wing, mounted atop the fuselage, affording unlimited downward visibility. We look forward with boundless excitement to the flight and a few days in Anchorage where I can show off the city of which I've grown so fond.

They drive to Seattle in their Nissan Pathfinder, leaving McCall early on the last day I'm flying fire-spotting missions. From the Seattle-Tacoma airport, they take a bus to Bellingham. It's a two hour and forty-minute ride. After my shift ends late in the afternoon, I climb aboard 17DL and take off. In the time it takes my parents to bus up to Bellingham, I've made my way from McCall in the Commander. I begin my descent under dimming, pale blue skies in an early evening twilight, embellished with thin wisps of pink-tinted clouds floating above the Bellingham Bay and the Pacific Ocean. We arrive at the tiny general aviation terminal within minutes of one another.

The Shamrock Motel sends a shuttle bus that deposits us back at their establishment in minutes. It's half a mile from the airport. The brown wood-sided building, unsurprisingly trimmed in shamrock green, nests off a quiet highway. It's surrounded by twenty and thirty-foot krummholz trees bent and deformed from large snow-packs and fierce winds. Its character seems a perfect fit for the beginning of our flight-seeing adventure. Its quiet and homey personality lend to deep and easy sleeping. Exhaustion helps too.

A telephone perched on a nightstand between our beds rings with a traditional bell from the 1960s. I don't think it's a novelty they put in for fun. All visible evidence leads me to believe it's just an antique that happens to fit the setting perfectly. The motel's front desk is making good on the courtesy wake-up call they promised. It's a real person calling, not an automated machine. I like this motel more and more. Concurrent almost to the second is an annoying electronic buzz from a cheap bedside alarm clock I'd set but not trusted. Blissful sleep ends at 4:30 a.m. in our shared room. A little foggy from several packed, adventure-filled days, all three of us rise and quietly shuffle through morning rituals, something we hadn't done in one another's presence since camping trips thirty years before.

I *dial* the 1-800 number I have for the FAA weather briefing service, which happily works on the motel's old telephone. The weather is going to be good for the beginning portion of the flight but will likely deteriorate along the more northerly segment. I file an Instrument Flight Rules, IFR, flight plan to Sitka and finish packing. Faces washed, breakfast bagels slathered with crunchy peanut butter and strawberry jam eaten, and teeth brushed, we board the motel's courtesy shuttle. A couple of minutes later, we're deposited at the front door of the small, cozy terminal.

Walking across the tarmac to our airplane, I feel wide awake, acutely aware of my environment. It's the kind of alertness that normally accompanies my cold morning runs. I consciously celebrate these feelings, knowing it's a good bet today will require a full ration of wits. As my brain tries to corral a thousand details that I want at the forefront of my mind, there's also soulful, childlike dazzle coloring every breath. I'm *beamed* as surely as if Scotty himself pushed the transporter lever, to summer campouts, earthworms wriggling deep in peat, yellow fiberglass fishing poles, and attached reels spun full of monofilament line. I'm certain for a fanciful moment that I even smell Zeke's Sierra Gold trout cheese bait.

A chorus starring a thousand crickets brings more youthful enchantment. Tiny whispers from a light, predawn breeze sing pianissimo in my ears, rounding out a symphony playing to my auditory delight. Sharpened eyes strain to discern the precise location of the ground for my foot's purchase against black asphalt blanketed by thin, crawling fog in the lightless night. The unmistakable presence of air ripe with an ocean's salt and marine life blend bring a seafood delicatessen to my olfactory receptors.

Arriving at the aircraft, I emplane my parents comfortably in the confines of the airplane's spacious cabin and proceed to inspect the aircraft's cold, dew-covered shell. As I circle the Commander, I remove each hold-down chain attached between cleats embedded in the ramp and eyelets attached below the airplane's wings, plus one under the tail. Their purpose is to thwart damage from potential maverick winds. Climbing into the pilot's seat, I complete my preflight preparations.

Outside's night sounds, now muffled beyond my senses, are replaced with music from electromechanical equipment coming to life in the instrument panel. Once all is prepared, starting the big Lycomings brings abrupt terminus to the quiet of the morning. With the low rumble of our engines humming their confident anthem, a wave of excitement seems to enfold my folks.

"Hey guys, I'm so glad we're doing this together. It's such a cool airplane!" I enthuse.

"Mom and I are really excited to be here!"

"Absolutely," spills out a little less eager but still earnest from Mom.

"It looks awfully dark and foggy out there. How do you know where you're going?" Dad asks.

"I just follow this taxi chart, plus I remember the layout well from yesterday. We'll just creep along slowly. You guys okay? Warm enough?" I ask.

"Temperature's perfect. I'll elaborate on the okay part in a few minutes," Mom says.

We all laugh, and it's clear they're both enjoying the beginning of our adventure.

I carefully navigate to runway 34 in the low, creeping fog, stopping short of the threshold to do my final checks. When I'm confident the engines are warm, magnetos are all working perfectly, and the oil channels to the propeller pitch governors are unclogged and filled with hot oil, I check back in with my parents.

"You guys ready? Seat belts snug?"

I watch my parents trade thumbs-up and big smiles.

"Yup," my dad says, "we're ready."

"Okay, hang on to your hats. Here we go," I announce.

I radio our takeoff intentions, in the blind, to local area air traffic. My broadcast finds the same audience present in empty forest, tree-falling analysis, and responds similarly—in silence. I proceed onto the runway centerline and switch on all our brilliant, luminous lights. Two hundred and fifty thousand candle power landing lights, rotating red beacons mounted on the top and bottom of the fuselage, and brilliant flickering white strobes light us up like a George Lucas fighter ship, and we begin our takeoff roll into raven-black skies. Thick seaside fog encroaches on the world from every direction, reducing visibility to barely enough to maintain adherence to the runway centerline. Gyroscopic effects and complex aeronautical forces nudge the nose leftward as force on the propeller blades is brought to bear during rotation. In the foggy darkness, I lose all reference to the ground for a moment during pitch-up. Ten thousand hours of flying experience leads me to unconsciously feed just the right amount of right rudder and aileron to counter it, and we leap into the air spot-on 344 degrees on the compass, the precise bearing of the runway we've departed. 17DL feels like an old friend to my fingers and feet, and we dance together like mates in a ballet. Our relatively light weight, with a total of only three people aboard, and cool, sea level air, allows a "homesick angle" climb catapulting us through the thin cloud layer in seconds, and suddenly, we're mesmerized by the spectacle of tens of thousands of brilliant stars blanketing the heavens.

Within half an hour dawn blossoms. Beginning with the faintest hint of light on the eastern horizon as the earth rotates a thousand miles per hour, the curtain rises on this sunrise play startlingly fast. At 8000 feet above sea level, the sky is mostly clear of contaminants, revealing clarity not often available to pedestrians fixed to earth's surface. The refraction of light through maritime air, heavily laden with water molecules, is thrilling to behold. The horizon first turns pale yellow, then morphs through a color wheel of pinks and reds soon blazing immodestly in shades breathtakingly bold. In just the right circumstances, dopamine is ferried to brain regions causing euphoric states. I'm in one right now. Whatever Creator is out there, this is His or Her most benevolent dominion. If there's a great Someone, I hope They're inclined to this kind of tranquility for the rest of the day.

CHAPTER 9

PIPELINE, CORPORATE, AND COMMUTERS
1981 ~ 1984

Soaring conditions last only as long as the sun is high overhead to accommodate intense heating of the earth, spawning rambunctious thermals on which gliders feed. Once the summer begins to wane, soaring pilots must seek new employment.

I have a background in low-level aerial patrol work flying a Super Cub to patrol powerlines for Utah Power and Light. I'm mostly looking for vandalism in the form of shot-out insulators. Once I catch a youngster climbing a lattice metal structure from which hangs three phases of power lines carrying 138,000 volts. This much voltage will happily jump from line to person if the path of least resistance to ground is through the person. I find a lot of shot-out insulators and quite a few broken supports on old wooden powerline poles, but rarely anything life-threatening.

I know this youngster is in terrible danger, and I clearly remember my own childhood that cared little for "Danger, Do Not Enter" signs. I'm a ballet artist with this airplane by now, and its movements are mere reflections of my thoughts. Under my wings in huge black print is written: POWERLINE PATROL. It's impossible to miss even by this shortsighted youth, who's clearly not blind. I repeatedly circle and dive on this young man until he realizes he's the focus of my effort. I don't know if he reads the advertisement under my wings or just realizes there's a plane aggressively warding him from his antics. In any case, he finally backs off and climbs down. That justifies every penny UP&L ever paid for this patrol, and to this day it's the only life I can, with fair certainty, claim credit for saving.

In late August, I get a call from Northwest Pipeline, a huge gas pipeline company based in Salt Lake City. They're looking for a pilot to patrol their pipeline network from the air, but very close to the ground. They need their pilot to be a certified aircraft mechanic so he can do all the light maintenance on the airplane in their hangar in Pocatello, Idaho. T, who's left his job working for the State of Utah and now mechanics full-time on their large fleet of executive jets, has recommended me. Fred loans me an airplane to attend the job interview.

After an amiable conference lasting about forty-five minutes, I'm offered the job. The interviewer, Wade, asks if $1900 a month plus daily per diem is an acceptable salary. I've never made more than $1000 and can't believe my good fortune. I sign the contract.

"REALLY! $1900 a month PLUS per diem?"

Fawn's as incredulous as I was.

"So we're moving to Pocatello? We've got to find a house. I've gotta find a school for Gretchen and get her enrolled. If we're renting, we need to find a place that allows cats. We need to reserve a U-Haul. What size? Boxes? We'll need Idaho driver's licenses, and we better re-register to vote."

Holy crap, I've got a fast-thinking woman for which I'm extremely grateful. Without her, I'd still be back on, "So, we're moving to Pocatello," but it wouldn't be a question. We're a good team, and Gretchen's adept at ducking out of the way when things get lively. Her primary job is to make sure Lily's present when it's time to roll. One of his favorite tricks—I'm certain it's on page one of the famous cat book, *How to Annoy Your Humans*—is to be right underfoot during all the hard labor of packing and loading and then vanish faster than herring down a Sea World seal's throat at the exact moment of departure.

Between August 23rd and 31st, Fawn and I manage to get married, depart our Driggs summer haven, pack belongings stored in Logan, and lease a home in Pocatello. I'm out on my first day of pipeline patrol while Fawn is trying to get moved into our new home and get Gretchen enrolled in school. By far I've got the better deal.

I fly that job for only three months even though I love everything about it. My airplane is a sleek, new Cessna 210, the fastest single-engine airplane Cessna makes, and while it's not certified for aerobatic flight, I've met few airplanes more responsive and spunky. This machine will drill barrel-rolling holes in the sky all day, and I delight in proving it whenever bored and high above the ground. Usually, I fly fifty feet off the ground at high power making about a hundred and ninety miles per hour. I don't need to go slow to look for "right-of-way" infringements. A big yellow backhoe headed for the line is easy enough to spot. From the air, the discoloration of the buried pipe's location is obvious. On the ground, developers that happen to miss the pervasive bright yellow "Do Not Dig Here" signs would be in for a nasty surprise if they happened to break the high-pressure line. That's why it's a federal law that all buried gas pipelines be patrolled from the air at least twice a month. It's a fantastically fun job, and I really like my observer, but I need multi-engine flight time to qualify for an airline job and am ever on the lookout for a gig flying a twin.

One day in late November 1981, Fawn gets a call from Prince. I'm out on the southern part of my patrol near Albuquerque, New Mexico. Prince has been selling high performance multi-engine airplanes to a client in Big Piney, Wyoming, for decades. Rod, the owner of Skyline Construction Company in Big Piney, is looking for a new pilot to fly him and his family around in his Cessna 421C, and Prince recommends me. Rod has become grudgingly aware that his current pilot, a retired international pilot also from Big Piney, has a drinking problem. Having been friends for more than fifty years, it's a hard observation for him to stomach. The idea of firing such an old friend weighs heavily on Rod, but his safety and that of his family win over the internal argument. It turns out this hard-drinking guy has been "medically retired" from his previous employer because of his alcohol problem. In those days, good will between pilot and employer mitigated the mandatory termination when one was in the throes of alcoholism. This man was simply "medically discharged" to save his retirement and reputation. Who cares if he kills someone as long as he's working for someone else.

Fawn is dubious. In fact, the correct word is furious.

"Move, AGAIN? We just got here! The ink on my Idaho driver's license isn't dry! Gretchen's just made a new friend at school. I LIKE POCATELLO!"

We both like Pocatello, and once again, my fast-thinking wife is way ahead of me. But she's partly responsible for the new job. When Prince called her, he asked her how much multi-engine and Cessna 421 time I had. Knowing more is better in the world of aircraft experience when it comes to job interviews and qualifications, and aware I need a multi-engine flying job, she generously inflates the numbers she finds. Prince doubles those when he talks to Rod. My numbers are all true and accurate in my logbooks, but by the time the information gets to Rod, it's more than a little exaggerated.

Fawn and I fly to Big Piney in a borrowed Cessna 172. Rod is a no-nonsense, tough CEO not easily sweet-talked. But he likes my honesty and the adoration I display for my bride and hires me, really us, then and there.

All Fawn's objections evaporate when she realizes what a huge boon this is to my career and sees the sleek airplane I'll be flying. Rod tells us there's a housing crunch in town because of the present oil and gas boom frenzy. He shows us a trailer park with a single spot left for rent. Rod knows the owner and calls him, saying, "Hey Bill, Spot 17's rented," then hangs up. Rod knows everyone in this entire part of Wyoming and is one of the wealthiest. He's widely revered. In fact, to his employees and most other people, he's kind of a tobacco-chewing version of the 4077th's Colonel Potter. He can be a tough old geezer, but generally he's agreeable, evenhanded, fatherly, and truly cares about the well-being of his employees and community.

Fawn goes straight to work on a trailer. She knows people in her hometown of St. Anthony, Idaho, who've been in the mobile home selling business for a long time. We visit them and walk away with a nice deal. Our brand-new single wide with a full arctic package will arrive in Wyoming, deposited onto Spot 17, just ahead of us. Rod's got a guy who'll put insulated skirting around it by the time we get there.

By early December 1981, the mammoth challenges of moving are behind us. Big Piney, reputed to be "The Ice Box of America," is exactly that. Friendly locals encourage us to get block heaters installed on our vehicles right away and keep them plugged in every minute spark plugs aren't igniting fuel in the cylinders. The next spot to the east of us is owned by a guy who drives a "hot oiler." His job is to melt wax deposits from wellbores. There are a lot of those around here in this *drill, baby, drill!* capital. He never shuts down. To keep his fluids warm enough to do their job, he leaves his big diesel rig chugging all night on the few nights he gets home. We've landed in a tough part of the country and will have to pay steep dues to get this Cessna 421 time, but it's a fantastic opportunity, and Fawn did more than she knows to make it happen.

We soon learn we live in a dual set of communities. Big Piney, population 500-ish, and Marbleton, a mile south, also population 500-ish. Big Piney was settled back in 1913, and the son of the founder thought he'd found the answer to drainage problems plaguing the town. He incorporated Marbleton a year later, but they never merged. To this day they enjoy unique, municipal cooperation, and that's exactly what we find here along with an intensely proud culture of rugged "can do." I watch Gretchen on some winter mornings walk off from our home to the bus stop. She vanishes in a blizzard not twenty feet away. This is the icebox life. Well, not all of it; nine months and nineteen days after arriving,

Fawn delivers us a newborn son, Jan Michael. We call him JM. She did most of that work too.

Twenty-nine months later, having grown hardy in this wild part of the west and skilled in flying multi-engine, high performance airplanes, I get a call from a man named Paul in Farmingdale, Long Island, owner of Trans East Airlines. He wants to hire me to fly for his airline. I'm ecstatic. An *airline* job!

I had two plain white poster boards tacked to a wall in our bedroom. With half an inch per line, I ruled in sixty spaces per sheet. That gave me blanks for one hundred twenty airlines that I entered in the left margin on each board. Moving across to the right I had blocks to show when I'd sent each a résumé, when and if they'd replied, when I sent an application, etc. It was a well-organized effort to track and divine some kind of airline job. About ninety percent of them were in the western US. But of course, with Murphy out on perpetual bail, I get a call from Long Island.

Paul is seeking a pilot who is also a certified aircraft mechanic. I fit the bill and am hired over the phone.

Fawn's as ecstatic as I am. After two years in America's coldest-sink, brownish-gray in the winter and greenish-brown in the summer, all snow flying sideways in blizzard winds, and winter temperatures rarely peaking above -10, we're ready to move. Long Island sounds *exciting*! "Airline" rings bells at the highest rung on my "hopes and dreams tower." We're outta here.

We hire a moving company to pack our belongings and drive them to Bay Shore, Long Island. It's late April 1983 when we arrive at a home I managed to find for us during a quick house-hunting trip I took a week ago. It's a small, two-room flat on the top floor of a three-story home in a multicultural neighborhood.

I take the job at less than half the money I'm making in Big Piney only because I'm going to be flying a turbine powered Twin Otter. I have to amass at least a thousand hours of turbine flying time to qualify for a major airline.

I'm flying out of the Marine Air Terminal on the northwest portion of New York's LaGuardia airport which is crammed between

Flushing Bay and Queens. Water from the bay laps at the fill upon which the runways are constructed, and due to their short lengths, many pilots refer to LGA as The USS LaGuardia.

Getting settled into our new home takes some adjusting. The incredible humidity is new and oppressive to us, and there's no air-conditioning in our apartment. A late sixties Italian couple owns the home and lives on the partially submerged ground floor. Their daughter and new son-in-law live on the second floor between the landlords and us. Their Italian fighting is nonstop, abrasive, and by no means G-rated. They always yell in Italian but swear in English.

Muezzins cry out Muslim prayers several times a day starting before daylight in our neighborhood. People seem frenzied, crass, and aggressive, and every moment is rife with clarity about the enormity of sacrifice we've made to come here. But one new, large notch is carved deep along my circuitous path to an airliner cock-pit. It won't be as fun as we'd imagined, but all things considered, we're glad we're here. TV, not a cornerstone of my life, lends to us one of the few sanguine anchors on which to grasp when we can get the rabbit ears adjusted just right. Seven p.m. brings the whim-sical voices of Sammy, Norm, Cliff, and Carla to this place where nobody knows our name.

I report to work, but I'm told the Twin Otter is in the paint shop where it's getting the company livery applied. Meanwhile, I'm told I'll be flying as captain on a Cessna 402, a smaller, unpressurized version of the plane I flew for Rod in Big Piney. I agreed to a pay rate in the Twin Otter of $600 per month starting as a first officer. I'm told that my captain upgrade into the Cessna will put my pay at $1000. That's half what I was making flying the 421 for Rod.

Early in May, I'm overnighting in a crew house in Hyannis Port, Massachusetts. There are nine of us on sleeping bags sharing the living room floor. The only furniture in the room is a small, rickety bedside table that holds a dim lamp. Wall-to-wall beige, cat-urine-impregnated shag carpet adds a slight softening to our bed but at the expense of a pervasive stench. Paul has bought houses near each airport to which we fly to serve as crew accommodations. It saves him hotel expenses, and he builds real estate equity in the process. He has no cleaning service and leaves the purchase of food and furnishings to the pilots. No one has taken it upon themselves to buy or bring cleaning supplies, so we live in ratty conditions. Our schedules are full, and no one has energy left to clean at the end of a shift anyway.

There's murmured conversation among some of the pilots. Everyone, including two women, is stripped down to underwear. Modesty is easily surrendered in a battle against the breezeless, unairconditioned, sweltering, and humid conditions in which we're trying to sleep. Someone asks me where I come from and what I'm doing here. When I relay the story Paul told me about the Twin Otter being in the paint shop, they all break up into raucous laughter. "Oh man, he fell for the old Twin Otter in the paint shop story!"

I've been duped into moving two thousand miles, cutting my pay in half with a cost of living appreciably higher than Big Piney's, to fly inferior airplanes. My judge of character proves mediocre at best, from my first encounter with Paul. I was willing to believe anything if it meant getting that elusive turbine time. I flew several days with a copilot who went on to become an FAA lawyer. Some years later he told me the FAA had been trying to shut Paul down for years, but no one would testify against him given his deep ties to the mob.

Early the next morning, one of the pilots, a guy named Bob, takes pity on me and tells me to check out a company on the other side of the Long Island Sound, in New Haven, Connecticut. It's called NewAir. They have real turbine airplanes, and Bob's confident they're looking for pilots.

One day in late June, when I get the Farmingdale scheduler on the phone to learn my day's schedule, she says, "Hey Andy, go ahead and take the day off." It's 7 in the morning. I haven't been home to Fawn, Gretchen, and JM for eight weeks. Within hours of my arrival at our Bay Shore apartment, I abscond with Fawn and the kids and drive to New Haven.

Neither Fawn nor Gretchen has any love for this little piece of hell on the south shore of Long Island, and at least Fawn's aware I'm working for a scoundrel who keeps me out *on the line* for weeks on end. We've shared a few phone calls in the past several weeks, but with my fatigue and crazy schedule, I've kind of lost track of my brood. Fawn's ecstatic for some adult conversation and news of a possible escape from this foreign pit of harsh people, weather, and traffic.

In just over two hours we pull into the New Haven airport's parking lot. NewAir has a company policy that no one gets an interview without an invitation. This is fairly universal and I expected it, but I'm willing to beg, prostrate myself, cry, anything to get them to make an exception. I plead that I don't have scheduled days off so can't plan. Inside, with my young family, Fawn at my side showing large, tired doe eyes, and kids shuffling quietly right behind, I tell the secretary my woeful story about getting swindled and coming all the way from Wyoming to fly a plane that doesn't exist. She listens with deepening concern showing on her face, disappears into the chief pilot's office for a minute and then comes to the door and waves me, just me, in. Gretchen, ten years old, and young JM, two, sit, fidget, and play with Fawn in the lobby, awaiting the conclusion of my interview. After a few minutes, I walk right past them with NewAir's chief pilot who's going to assess my flying skills right now. I sneak a desperate, hopeful look at Fawn as we pass. She returns it with one of confidence. I needed that. I impress him enough to get the job. We have until July 5th to get settled in Connecticut, and for the fifth time in two years, we pack up and move. Fawn has no apprehension and packs like we just got an early release from a Siberian Gulag. She seems as relieved as I am, and we share a lot of happy glances and hand holding driving back to our Italian horror house. We have a big celebration dinner, tune in an extra staticky version of Cheers, and go to bed exhausted but happy.

I go to Connecticut one afternoon after flying a full day for the crook who tricked us into moving east. I haven't yet told him we're moving across the Sound. One of his pilots is taking a plane from Islip airport, smack in the middle of Long Island, to New Haven, and I bum a clandestine ride. I rent a car and search for a home. New Haven is totally out of our price range. My starting salary will be $600 per month. I find a home just off Interstate 95, Rural Route 97, which serves the commercial trucks that bring groceries and supplies into Norwich by the back way. Our tiny, stand-alone New England clapboard house is fifty-six miles east of New Haven. Rent will be $600 per month. I tell Fawn I'll take care of rent; she'll have to find a job to pay for utilities, childcare, groceries, and gas. Despite our strong alliance, I'm betting she's pretty sorry she married me at this point.

While Trans East Airlines has been a bitter disappointment based in a lie, it was nonetheless an airline with a published schedule, and I flew every day in and out of busy East Coast airports building twin engine time quickly. It looks pretty good on my résumé. Airline Number 1 is gladly dispatched from my list.

We settle into our new life in Connecticut, and I start work for Airline Number 2. Ground school and initial flight training is in New Haven. I drive there in my blue, 1978 Toyota Hilux pickup truck and sleep in its open, six-foot bed at night. Early mornings find me slinking into the airport restroom, with my Dennis the Menace hair and sweat-encrusted body, to wash up and change into clean underwear and socks. I can't afford the gas and tolls to commute home. By the end of a week, I'm qualified in their accelerated training program whose bulk will be forthcoming on-the-job training. I feel ultra-fortunate to get assigned to the only copilot slot not in New Haven, but instead at a tiny, four-pilot mini base in Groton—half an hour closer to the house we found in Norwich.

Every few days I get home when my schedule ends early one afternoon and doesn't start until noon the next. Otherwise, I'm sleeping in the back of my truck in Groton Airport's parking lot hoping to eke out six or seven hours of sleep. But finally, after more than six years with my nose to a particular coarse grindstone, I'm flying turbine engine, nineteen-passenger airplanes, practically assuring my dream future as an airline pilot for a major airline.

After only three months, I upgrade to captain with my pay increasing to $1200 per month. For once my timing is good. Most first officers at NewAir spend over a year before they upgrade. It's not based on skill; it's based on expansion of the airline and attrition out the top. No one leaves when no airlines are hiring. It can be very stagnant, but NewAir is growing. We got lucky. We believe we can now join mainstream America and apply for a credit card. It takes a few tries, but we finally qualify and within a few weeks receive our brand-new card in the mail. With it, we engage a long-time fantasy—grab two shopping carts at the Stop and Shop in Norwich and fill them both to the brim with reckless abandon. Walking out the door, we see "Seasonal Summer" goods advertised on a huge stage. We barely fit the new gas BBQ grill into our Ford Escort station wagon. We return a day later with a newly purchased and installed roof rack to pick up a sixteen-foot Coleman canoe, the other impulse purchase. We settle exuberantly into front row seats on the American Dream tour.

We feel like we've arrived, though we still qualify for food stamps.

One year later, I get a call from Eastern Airlines. Airline Number 3. A career.

CHAPTER 10

SOUTHERN COAST
OF ALASKA
SEPTEMBER 18, 1994

F our hours and forty-three minutes after takeoff, we complete an uneventful instrument approach and landing at Sitka, Alaska, picking up just a trace of ice during descent through the clouds. Even after intentionally skipped coffee that morning, I walk with conspicuous haste to the restroom. Modesty and common decency disallow the coffee can on the return flight. There are some great perks available to we who fly 747s around the world. On-board washrooms rank high among them. More will evolve into sharp relief soon.

After finishing up in the lavatory, where my folks linger, I find the customer service counter and order my fuel tanks topped off with 100 LL avgas. Then I find my folks, and together we stroll down to the airport's newly modernized passenger terminal for lunch. While waiting for our meals, I walk down to the Flight Service Station to get a weather update. From Sitka to Anchorage, along the coast, the forecast calls for various layers of clouds, light winds from the west, and light to moderate ice in clouds and precipitation between six and twelve thousand feet. This is typical coastal weather for this time of year and though not adverse enough to keep us on the ground, my heart sinks knowing my parents will likely miss the spectacular views I'm hoping for. I file an instrument flight plan with a cruise altitude of 14,000 feet to keep us above the icing conditions and head back to the café to enjoy a big lunch.

Airport food is not typically something a person will go out of their way for, but Sitka's airport restaurant breaks all the stereotypes. My dad gapes at the menu. "Is this a typical airport menu?" My mother bends toward us, clearly curious for my answer.

"Absolutely not," I declare. "I've seen some okay fare but mostly just fast food like we sold at Watson."

"You impugn the haven of your youth with such recklessness?" Mom says with just enough buoyancy to signal diplomacy.

"No, Mom," I defend, "I meant no insult to our lodge's menu. I can still taste the burgers, ham and cheese, and roast beef sandwiches that fueled my youth. Nothing was ever tastier. I just meant it seemed more like fast food than fine dining."

Never one to pass up an opportunity for a little scrap, she continues, "Even after Tim returned from chef's school? Remember, the one that took him all the way to Paris to study the intricacies of gourmet food preparation? Surely you remember the exquisite chowders, soups, and stews he concocted. That was NOT fast food."

Mom's rant, measured as it was, drove my father to bury himself deep in the big wall-mounted menu, leaving me to fend for myself. He'd fielded enough battles with her in their forty-four-year marriage and let the more frivolous ones die from one-sidedness.

"Easy, Mom. I'll never forget what happened to our menu after Tim returned. I couldn't believe such delicacies were possible from the ingredients he had on hand," There, I think, that outta calm her down.

"Actually, he used to give me a list of special ingredients he needed to make those dishes. We spent a lot of money for those upgrades," Mom adds.

I'm not exactly hitting it out of the park here so just concede that Watson's late years' menus were several steps above *fast food*, and we go back to gawking at the menu here.

After fifteen minutes, as we're strolling the memory freeway of our Alta years with impassioned animation, our meals arrive. Dungeness crab, prawns, shrimp by the dozen, and Caesar salad covers every square inch of our red-checked draped table. In another minute, our waitress brings several half ears of corn-on-the-cob, apologizing for forgetting them. I wonder what they expect of the wait staff here. I double-check and verify she only has two hands. I'd added 15% to the tab when I paid at the cash register but leave another $10 bill under a basket on the table after we're done.

"I guess that cinches it—we're on vacation," declares my dad. "Who eats like this at home?"

I have some five-star restaurants I can't wait to show off in Anchorage, but I—well, all of us—are kind of shocked at the "airport" meal we just devoured.

"Why don't you guys just relax for a while? It'll take me a few minutes to preflight the plane. Just hang out for ten or fifteen minutes and then come on out. I'll have it ready by then," I say.

They're happy to comply, but my mom smart alecks me good-naturedly. "If you decide to leave us here, just put my purse out on the ramp. We'll find a motel nearby and come here morning, noon, and night for meals. In fact, if they've still got your credit card information, we'll just charge everything on it!"

And people wonder where I get my wise guy demeanor.

I smile and excuse myself. With 17DL nearing the end of its maintenance cycle, I elect to take some extra time inspecting it. I want to be ready for takeoff as soon as my folks arrive.

I joke to the fuel truck driver who has just topped our fuel tanks, "You can say you fueled that doomed airplane as you read about us in the paper tomorrow."

He shrugs and offers a stifled laugh, cocking his head northward. I don't think he sees much humor in my joke. I suspect he's read about enough disasters in weather along this coast to take it deadly serious.

I must have been trying to convince myself that my "airline pilot" status and vast experience protect me from the horrors of bad weather in an ill-equipped airplane. What am I thinking? That weather to the northwest is no joke. I'm suckering into the most dangerous phenomenon known to aviation, responsible for more airplane fatalities than all other causes combined—"get home-itis." With my folks secure in their seats, I shout "CLEAR" out the door and start the engines.

At 11:06 a.m. Alaska time, we lift off eastbound from Sitka and retract the wheels aerodynamically into their wells. Banking right takes us away from jagged high terrain inland and puts us instead over channel water in dark gray clouds, overripe with moisture. Two minutes later, we're making good a northerly course for Yakutat.

Moments ago, my "good angel" tried to poke some sense into my head about this flight, but I managed to sidestep *him*. Now I'm looking for some way to rationalize my choice. The rascal inside me grabs the only low hanging fruit in sight and pumps up my ego with thoughts about how much I enjoy this kind of exciting adventure. How flying an airplane in inclement weather in the wilds of Alaska with six hundred miles of mostly wilderness between us and Anchorage is a perfectly rational idea of which I'm fully capable. My parents, non-seasoned fliers by any definition, sense my elation and confidence which notches up their own ability to enjoy the flight. Nonetheless, I get a short lecture from my mother on not looking so serious if things are going so well. Consciously or un-, my mom sees something darker in me than I'm admitting, even to myself.

Her probe, however, does point to a large part of the fulfillment of flying, especially in crummy weather—it's tricky business that involves years of care, training, and practice to survive. Anything requiring such an investment pays large dividends in gratification as time passes and competence is gained. In this model aircraft, the first Air Force One, with my parents on board, I can hardly be more delighted, so says the horned apparition sitting on my left shoulder, unless the clouds disappear, and the mountain and sea-scapes become visible under dazzling sunlit skies.

Eleven minutes after takeoff, we break through a stratiform cloud top at about 11,000 feet. It spreads in all directions so flat it mimics a smooth sandy desert. The sunshine I've been praying for is at hand, shining down on the retreating cloud layer. It had been a hundred different shades of greenish gray from below and within the clouds, but now the sun blazes snow-white, too bright for my dilated pupils. My irises' aperture can't shrink fast enough to thwart the painful bombarding light. I'm almost blind and fumble for my dark glasses, finding them perched on my forehead, forgotten in the long slog since I last needed them. Dropping them to the bridge of my nose brings immediate relief, and now I can fully enjoy the grand spectacle out the windshield. I turn off the pitot and fuel vent heaters since they're no longer needed.

I request a clearance to level at 12,000 feet since I'm above the clouds. Lower is better since we don't have supplemental oxygen. I elect to save higher altitudes for later if I need them. Engaging the autopilot unburdens my busy brain, greatly expanding my situational awareness which has been constrained by the focus I've had to invest in hand flying the airplane through the thick clouds below. I'm now free to enjoy the beautiful day and company of my folks who are enjoying the new flight conditions as much as I am. I can also dedicate a lot more attention to planning and navigating. The forecast weather almost surely awaits somewhere ahead, and I'm enjoying this time to consider as many possibilities as I can about how to deal with it.

Just shy of an hour after leveling off, I start to see outlines in the distance of large clouds thickening heavenward. My present heading looks like it will take me right into them. As they get closer, I see some are cumuliform type clouds, those beautiful, billowy, cauliflower-shaped things that look like cotton candy.

This type of cloud offers the most hazards to airplanes. While delightful to watch from the ground, these innocuous piles of rising water harbor a lot of peril within. Fed by updrafts, water vapor rises with the air and cools during ascent. At a certain temperature called the dew point, the water vapor changes into tiny droplets of liquid water. This simple-sounding mutation gives rise to a principle taught in high school science classes called the latent heat of vaporization. There's a fantastic release of heat as the component parts of atoms reconfigure into this lower energy state, and that release warms the adjacent air rapidly. Warming air makes the ascending column rise faster, which transforms more water vapor to liquid, and soon, a full-blown thunderstorm forms. There are all kinds of ways for this process to burn itself out, but in any case, once it's developed enough to make cotton candy, the up and down drafts alone make flying an airplane within a bad idea. No matter how exaggerated the physics get that intensify the storm, it always ends when the water droplets grow too large for the updrafts to buoy. Then the whole parade turns around and barrels earthward in a massive downdraft. With columns of rising and sinking air particles rubbing against each other at over two hundred miles per hour, the shear zone develops a huge electrical charge and lightning then pounds the earth, neutralizing the differential polarity.

I've seen my share of this kind of weather and want no part of it, especially in an airplane not equipped with protections against ice and no radar to see inside the cloud. I put in a call to Air Traffic Control requesting a deviation west of course to avoid this ominous-looking storm. They approve my request, and I immediately turn thirty degrees left.

One of the most useful utilities in recent years for aircraft navigation is the ability to precisely determine one's position anywhere on earth. With Global Positioning Systems, GPS, pinpoint accuracy is cheap and easy. Precise navigation to anyplace, anytime, with no ground-based navigation aids, becomes a cinch.

A GPS for recreational use is not expensive nor is the kind installed in an airplane to assist fire-spotting missions. But one blessed by the FAA to get your commercial airliner, loaded with paying passengers, to and fro costs magnitudes more. 17DL, as is true of Doug's other two airplanes, has GPS. We use it every day in fire-spotting and fighting missions. It's not FAA certified for aeronautical navigation. When I file flight plans, there's a place to input an "equipment suffix." This tells the FAA what navigation equipment is on board. They only count the certified stuff.

To check a hunch, on our new course, I program in the coordinates for Johnstone Point, a VOR used for ground-based air navigation. It's located on Hinchinbrook Island off the east shore of Prince William Sound, made famous by the Exxon Valdez. As I suspected, we're pointed directly at it.

A VOR is trustworthy for air navigation only with considerable limitations. The "V" in VOR stands for Very High Frequency, and that spectrum of radio waves is limited by line-of-sight. From typical civilian airplane cruise altitudes, the curvature of earth sinks objects upon the planet's surface below the horizon in around two hundred miles, hence the restrained usable range. I'm about twice that distance from Johnstone Point.

I call ATC requesting a clearance directly to Johnstone Point. I should realize it's beyond legal navigation limits for my airplane, but I call anyway thinking maybe they can keep me on radar and that maybe different rules apply up here in the wilds of Alaska. Of course, they can't approve my request, and my flimsy logic evaporates immediately. In fact, they tell me I'm about to leave the lateral limits of their radar coverage and must turn right and re-intercept my flight plan route within twenty-five miles. I can see this turn will point me toward the churning coastal weather I had turned away from a short while ago. On my present course, which would take me far out over the Gulf waters, I get a great shortcut and avoid that dangerous weather system east of us.

Two choices stare me right in the face. Cancel my IFR flight plan and proceed visually using any means of direction finding I want, or stay on my instrument flight plan, return to my filed route, and take my chances with the weather. I'm torn, wanting to stay closer to the coast and remain tethered to safety nets offered by ATC. I also fear the weather I suspect is obscuring mountain passes ahead, near Whittier, and don't want to get stuck trying to duck under low clouds in mountainous terrain.

I choose to stay on my IFR flight plan and make the sweeping right turn that will put me back on my filed route. Established on my new heading, I see we're pointing right into the thick of that threatening storm ahead.

CHAPTER 11
EASTERN AIR LINES
1984 TO 1989

Colonel Frank Borman does an admirable job commanding Apollo 8 on a mission to the moon, but his leadership skills pale mightily against Eastern's legendary maker, WWI fighter ace and team-builder extraordinaire, Captain Eddie Rickenbacker.

My first and only encounter with Colonel Borman, CEO of Eastern Airlines, is on October 10, 1984. In the company of thirty-three other new-hire pilots, the first group of pilots hired at Eastern in five depressing years, Frank walks into our lecture hall-sized classroom in Eastern's training center in Miami and utters these unforgettable words into the podium microphone. "Gentlemen, the good old days are over." I don't remember anything else he said. This is a gloomy way to start the airline career I've dreamt of for a lifetime.

Six weeks later, I graduate from training, and six months after that, get a letter in my company mailbox. It's from the director of Second Officer training for the Boeing 727 stating that due to the outstanding level of my performance during my check ride back in November, I'm being invited to join the training department as an instructor. I mull the idea over. Joining the instructor/management ranks will lose me valuable time on the *line* flying actual trips, but I'm convinced I've finally landed at my career airline and feel I should take advantage of every opportunity. Accumulating hours for my résumé no longer plays a role in my career path.

In August 1985, I arrive in Miami for instructor training. In the contract between Eastern Airlines and Eastern's Pilot's Union, there's a clause that says nobody can be an instructor with less than one year on the property. It doesn't say a probationary pilot can't work for the training department. He or she just can't teach. I find myself flying "blue side up" in the simulators until my year's probation ends. While new captains and first officers are training in the flight simulators, with engines blowing up or lighting on fire, hydraulic systems bursting and failing, cabin and cargo fires spontaneously igniting, and cabins explosively decompressing, somebody needs to be sitting in the "second officer's seat" also known as the flight engineer's seat, orchestrating the handling of the emergencies. That's my new job. It's nothing less than repetitive plunges into the most horrifying emergencies possible in the airplane—the very exercises I'd done so well during my own training. By the end of six months doing these stunts over and over, I can do them in my sleep.

After my own probationary check ride, the simulator evaluation all new hires must successfully complete before advancing to a tenured position, I'm ready to begin teaching and am well prepared given the vast exposure I've enjoyed in my "blue side up" position.

Unlike flying the line, instructors advance based on performance, not seniority, and my career path seems to advance steeply. Soon I'm in Check Airman school learning to give check rides instead of just teaching. Another year yields an invitation to become an FAA Designated Check Airman, a position that charges me with passing or failing applicants for their FAA Flight Engineer's license. In April of 1986, I'm awarded a bid for a First Officer's seat meaning I can go back to a pilot's "window" seat. Flight Engineers face sideways looking at a vast array of instruments, switches, dials, and gauges. They ensure all systems are operating normally, manage fuel, heating and cooling, cabin pressure, and become the main coordination element in emergencies. It's a fun and demanding job, but it's not flying and does little to sate a pilot's desire to fly. It's a mandatory starting point for every pilot hired by a major airline. Working in the training department pays a lot more and gives me far better control of my schedule. I spend eighty percent of my time in Miami teaching and checking. The benefits are irresistible, and my family life advances at least a decade beyond my "line" seniority.

On January 28th, 1986, I'm driving to Bradley International Airport fifteen miles north of Hartford, Connecticut. This is the airport from which I commute to get from my home in Norwich to Miami. Upon intercepting Interstate 91, northbound out of Hartford, I notice most oncoming traffic on the southbound side of the interstate has their headlights on. This is something I've never noticed before. I turn on the radio to see if there's any news to explain the oddity. At 11:38, just a few minutes ago, Christa McAuliffe and six other astronauts on the Space Shuttle Challenger "touched the Face of God," Ronald Reagan's words, in the year's first disaster, and people are asked to turn on their headlights to honor the lives tragically lost. I join the memorial and soon find tears streaming down my cheeks in tune with the national sadness.

Eastern's moniker seems official by mid-summer—"Financially troubled Eastern Airlines." Deregulation is giving license to new entrants into the airline business operating with business models that make profits impossible for established legacy carriers like EAL. Our CEO, Frank Borman, demands concessions from the unions across the board. Corporate survival is at stake, a claim easily corroborated. Pilots and flight attendants accept the stark reality and take a twenty percent pay cut that becomes effective the same day my twenty percent pay raise for upgrading kicks in. I end up with no raise but, looking at it from a glass-half-full viewpoint, don't suffer a pay cut either.

The International Association of Machinists, or IAM, under Charlie Bryan's leadership, represents Eastern's mechanics, cleaners, and baggage handlers. He holds out, refusing to budge on wages. Soon a strike looks likely. Most people disagree with Charlie's obstinance, but other circumstances make the looming job action minimally appealing. The strike is set to begin at one minute after midnight on March 24th. I'm teaching a "Period E" simulator session on Sunday, the day before, whose hours straddle the midnight hour. I'm told by union representatives that I'm allowed to finish my sim session even if a strike is called but must leave the property and not return afterward. The period ends at 2 a.m. After debriefing my students, I walk to the north gate en route to my crash pad just across 36th Street and ask the guard at the kiosk if a strike was called. He excitedly tells me no. He quickly adds that "some guy named Frank Lorenzo bought the airline." While I can't put this blow in the same category with the Challenger disaster, it rates an honorable mention in the department of calamities. It's only March. I pray the year's complexion doesn't continue to sour.

Lorenzo is well-known in the airline industry and looked upon by all rank-and-file workers as the anti-Christ. His ideas are based, at least in part, on Herb Kelleher's start-up, Southwest Airlines. Herb believes the pyramid of most business foundations is upside down. He espouses that if you treat your employees as the number one asset atop the scheme, they'll work hard, do a great job naturally attracting customers and, subsequently, investors. Lorenzo takes the opposite tack with adversarial tactics against his workers. Both models make money for the investor class. But Kelleher's makes money for everyone and makes flying cheap for customers. Lorenzo's "Peanuts" fares make flying low cost as well, but one company after another under his watch liquidates, putting tens of thousands of employees out of work while making Frank a very wealthy man. The countdown to perdition begins at 12:01 that March night, and we all know it.

Titanic battles wage between Lorenzo and our unions, as is this Harvard graduate's style. The price of food in the employee cafeteria doubles, and I notice the marble being removed from the walls of Eastern's terminal at JFK one day when arriving for my flight assignment. Lorenzo creates a holding company for fuel purchase, purportedly to leverage huge buying power and save money. The penny a gallon he charges for the service raises Eastern's fuel bill by over a million dollars a day. It goes right into Lorenzo and company's pockets. His conniving is blatant and multifarious and continues until the IAM's contract finally runs out. That gives them license to strike after all due process expires. All other Eastern unions can legally join the strike in "sympathy." On March 4th, 1989, a mammoth strike begins against Lorenzo. I walk the picket lines for a few months, but it soon becomes clear Lorenzo is going to take Eastern down. I'm never coming back and say farewell to Airline Job Number 3.

CHAPTER 12

INTO THE STORM – 75 MILES SOUTHWEST OF YAKUTAT SEPTEMBER 18, 1994

Without weather radar, I am blind to degrees of precipitation in the storm ahead. Radars work by returning signals from energy beams shot from an antenna, that bounce off things in their path. With weather radar, those "things" are raindrops. The bigger the drops, the more powerful the return and the brighter the picture "painted" on the radarscope. I can see none of this, and ATC has poor weather radar coverage in this area. I'm now flying by Braille.

Feeling committed, I request and receive a clearance to climb to fourteen thousand feet. According to the weather reports and forecast I got a couple of hours ago, that's above the icing. I turn on my pitot and fuel tank vent heaters and venture in. I don't feel good about it, but acceptable alternatives elude me. I'm not the first, nor will I be the last, to make this grave error.

Soon we begin picking up just a trace of ice, but it's "burning" off as fast as it's building from a process called ablation. No sweat, I can fly in this all day. At about three miles a minute, we're covering ground fast, and what lies ahead weather-wise is increasingly

uncertain. I can see the ambient temperature on my instrument panel, and turbulence gives me a good read on the strength of up and down drafts, which, so far, are light. I can also monitor icing on the wings from my seat. I continue hoping this icing encounter will be brief and remain insignificant. I'm trying to keep a big-picture awareness of how trends are developing.

ATC calls and directs me to contact them on the next sector's frequency in fifty miles, just shy of twenty minutes from now. I note the time is 12:22. I'll start attempting contact on the new frequency at 12:40.

CHAPTER 13
AIRLINE NUMBER 4 –
AMERICA WEST AIRLINES
1989 ~ 1991

Financial strains combine with growing domestic disputes that lead to divorce. It's probably fair to characterize this dissolution as about as amicable as they get. In the end I agree to pay child support 'til JM is through with high school, extending the judge's "18th birthday endpoint" by nine months. I feel desperately poor. I'm jobless, embarking on a two-thousand-mile move, and out a few months' worth of attorney's fees, but somehow I will manage my fatherly obligations.

After the final court hearing legally completes our severance, I take Fawn out to breakfast. Fawn has given up trying to "talk sense into me," so our conversation over scrambled eggs, hash browned potatoes, bacon, and two or three cups of black coffee is sedate. The fight is drained out of both of us, and it feels like healing must begin. No, *should* begin. I really need to let go of trying to control everything—that much I've learned. There's plenty of blame to go around coupled with a lot of unanticipated life changes; we both agree on that to greater and lesser degrees. What we completely agree on is that it was Camelot for a few precious years, that we still both drink our coffee only black, and that the worst casualties of this will be Gretchen, now sixteen years old, and JM, merely eight. Mostly young JM who's grown up masterfully skilled at hiding his feelings.

"I know I'm leaving you with a terrible burden, Fawn. But everything feels unalterable at this point. I know you've heard this too many times, but I'm gonna say it again anyway. If I don't get out of the east, I'll wither away to nothing. For years and years I put this airline career distantly ahead of every other consideration in my life. Where I lived hardly mattered compared to the job I found. I've come one hundred and eighty degrees to that, now realizing where I live means infinitely more than any job. I've gotta get back to my mountains." I trail off feeling like I'll cry if I try to say more.

Smiling weakly, Fawn interjects, "Yeah, I know all that, but you're still an asshole." The dam is broken, and we spend an hour reminiscing, laughing, and crying together. It's as good a rainbow as we're able to paint on this chapter's ending.

It's now more than three decades later. Fawn has been married to a wonderful Italian man nearly all that time, but I still feel bad about the suffering and hardship I left in my wake. Recalling these memories assures tears of sadness and glass-sharp fragments of guilt that slice deeply into my emotional bearing. That last day on Dudley Street remains vividly etched in me. Standing at my car, U-Haul attached, I wait. My heart feels like it's breaking. Fawn is intentionally not home. Gretchen waits inside. The big yellow school bus stops across the narrow street, and JM launches off the bottom step yelling "Daddy, daddy!" high hands trailing colorful, paper crafts he made in school. I put on a big smile and yell, "JM!" and wrap my arms around him, lifting him three feet off the ground spinning joyous circles. Crushing pain nearly cripples me, but I fight to keep the display alive, willing tear valves to stay shut. Still they leak as we *tour* my basement workshop, empty but for a small workbench with a little hammer and screwdriver left for him. Our words echo off stark concrete walls lending horror movie effects to this overwhelming playact. Hoping to impart a sense to him of being the new *man of the house,* I find the ground infertile, and my words blow away rootless with the dust. JM is fully aware of what's going on yet performs with equal conviction as if all's well and it's a happy day. This remains one of life's unhealable wounds.

Motoring away in my leased, bright red BMW 325, I'm bound for Park City, Utah. The relief of leaving the east coast, knowing I'll never again drive to work on Interstate 95, brings comfort enough to blight some of the guilt stuck in my heart.

From an eighteen hundred square foot home packed with furnishings, entertainment gear, tools, and an eight-year dissolved marriage, I'm down to what's in my car and a tiny trailer. I find a bedroom to rent in a small home right across the street from Park City's high school. I run. I run a lot. It's the only thing I can afford, and the hilly mountains near my home provide the perfect escape from the abyss of depression upon which I frequently teeter.

I find carpentry work in Salt Lake, twenty-five miles west, employed by old childhood friends anxious to help me get back on my feet. But it's time to get back to an interrupted career, and I'm sure if I can just find one more airline job, it'll be my last. I set my sights on America West Airlines based in Phoenix, AZ. They're a fast-growing, brash new airline company going head-to-head with Southwest Airlines. I figure if I send them a letter every day, they'll eventually succumb to my peskiness, and I'll get an interview. I don't quite manage a letter a day, but after twenty-eight of them over a couple of months, I get the desired results. Eight months and eighteen days after going on strike at Eastern, I get my new airline job.

They have a fleet of more than a hundred Boeing 737s, fifteen Boeing 757s, and a dozen twin turboprop De Havilland Dash 8s for short haul flights. They have also just leased two Boeing 747s from KLM out of Amsterdam. The first has yet to arrive. This time, the planes really are in the paint shop.

This is the first airplane AWA has ever owned that has a flight engineer position. In their hiring process, they're specifically on the lookout for pilots with Boeing flight engineer experience. I'm precisely what they're looking for, so when my phone rings in mid-November, they tell me I've got the job and will be starting as an FE, flight engineer, on the B747. I'm ecstatic. It's three days until my thirty-fifth birthday. This gift takes the cake for best present ever.

After six weeks of training, it's time to start flying. Seniority within your new-hire class at AWA is random, pulled from a hat. I fall toward the bottom of the list and that puts me on reserve. I don't get assigned trips. Instead I spend several days a week on standby in case they need a new FE at the last minute. I live in Park City and can't afford a crash pad or motels in Phoenix, the only base AWA has. I get up at 4 a.m. every day I'm on reserve, put on a fresh uniform and, with a packed bag, head to SLC. I take our 6 a.m. flight to PHX arriving well before my duty cycle begins. At 5 in the afternoon, if I haven't been used, I fly back to SLC, drive to Park City, and repeat. It's a terrible way to make a living, but my choices are limited given my financial and seniority status. New-hire pilots make a pittance. This is standard throughout the airline industry. That first year is kind of a torture test. If you'll suffer it, you get to enjoy significantly better benefits later.

Most of the other reserve pilots didn't just come from a bankrupt airline, a failed marriage, and a two-thousand-mile move. Most of them have moved to Phoenix and wait at home for the phone call if they're needed. By contract, we have ninety minutes after the call to report for duty at the base. On two occasions, I'm called out but I'm in the pilot lounge in uniform chomping at the bit to get a trip. In both cases I was on the flight deck within minutes, and the flights left right on time. The only flights the 747 does are to Honolulu, and vacationers don't want to be late.

This gets management's attention, and some sterling letters land in my file.

With my spare time wandering the halls of the base, I become acquainted with a lot of management people. The FAA is unhappy with the lack of a management pilot atop the ranks of the 747 flight engineers, so a new Chief FE position is open for bid. AWA is a non-union airline, so bids for such positions are awarded by merit, not seniority. With my good standing and background in management in Boeing FE operations, I get the job. It comes with a raise and infinitely better control of my schedule.

The first order of my new job is to rewrite the Aircraft Operating Manual, a several hundred-page manual describing precisely how the airplane works and how we will operate it. Presently we simply have an old Pan Am manual brought to us by the ground school instructor they've hired, an ex-Pan Am instructor. I'm to write the new manual so it matches the operating philosophy specified for all other AWA aircraft to as great a degree as possible.

The only English class I ever enjoyed in college was called "Technical Writing." It was great preparation for this mammoth task. Concurrent with my writing duties, I'm to form standards by which we train and execute every aspect of the job. I probably spend an average of nine to ten hours a day, but they're hours at my home in Park City. It becomes unusual that I need to be present in PHX with the widespread use of FAX machines. I finish the project in a few months and then take on the task of standardizing how all the simulator training is done. I travel constantly to our simulator training center in Newark, NJ. I also do standardization rides and line training in the airplanes back and forth to Honolulu. In the last few months, we've taken delivery of two more 747s from KLM, bringing our fleet to four.

These 747s are supposed to be flying lucrative trips to Japan. Initially, management imagined we'd be flying them to Tokyo's Narita airport. Then they found out the waiting list for a slot in NRT was years. They finally got authorization from the Japanese Civil Aeronautics Board to serve Nagoya. Delta Air Lines had recently been awarded a route from Portland, via Honolulu, to Nagoya. They were operating it with a more economical MD-11. We were flying PHX, HNL, NGO with nearly empty 747s. Delta's reservations network and acumen for international travel dwarfed ours. Almost exactly concurrent with our authority to start flying to Japan, the first Gulf War began. Add to AWA's financial strain of operating these 747s an FAA mandate that we leave our jumbos on their existing progressive maintenance schedules, meaning they had to ferry to Amsterdam from time to time for KLM to do the heavy maintenance, and those behemoths are putting quite a dent in the company's bottom line. Likewise, competition from Southwest and other airlines in this time of economic contraction is hitting us hard.

Rumors of financial struggle begin to circulate the employee ranks. In the fall of 1991, I start receiving phone calls from a recruiting company staffing pilots for contracts with Japan Airlines. They want status reports on some of the flight engineers working for me. Obviously, people are beginning to jump ship. I field these calls for about a month and realize I probably ought to climb onto this exodus. One day when the recruiting company calls, I ask if I can get an interview. The next Tuesday, I'm at a long table in a conference room in Los Angeles seated with two English-speaking recruiters from IASCO, a Foster City, CA, crew leasing company, and six Japanese gentlemen from Japan Airlines. Two weeks after that I fly to Tokyo for a flight evaluation. One of the more comical instances of my career is this evaluation flight, done in a simulator that convincingly mimics flight in an actual airplane. I'm the only non-Japanese person in the simulator. There's a captain, first officer, simulator operator, and three evaluators aboard. We get through all the briefings, little of which I understand, and line up on a runway at Tokyo's Haneda airport. The captain applies takeoff thrust, and we blast down the runway and into the sky. My job is to demonstrate competence at the massive flight engineer's panel decorated with hundreds of switches, buttons, and gauges.

747 Flight Engineer's panel. Author pictured.

Modern day simulators are perched on enormous hydraulic jacks that precisely follow control inputs from the cockpit, so the thing literally tips up skyward on takeoff. As soon as the first officer retracts the eighteen-wheeled landing gear, I hear click, click, click, click, click, click. It's the sound of six Bic lighters lighting six cigarettes. This is when I learn that nearly every man in Japan still smokes, and while JAL's rules prohibit smoking during taxi and takeoff, they're free to smoke once airborne. They treat the simulator just like a real airplane and faithfully follow the company's rules. Once airborne, every single one of them lights up, and my eyes begin to water from forest-fire quantities of smoke. I survive only because I've been instructing and checking other engineers on this airplane for two years. I know it intimately, and JAL's hiring guidelines allow me to use the company procedures I'm accustomed to. On January 15, 1992, I start training at JAL, Airline Number 5, and say goodbye to bankrupt America West.

CHAPTER 14
DIVE FOR LIFE
SEPTEMBER 18, 1994

Our freezing tomb dims by the second. The cloud mass is getting thicker, now the dark purple of a mature black eye. The braying of ice-filled air beats against our airplane and into our eardrums in unrelenting terror. There's no question now that we're in a dive for life, and like a nightmare, no matter which way I run, the cloud gets thicker and ice gets worse.

Screaming through 10,000 feet I wonder, is this vicious din retreating? A check of the outside temperature reads +11. Only 21 degrees to go to get to freezing, clearly trending the right way. Still no tell-tale sign of this dense monster thinning. It's as dark and cold as Alta's abandoned mine shafts in our confines.

Eight thousand feet, temperature 18 degrees. The outside color is changing. More purple, less black.

Six thousand feet, temperature 25 degrees, purple waxing toward iron-gray, concentration intent—SURVIVE!

I can think of nothing else to do but steady our dive, watching and praying for hopeful signs.

BAM! A chunk of ice separates from one of the propeller blades and slams into the side of the plane six inches from my mother's head. A terrible vibration feels like a washboard dirt road at twenty miles an hour in a truck with no shocks and one flat tire. It's hard to focus with all the vibration. One blade now weighs a few ounces less than its companions. BAM, BAM, THUD, BAM! It sounds like we're under assault from machine gun fire. Mom and Dad duck instinctively. I try to yell over the shocking refrain that this is good. "Hang on, we're shedding ice!"

Four thousand feet, 32 degrees. Ice still flinging wildly off the propeller blades and bashing at the airplane like a SWAT team trying to slug through the fuselage. Mom is now doubled over. I can feel the bulge of her head pushing into the back of my seat. In addition to being terrified, I'm heartbroken that I am putting her, them, us, through this. All my machismo is gone. There's no more joking about flying prowess. The illusion of invincibility is long gone with nothing but remorse left in its place.

Three thousand feet, it's definitely getting lighter. Iron-gray turns perceptibly to pearl. Outside air temperature is 34 degrees. Ice begins to break away from the wings. The propellers have shed clean and the vibration is gone.

Two thousand feet. The ice on the windshield is peeling away in book-sized chunks starting in the middle and working outward. From the corner of my overworked eyes, I can see my father watching intently, brave enough to bear witness to this climactic ending, maybe of his life. It's 36 degrees.

There's a lot of potential variation between indicated altitude and actual altitude. Barometric pressure and temperature changes can swing wide the berth separating them. While the altimeter reads eighteen hundred feet, we might be lower. A lot lower. I think I see a flash of the sea. Our wings are clean. I feel confident I can pull some "g" force on the airplane with harder back-pressure on the yoke with no danger of stalling. I begin a moderate pull up. Our bodies feel half again their regular weight as I load up the wings and arrest our descent. I retract the landing gear. The cacophony retreats, and I spot an angry, white-capped, blue-green sea a thousand feet below. I can see we're below a ragged cloud base spitting wide swaths of rain here and there. The danger of icing is past, and we're now flying visually below the cloud with plenty of margin between our belly and the choppy gulf. My relief seems reluctant to burst through a membrane of shock. Minutes ago, our frantic dive and death's resolute, obstinate path seemed all but certain to merge. Panic was knocking loud at my mind's door. Only merciful bursts of adrenaline fostered enough wit to allow logic to reign over terror. We'll live to tell this tale.

For what seems a long time, library-quiet pervades the confines of our cocoon. Only the purr of those Lycoming engines rends the silence. Deep contemplation seems to visit each of us. For me, I can't believe how close I just came to extinguishing our three lives. Our burial at sea would almost certainly remain merely conjecture as little chance exists our remains would ever be found. What great care, I surmise, it takes to avoid deadly misfortune.

But it's time to continue living, and I'm still in charge of that. I turn off the heating elements that sustained our lives through the tenacious ice storm in which we've been encased for the last twenty minutes. I still have a battery to baby, though it's not necessary, as it is in automobiles, for our twenty-four sparkplugs to continue firing. That critical function is entrusted to magnetos, mounted on and driven directly by the engines. These grapefruit-sized accessories create their own energy through a microcosm of springs, wire coils, and permanent magnets.

I look next at the ammeters whose needles still rest sleepily on zero. I repeat steps to reactivate them, and finally ice-free, the field relays accept electrical current and they both zing back to life.

My battery begins recharging immediately, and my dead instruments tuck their red warning flags back inside their cases and resume operating normally.

I can't see land on any horizon, but know it lies not far east, and I bank right to point north of that direction. In a few minutes its blurred anatomy begins to appear, barely discernible, through light rain. Upon reaching the coast, I turn left following it north-west. In five more minutes, Yakutat appears ten or twelve miles ahead.

Static in my earphones tells me the tangles of wire and transis-tors in my radios have re-flooded with 28 volts of electricity. On the frequency on which we'd tried to check in fifteen minutes ago, I hear an American Airlines flight repeatedly calling us in the blind: "November-one-seven-delta-lima, this is American 7474, do you read? Over." Anchorage Center, having lost radar and radio con-tact with us elicits American's help in searching the airwaves for us. Their high altitude gives them far greater VHF communications range than the ATC guy on the ground. I respond professionally, but my insides are doing backflips. "American 7474, November-one-seven-delta-lima reads you 5 by 5. Go ahead please."

"November-one-seven-delta-lima, Anchorage Center has been looking for you on 125.5. They need to know your position and altitude, over."

I explain our electrical failure, icing emergency, my subsequent emergency descent, and present position and altitude. Through AA7474, Anchorage gives a new clearance to climb to 4,000 feet and check in on 124.85 in five minutes. Once radar contact is re-established, they'll give me directions regarding airways naviga-tion. I acknowledge, turn the pitot and fuel vent heat back on, and begin a climb back into the clouds believing 4,000' to be below the icing hazard. Even with no ice, merely penetrating into the cloud causes both alternators to fail almost immediately. I urgently reverse our climb to descent, this time knowing full details of what lies below. Once in the clear, my field relays easily reset, and I'm back to a fully intact electrical system. I realize we're stuck with visual flying for the rest of this trip. Doug's mechanic can sort out 17DL's electrical problems once we get back to Anchorage.

I advise AA7474 we're unable to fly on instruments and tell them to relay to Anchorage Center that we'll proceed visually to Anchorage International. The American flight relays Center's request that I set my radios to convey I'm flying visually and switch to the local air to air frequency to listen for other VFR traffic in the area. Before severing communications with American, I give them an ETA for Anchorage and tell them I can't count on my alternators and, hence, my radios. I asked them to pass my information to Anchorage Center and have them forward it to Anchorage Tower. Forewarned with my ETA and possible radio outage, they can be ready with light signals to clear us to land once we're in range of the airport. I offer heartfelt gratitude to American for their help and sign off.

By now the shock is waning, and subdued conversation begins after the dispassionate communications settling our immediate business. Not entirely dispassionate. The inflection I hear in the American pilot's voice is noticeably laced with surprise and solace. They had been trying to raise us for more than ten minutes. Images of catastrophe are easily conceived in this environment.

Yakutat has a good airport and maybe even a decent electronics technician. Aware that IFR flight is no longer an option, we have a decision to make, and I put it to vote.

"Hey Mom 'n Dad, I know we just went through a rough ride and a good scare. Now that we're safely out of all that ice, I've been able to reset the alternators and everything's back to normal. You can feel the heater's kicked back on so you'll probably be peeling some layers soon. We just passed Yakutat and there's a good airport down there. Maybe even a good avionics technician. We can turn around and be on the ground in just a few minutes. We could take a break, see if there's a mechanic, and maybe grab some food. Or we can head home. I just checked the GPS, and we're only about 370 miles from Anchorage. With maneuvering to get through the mountains, at our speed, we can be there in about two hours. We have about three and a half hours of gas remaining. What do you guys wanna do?"

"Do you think there's a bar with good Scotch down there?" my mom only half-jokingly asks. My dad smiles affirming he's of a similar mind. I'm taking a sabbatical from alcohol but totally relate to their current mindset.

"I kinda doubt it. But I can have you in my kitchen with a roaring fire in the fireplace in about three hours. I know you packed your booze, and I wish it was accessible. This is no airliner, and I'd be happy to let you mix drinks right here 'n now. But I fear we have some more bumps ahead, and it would look mighty bad for me if we showed up in a plane smelling like whiskey."

"Let's head for your place—all ahead full!" shouts my mom recalling some apropos nautical adage.

It's unanimous; we're heading home.

Our lungs gulp oxygen now with the aid of full atmospheric pressure, absorbing it like a Sahara pilgrim who's just discovered water. Our arteries quickly flood with normal levels of oxygenated blood, and we begin shaking off sense-dulling lethargy. My folks believe I just saved the day, discounting that it was my foolishness that nearly killed us. I warily accept their praise only because my ego needs time to absorb a full accounting of what I've done. There's another aviation axiom that states, *Good judgment comes mostly from experience and most experience comes from bad judgment.* I'm living testament. This experience changes me for life and gradually dumps my ego to a new station more conducive to an aviator's long life.

When within two hundred miles of Johnstone Point, I receive its electronic highway information and easily beeline straight for it. The serenity of the Prince William Sound, sans Exxon Valdez's eleven million gallons of crude oil, appears sublime ahead. Views in all directions are spellbinding, and I get to show off, after all, the wilds of Alaska to parents responsible for my privileged life.

We fly through several mountain passes with no more than a couple of wingspans separating us from the ground. Twice we pass oncoming float planes heading the opposite way, also hugging the terrain to get passengers to planned destinations. My nap-of-the-earth flying skills serve us effectively, now allowing confident low-level aviating, The terrain whisks by below eliciting amusement park excitement coupled with staggering scenery. Even my white-knuckle mother thrills in the excursion.

Twenty minutes from Ted Stevens International airport, Whittier passes below our nose, and we clearly see a late season Princess Cruise ship readying for sail to Vancouver. I hope they avoid sailing below flying ice blocks dropped from foolish airplanes.

The next several minutes gift us with breathtaking views of deep canyons honeycombing granite mountains that crawl with live glaciers. Now topography approaches of which I am well acquainted. Portage Pass and the Turnagain Arm soon sail below, and after that, Girdwood at the base of Anchorage's ski area, Alyeska. We marvel at a new aerial tramway scaling a steep cirque on this alpine sanctuary, and I know we've made it home.

Ten minutes later, we arrive over the outer limits of Anchorage neighborhoods. I pull the power back to slow as the airport races toward us.

The tower is expecting me to be NORAD, no radio, so flashes a steady green, "Cleared to land" light signal aimed precisely at the Commander. Our alternators failed again several minutes ago and will no longer accept field energizing current. That trusty battery, however, has life enough to allow two-way radio communication, and I call the tower to advise.

I wonder if they're disappointed. It's so unusual to need such antiquated communications equipment in this modern age. I'll bet they needed to read up on light-signal codes to prepare for us and may have been looking forward to an actual opportunity to test rusty skills.

They clear us to land on runway 25R, the same runway, opposite direction, I'd departed six days ago in 999GB. My heart soars when, three hours and fifty-six minutes after departing Sitka, our tires screech onto the black asphalt. Both of my parents cheer, clap, and shine in dignified repose. I rollout to taxiway Mike to simplify my taxi routing back to Lake Hood where Doug's hangar stands waiting.

Three days later my schedule installs me into JA8160, a cavernous Boeing 747, to haul a couple of hundred thousand pounds of cargo to Tokyo in furtherance of international commerce.

In the meantime, my parents and I revel in celebration for a couple of tranquil days exploring the frontier feel that Anchorage offers. As promised, we're ensconced in my home, securely affixed to the ground, by early evening that first day, and a few cocktails work their magic, melting away stresses I orchestrated earlier. In the morning, we barnstorm Anchorage with energy widely familiar to survivors of near-death encounters. Starting with a drive along the Seward Highway to Alyeska ski resort, we see the fathomless spectacle of the Turnagain Arm from a few feet away and then ride a tram to great heights on the mountain. During ascent we pass over a mother grizzly and her two cubs, something I've never seen. This is precisely the show I had in mind.

Returning to the sprawling canvas of Anchorage, seemingly spread endlessly in all directions, we visit a particularly close friend high in the Hillside neighborhood. Larry's views are spellbinding in every direction. The price of the perspective includes building codes requiring 250-mile-per-hour roofs to tolerate the venturi accelerated winds screaming off the Chugach mountains upon whose flanks we're perched.

"Hi, Neef and Shirlee. We knew Andrew before he decided to mimic marathon runners with his scrawny new body," Larry chortles. He loves ribbing me about all the weight I'm losing in a health campaign I've engaged. My folks are deeply taken with him and his quirky humor as is nearly everyone who gets to meet this hard laughing, Vietnam surviving, transplanted New Englander.

A nearly empty bottle of Tramin Pinot Grigio and a freshly opened bottle of Kim Crawford Sauvignon Blanc adorn our elegantly set table at Simon and Seafort's restaurant this evening. Dazzling views overlook waters of the Cook Inlet where the Knik Arm wanders northeast diverging at right angles from Turnagain. Baked sea bass for Dad and me and boiled lobster tail for my mother brings a new peak to the concept of fine dining for all of us. "So Mom, *this* is what I was trying to describe when we had lunch at Sitka yesterday."

Drawn butter cuts glistening streams down from both corners of her lips as she cherishes the prized meal with such euphoric delight she can't be bothered with anything but a smile, uncaring about whatever coats her chin. Finally swallowing and wiping the delicious butter with an aloe vera infused wipe, she offers assurances that nothing she's ever eaten can match this exquisite delicacy. I knew she'd *get it* if we survived long enough to get here. My dad is equally entranced, and our silent table bespeaks the epic nature of the cuisine on which we feast. The colors on the sea in the endless twilight, ambiance in our shared, cozy booth, and the love we're sharing bring a trifecta of unforgettable perfection to these moments only lives so intimately tangled, with nearly simultaneous conclusions, can contrive.

Day two finds us walking downtown where hanging flower baskets adorning every streetlight bring civic awards to Anchorage each year. We make our way to 2nd Avenue at the northern end of the city and follow it west to the Tony Knowles Coastal Trail. This eleven-mile jaunt stays constantly populated with outdoor enthusiasts. Part of it fronts "Earthquake Park" where an entire neighborhood fell into the sea in 1964's massive earthquake. An invigorating walk is overly taxing for my mother, so I leave them at a picnic table and run back to fetch my Isuzu Trooper for ambulance duty.

At day's end, I drive them to the airport to board their Alaska Airlines red-eye flight to Sea-Tac airport, where they'll pick up their Pathfinder and drive eight hours home to Victor, Montana, and resume lives in the mellowing years left to them.

There's something empowering and deeply humbling about facing death at such close quarters. Something of great value, though I'm happy to wait a good long time for its next visit. My parents have both faced that reaper for the last time since then, but maybe, after our ride, it was less fearsome. I was with each of them when they passed, seven years apart. In both instances, I thought of our terrifying ride all those years before on that autumn afternoon and wondered if they remembered that old scythe carrier when he appeared, from that frenetic day. "Hey Death, what's happening?"

Both my mother and father later admitted they thought we were going to die in that wild dive from the sky. That our mad dive would end in a gigantic splash, and we'd be snuffed out together in the freezing waters below. They both shared that it was somehow not the terror they'd always imagined. That they'd been ready and if they had to die, why not in the company of those they loved. It was almost comforting, they said.

My soul has some climbing ahead to reach the elevated levels theirs achieved by the ends of their lives. That humbling day so long ago added some valuable arrows to my quiver, and with them, I intend to aim better. While my lifestyle is unlikely to enter a meek or mild stage anytime soon, wiser eyes and a faded ego should guide me to safer harbors and smoother sailing in the future. With deep reverence and abiding honor for their memories, I hope my folks sit in lofty perches somewhere, enjoying the view. In whatever lies "after," I don't expect they've settled down much either. It's not their way. In that place, I hope they think to check on me from time to time. I could use some of that poise and discernment they demonstrated in their corporeal bodies. I'll watch carefully for a little nudge and turn that direction in grateful compliance. Just as in life, I look forward to that light-handed push toward brightness, and a more cushioned stroll down the byways of my life.

CHAPTER 15
JAPAN AIRLINES – AIRLINE JOB NUMBER 5
1992

Concluding a long period of revolutions in Eastern European Bloc countries, President Ronald Reagan *invites* Soviet General Secretary Mikhail Gorbachev to "tear down this wall." On November 9, 1989, down comes the first domino—The Berlin Wall. The entire Iron Curtain collapses in its wake ending a cold war that's lasted since the end of WWII.

During the Cold War years, NATO aircraft are denied permission to overfly any Soviet soil, requiring them to fly circuitous routes over polar regions. No aircraft from that era had the endurance to fly nonstop between Asia, Europe, and the US mainland. Subsequently, Anchorage became the universal midroute "gas station."

After the Iron Curtain falls, passenger flights can navigate across Siberia and make these flights nonstop. Cargo, per square foot, weighs many times more than passengers. It's more economical to cram the jet's mammoth caverns full to the brim with cargo and put less fuel in the tanks, so to this day, cargo flights fly the longer polar routes and stop for gas in ANC.

JAL has decided to establish a crew base in ANC to facilitate their profitable cargo enterprise. Given their distaste for both icy flying conditions and *gaijins,* a derogatory term for non-Japanese, they staff the new base with us which was the motivation behind the huge new contract for foreign pilots. It's why I have a job.

I'm employed to haul a hundred tons of freight at a time between Anchorage, Frankfurt, London, Paris, and Tokyo. It's a dream job complete with extraordinary perks.

JAL doesn't particularly like employing non-Japanese but can't recruit and train their own countrymen as fast as their airline's expansion demands. The arduous seven-month training course in Tokyo inducts me into a culture more severe than I'd imagined. I suspect its roots evolve from the Samurai nobility of medieval times.

Challenges are intentionally harsh in friendless student/Sensei intercourse, more so given I'm from the country that dropped atomic bombs on them. I swallow unending humility, brave vision-blurring hours of reading, and suffer endless memorization exercises to matriculate through the rigorous syllabus demanded daily. I'm afraid of my teachers as is their intent. My first Japanese words get polished quickly—*Gomen nasai,* meaning "sorry," *I'll study harder next time.* Any foreigner intending to get through this program knows and repeats this mantra often. Contract pilots are fired almost daily for invisible infractions. I'm ensnared in their web but realize well its bounty. I'm willing to endure a lot of drudgery to succeed.

There are considerable rewards during this difficult academic venture, however. Near my hotel in Narita, a rural enclave forty miles from Tokyo's urban prefectures, I discover jogging paths among rice paddies complete with stooped, seemingly ancient women bent over, knee-deep in ponds, long sleeves hanging open, tending crops.

Rice paddies set between rolling hills, accessed by service roads just wide enough for golfcart-sized farmers' vehicles, leave off where a quiet neighborhood begins. Set back a dozen yards off the street, I come upon a prize few non-Japanese have ever seen. An architecturally magnificent framework rises from an exquisitely crafted stone foundation. I'm astounded to realize I'm witness to a traditional Japanese-style, post and beam home under construction. I'm mesmerized by laboring carpenters, walking and working the structure like spiders confidently dancing their webs. The scent of Hinoki Cypress, returning to Japan after over-harvesting during WWII, wafts from skillfully cut and chiseled timbers. I'm awed to watch, realizing the skills of these sukiya-daiku, or residential carpenters, are learned from masters over decades.

As I gawk in fascination, work stops and all eyes are on me. Not many gaijins around here, and I'm eyed with suspicion. I feel like I've interrupted a sacred ritual and resume my run, sorry for not being able to spend the day with these master craftsmen. But the discovery is unforgettable, and my stays in Narita are frequent. The sukiya-daiku never invite me for tea, but their disquiet at my presence ebbs in time, and I get as close as a gaijin can ever hope to watching an edifice of precision joinery, not a steel nail or spike ever used, become a breathtaking home. This is only a sampling of the culturally unique awards I receive during my years with JAL.

After training in Tokyo, I return to Park City and pack the few belongings I have and begin a three-thousand-mile road trip to Anchorage. First stop, St. Anthony, Idaho, to pick up my ten-year-old son, JM, at his grandparents' home. We make a week's adventure out of the expedition every day, plugging cassettes into my *new* used Isuzu Trooper's tape deck. The Indigo Girls seem to be taking first place in the *choice of the day* department, and luckily, I have two of their longest albums and neither JM nor I tire easily of repetition. I start every morning's drive with "What do you wanna hear?" and every day I get the same answer—"The Girls!"

At the Canadian border, a Mountie asks us a handful of questions. Everything's going fine until he directs his gaze at JM and asks, "Son, does your mom know where you are?" JM looks at me, unsure how to answer. The Mountie notices this immediately and invites us to park "right over there and come with me." JM's terrified. I'm not sure how this is going to end. We get a private audience with the supervisor who needs to determine whether there's a kidnapping in progress.

Our innocent natures and plausible story soon convince him nothing nefarious is taking place, and he elects to let us pass. He cautions that in the future, if I do something like this again, I get a notarized note from JM's mom assuring authorities he's traveling with her permission. He also warns us that Canadians are easy, but US border authorities, not so much. We're promised a likely unpleasant standoff with border inspectors when we re-enter the US in Alaska. Pondering my missing note from Fawn, I begin wondering, if you add innocent, silly, reckless, and stupid, how many mistakes are possible in one human lifetime?

The adventuring along the Alcan Highway is a magnificent highlight in both our lives, but its end point is approaching as we near the Alaskan border and we both begin to worry what's going to happen. Finally, we arrive and are number four in line to speak to the customs officer who's standing outside his kiosk on this beautiful, bluebird day.

"Daddy, what if that man doesn't let us in? I'm kinda scared," JM whispers.

"I'll tell you what, let's just be nice and truthful and see what happens. I'm quite sure there won't be a problem. And if he asks, you can tell him Mom knows you're with me on this trip," I suggest with more bravado than what's truly cooking inside.

Arriving at the front of the line, I put down my window and offer the crisply uniformed man both my driver's license and passport, intending to be as cooperative and forthcoming as possible. I'm guessing he's in his midfifties and looks very conservative with a military haircut and clean-shaven face. His name tag says Officer Bradley. He surveys the car and us, then calmly asks:

"Mr. Walker, what business brings you and this young man to Alaska?"

"Well, Officer Bradley, my son, JM, and I are traveling together on a relocation adventure. I'm moving to Anchorage which is my new base. I'm a pilot for Japan Airlines," I explain.

Now he's perplexed as it's clear I'm not Japanese so why...

I offer, "JAL is starting a new pilot base here and has hired about two hundred pilots to staff it. You'll be seeing several more of us arriving in the coming weeks."

"I see," he says. "Hello, JM. I'm Officer Bradley. Is this your first time to Alaska, and where's your home?"

JM really doesn't want to screw this up, so he answers directly albeit it with almost hoarse tremolo infused in his voice. He's scared. "Sir, this is my first trip to Alaska in my whole life, and I live in Connecticut with my mom and sister."

I'm so proud I could pop. JM has been comfortable calling people *sir* and *ma'am* from his earliest speech, and that habit just paid handsomely.

Now Officer Bradley turns his attention back to me.

"Mr. Walker, I need you to hold your hands out the window where I can see them." *Holy cow*, I think. *Does he think I'm packing a gun? Is he gonna cuff me?*

Puzzled, I comply. He studies them for a few seconds and tells us we're free to go. Whew! Boldly tempting fate, I ask him about this curious check. His disarming smile settles my jitters, and he explains that it stems from thirty plus years of border work.

"I've learned to assess the honesty of people's claims by the perspiration on their hands. It's almost foolproof."

Both JM and I smile and wish this kind man a great day as we motor across the border into Alaska, USA. We're grateful today wasn't Bradley's day off.

On August 19th, the day after Mt. Spurr erupts sending inches of volcanic ash down on hundreds of square miles in the vicinity, JM and I pull into Anchorage's city center. Even with the recent celestial litter rained by mischievous gods too bored to find something better to do, it's as pristine and enchanting as anyplace I've ever seen. I form an instant bond with the city—kind of like a crush. It lasts. It's still there.

We find a motel and get settled in, then go exploring. For two days we amble around the city. It's tempting to say "the city and its surroundings" but that would be technically inaccurate. Anchorage is the fourth biggest city in America following Sitka, Juneau, and Wrangell. Apparently, Alaskans are loath to be dividing up their municipalities, so they just let 'em run. Anchorage is 1,961 square miles, making it about five times the size of Dallas. We go to every museum we can find. The one celebrating Alaska's earthquakes ranks as most spectacular of all. The proprietor suggests that if you feel nausea during the flight movie, simply close your eyes. It's shocking how real the low flight down Alaskan rivers is and how deeply your stomach gets involved. He also warns we'll be getting a taste of Alaska's 1964 earthquake, a 9.2 magnitude, the second largest ever recorded. We'll only get 5.0, but you must wear a seatbelt. When the tremor hits, you're glad you did.

A few days pass too quickly before I must put JM on a flight back to his home in Connecticut. I've never seen him so animated so many hours and days in a row. He's loved every minute and expresses it, unusual for his normally quiet nature. "This is the BEST, Daddy!" I've heard him say a dozen times in the last few days. Our mutual sentimentality diminishes as departure time approaches. We both shy from getting too emotional at the last minute as if denying our hurt will make it go away. It doesn't, but it's just how we've always addressed separating, clear back to that remorseful day on Dudley Street.

After losing sight of him making his way down the jetway, I go home and mope around for a couple of days, assuaging my loss and reliving the memories with great fervor. Soon enough it's time to get to work, and those happy memories settle into the background of my life.

The whole ANC cargo base plan doesn't go quite as efficiently as planned, so JAL decides to thin it considerably. Their Honolulu base is thriving, and they decide to shift a bunch of assets from ANC to HNL. I'm included in that reallocation.

In April of 1995, only two years and eight months after engaging this love affair with Anchorage, IASCO sends movers to my home, and I board a plane to Honolulu, my new base. It's a sweet gig as most would agree, but my heart lies in the last frontiers of Alaska.

I settle in quickly on the Windward side of Oahu and find a great little cottage half a block from the snowy white beaches of Lanikai. In a particularly buff stage of my life, I seek out an aerobics studio. There's one two miles away in Kailua, and one of its instructors knocks Anchorage well into the background of my heart. "Yeah, this place won't be so bad," I decide.

Kimberly and I become close, and a romance evolves. She's a veterinarian and deeply spiritual, in a really cool way. She's eleven years my junior clocking in at twenty-nine, and would likely put the entire Barbie line out of business if Mattel could only see her. One day when I'm checking in for a trip at the HNL airport, Jean, the secretary, shares that "last night I had a dream with your Kimberly in it." In mock jealousy I demand, "What are you doing with my flame in YOUR dreams!" The chief pilot overhears the exchange and emerges from his office declaring, "Andy, we ALL have Kimberly in our dreams," then smiles and returns to his office. A year into our liaison, she talks me into taking a trip to Kauai which turns into a cottage on a little inland lake on its north shore. There my girlfriend finds the life she's been seeking, and soon I find myself moved far onto the periphery of her regard.

As if written into my life's script to save me from too much despair, JAL decides it's time for me to upgrade from flight engineer to first officer. That buys me seven months in Tokyo pedaling as fast as I can to stay afloat, and Kimberly drops off my radar.

With training complete and a brand-new Japanese-issued Boeing 747 Type Rating added to my collection, I decide to move as far from Kauai as the island state will allow. The Big Island's Kamuela puts 289 miles of separation between us. Everything's going great except for the smoldering hole in my heart. Phone calls and emails shrink the berth separating us to zero. Maybe absence made her heart grow fonder, or she wasn't a hundred percent good with the full split. Whatever it is, her words and tenor say, "why don't you come back to Kauai."

Two years in Kamuela have strengthened my character. I feel more complete and confident but, in quiet times—bountiful in that I live alone—I feel a strong tug pulling me, like a tractor beam, constantly toward my Kauaian animal doctor. My phone rings with Kimberly's special ringtone more and more frequently.

"Hi, Andy," her honey-rich voice intones, immediately warming my heart. "Just checking in wondering how you're doing. Are you home for a few days? It's beautiful here on Kauai today. Do you think you'll ever come over to visit?"

I can't resist her charms. Our conversations feel romantic, and I feel invited to call her whenever the urge strikes. It's a lot. Eventually I feel persuaded to visit, and that quickly ripens into a move. We've decided I should come back to help her and an old friend of hers build a temple. I'm deeply intrigued. For one thing, it'll get me back into Kimberly's world where I can enjoy a flame that's never really extinguished, and the temple's architecture will closely mimic Japanese building styles—something I really yearn to be part of.

There are modest flickers of romance going on between us, but it's stymied and unfulfilling. Numerous obstacles impede its flowering, primary among them, her friend David, who has been her spiritual guide for years. It was only with his assent that Kimberly ever "explored" a relationship with me in the first place. David and I have a lot in common, but he knows about the strong feelings that exist between Kimberly and me and seems threatened by them. He carefully guards against us having alone time. His efforts stifle the romance, and I've come to feel duplicitous just feeling the way I do. Our trinity is often strained, tranquility fleeting. I find Crosby, Stills, Nash & Young's "Triad" weaving through my thoughts, questioning *what's the harm in going on as three* increasingly, and realize how much easier it is to sing than live. At least the temple project is incredibly fulfilling, and that makes up for some of the disappointment of our languishing liaison.

I have felt like a bastard stepchild at JAL for years. We gaijin are never really part of the JAL family. We're more like "Mikey" from the cereal advertisement. Give us the crappy stuff, we'll "Like it." I don't, and their abuse seems to be bolder lately, showing up most recently in unbearable schedules.

While JAL's pilots have a strong union representing them, contract pilots have none. Years ago, a group of IASCO flight engineers attempted to organize, and they were all summarily fired the moment word leaked. I assume JAL and IASCO get away with this through some complex interpretation of international labor laws.

In April of 2000, JAL unilaterally adds a new flight pattern to IASCO's Honolulu flying. It would be completely illegal under US rules and would be laughed off the table by the Japanese unions. Springtime still poses powerful jet stream winds to westerly flights, so the HNL to Osaka trips typically take about nine hours. I live on the north shore of The Big Island giving me a half hour drive to the Kona airport. Allowing for all contingencies, I must awaken five hours before scheduled departure time. I'm in the majority of contract pilots in choosing to live on outer islands because of the lower cost of living and a more authentic Hawaiian lifestyle compared to the megacity feel of much of Oahu.

By the time we land, my day is fourteen hours old. Normally we would be bused thirty minutes to a hotel in Osaka to begin a thirty-two-hour layover. This is an ordinary duty period for international pilots for which none would complain. But our new pattern has us stay at Kansai airport for an hour and a half to catch a ride to Haneda, Tokyo's domestic airport, on All Nippon Airways. It's a two-hour trip including boarding, disembarking, and taxi time. At HND we pull our bags, packed for a six-day trek, to a bus stop and wait half an hour for a bus that will take us to Narita, Tokyo's international airport, from which we'll be flying to Bangkok tomorrow evening. The ride is one hour and fifteen minutes. At NRT we disgorge with our baggage and make our way to another bus stop where, after twenty minutes or so, we board another bus that will take us to the Nikko Narita, our layover hotel. We drag into the front desk about midnight to check in with a twenty-hour day creeping behind us.

I confront our chief pilot back in HNL about this arduous schedule noting that, legal or not, it should never have been accepted. He confirms his steadfast agreement but has no real authority to intervene on our behalf. JAL, he assures me, is insistent. In this moment, a latent seed of discontent finally opens wide within, directing me to begin serious plans to leave Japan Airlines.

I've been commuting from Hawaii's outer islands for six years to Honolulu where my JAL flights originate and terminate. I fly mostly on Aloha Airlines and have learned they have major growth plans. I could go to work for them and expect to be a captain in just a few years. It would solve a lot of uncomfortable problems I brook with JAL.

Except for Trans East and NewAir, it's never been my idea to leave an airline. They fail, I find a new job. But I'm realizing I really want to leave JAL if I can replace it with Aloha. The airline is hiring in big numbers, and seniority is everything in the airline world. I'm three months from finishing the three-year contract I signed with IASCO to fly for JAL. I know four pilots that have left the contract early and were never punished, even though the contract says we owe them $17,000 for the breach.

CHAPTER 16

ALOHA AIRLINES,
CAREER AIRLINE #6
CIRCA 2000

I shoot an arrow and hit the bull's-eye. Aloha hires me almost immediately. I call IASCO to say sayonara.

"Hey, Jean,"—she's the Kimberly dream thief—"I just got a job offer from Aloha, so I'm giving you two weeks' notice."

There's a long silence. Jean's probably trying to decide whether I'm kidding. I'm not and she soon realizes it.

"Can you hang on a minute?" she says in a voice much smaller than usual.

"Sure," I say. I'm as uncomfortable as she is. I hate this, but I can't figure out any easier way to do it.

The head of the contract department at IASCO in Foster City, CA, picks up the line. "Hey, Andy. Seriously, you're leaving?"

"Yeah. Sorry, Bruce, but this opportunity with Aloha has landed at my doorstep, and the last I heard, the Japanese are refusing to consider any ex-flight engineers for upgrade to captain. I'm afraid that's a deal breaker for me."

"Okay, Andy, but you know about the breach of contract penalty, right? You need to send me a check for $17,000, okay?"

"Okay, Bruce, will do. See you later," and I hang up. I've already talked to a contract lawyer who's assures me the contract "is full of holes and unenforceable." Why, I wonder, am I still so scared?

They're not happy, and my action has caught them by surprise. I'm a nine-year IASCO guy with a sterling record. I'm well liked and before upgrading to first officer was even offered the chief flight engineer position on the 747 in the HNL base—a mega honor in this Japanese hierarchy. But things have been deteriorating between JAL and its contract pilots for some time, and I'm not the only one itching to go. The US airline industry is recovering from a long, deep slump and jobs are opening up with *home team* major airlines again, and several of our ranks are looking outward. Both JAL and IASCO seem to be aware of this troublesome trend so somewhere in the upper ranks, it's decided to stop the leak. I'm to be made an example of.

I complete training and find tremendous satisfaction in flying Boeing 737s on these mini-interisland flights that average sixteen minutes. I'm on "probation pay" again, netting about $1500 per month. Four months into my first year, I get a letter in my company mailbox from the Sheriff's office. It's a copy of a court order IASCO has secured to garnish my pay in the amount of 25% of my pre-tax pay. Ouch!

My lawyer advises me not to worry. He's going to fight this onerous punishment and defend my defection. Being a very close friend of a friend, he's agreed not to charge me until the battle is over. I pay for a flight and hotel room on two occasions when he has to fly to LA to address the court on my behalf. Otherwise, it's cost deferred, like Home Depot's special financing. His crowing seems a little inflated, especially when I learn IASCO has thrown their entire legal team at this prosecution. One motion after another comes and goes, and I trust my guy with the white hat to wreck the other side. At the end of a year of arbitration, I lose. The *judge* decides I not only owe IASCO the $17,000, but also all court and lawyer fees for the other side. My new burden is $55,000. I'm so screwed.

My contract expert assures me that arbitrators always rule on the side of the corporation. He wants to appeal, where a panel of real judges will surely rule for me. I bite. Proceedings drag on and on.

One evening, I get a call from a very close friend, Chris. He's still flying for JAL and has just landed, looking forward to a long layover on Oahu. I have a day off tomorrow, so I jump a flight to HNL and drive downtown in a car I keep in employee parking. We go for a run in the afternoon sun and reminisce about old times. He still lives in Anchorage so I'm, of course, jealous. We mill around soon finding ourselves at Duke's, a favorite beachgoers hangout with great drinks and fantastic seafood. Stuffed and filled with the giggles, we amble back to the hotel where a foldout couch is my bed, and I find refuge under its sheets promptly. We're both beat.

At 4 a.m. the phone rings.

"Hey, Chris, you better turn on the TV. They've just attacked the capital with missiles!" Cynthia, Chris's wife, is calling from Anchorage, relaying reports she's hearing on the morning news. It's September 11, 2001. The world changes forever.

I'm stuck on Oahu for a few days. Everyone in the world is stuck for a few days.

When the dust settles, I'm "juniored" into the 737-700. This is the bigger plane Aloha uses to fly across the Pacific to the west coast and on to some inland destinations including Las Vegas, Reno, and Sacramento. The more senior pilots want to fly interisland because they're home every night, and every day includes enough time off to go surfing, run a business on the side, or whatever. I go to the -700 reluctantly. Before Aloha, I'd spent the prior eleven years in Boeing 747s flying very long-haul international flights. I was loving the short flights my new life offered. But it wasn't a choice I got to make.

I realize that if I lose this appeal, the sanction against me will be astronomical. Some easy research shows that Nevada is one of the best states in which to declare bankruptcy. I call a bankruptcy attorney there and set up a meeting. My seniority allows me to get nearly any schedule I want, so I pick up some LAS flights to facilitate lawyerly meetings.

After I explain my situation, this guy suggests that I move to Vegas and buy a home. He wants me to furnish it lavishly and buy everything I want on credit. He wants my debt to be as large as I can get it. This puts me in a position to bargain with IASCO if the appeal doesn't go my way.

In record-breaking time, I bow out of an exploding living situation on Kauai and buy a beautiful home in Summerlin, on slopes west of Las Vegas, for $270,000. Following instructions I find exceedingly decadent, like eating four chocolate doughnuts in a row, I buy a new car, furniture, entertainment center, and every kitchen gadget on the market. I'm in deep debt. I lose the appeal. The judges won't even take the case it's so poorly presented. I owe IASCO $110,000.

Before declaring bankruptcy, I call my uncle, a retired attorney, and tell him the whole story. His only question is, "Are you friends with this Bruce guy at IASCO?"

"Yes," I honestly reply.

"Good. Call him and get the f*@#king lawyers out of the picture. Make him a deal."

Minutes later, I'm on the phone with Bruce. He's as pleasant as he can be and tells me he wishes I'd listened to him three years ago when this all began.

"I get it, Bruce, and wish the same thing. But I had an expert contract lawyer who advised me otherwise. He sounded competent. He'd read the contract and assured me it was full of holes, and there was no need for me to pay."

"And what happened?" I can hear Bruce smiling.

"Well, Bruce, he came highly recommended, and he spoke with so much authority about the contract's 'grievous inequities.' I remember he used those words. I thought this is my guy! I know other pilots that left early and never paid. It's simple, Bruce. I didn't want to part with that money, and I found someone that said I didn't have to. He turned out to be kind of blustery, especially against the team IASCO put against him. Of course, in hindsight, I wish I'd have just paid you," I explained.

I've carefully done my math. I tell Bruce I can pay $50,000. If he can't accept that, I'm going to declare bankruptcy, and the courts can work out IASCO's share. He says, "I'll call you back tomorrow." He does. They take the deal. I pull every penny of my savings plus five grand I borrow from a brother and send them a check. My garnishment not only disappears, but the most recent deduction is also put back into my bank account. We both act in good faith, like friends do, and a million-pound gorilla is peeled from a three-year ride on my back. I never get a bill from my contract lawyer friend of a friend.

Ten months after moving to Summerlin, in the peak of a housing bubble, I sell my home. I'd never have been here and bought this home in the first place had it not been for the legal troubles hanging over my head. I put it on the market at $405,000. By day's end, it sells for $410,000. I walk away with $140,000 for my trouble, netting $90,000 after paying off my IASCO debt. Sometimes you get the bear, sometimes the bear gets you. It looks like this time, I come out with the trophy.

CHAPTER 17

BLUE SKIES DARKEN

After twenty-five years away, I move back to Salt Lake City, my birthplace. I'm making good money and buy a brand-new home, furnishing it with all the stuff I bought in Vegas. I commute to Hawaii on Delta Air Lines. Commercial pilots have "jumpseat" privileges, with few exceptions, among other US airlines. These have been negotiated into pilot contracts for decades, allowing us to commute free. I have little competition out of SLC for jump-seats to HNL so it's an easy commute.

While we had a bit of an economic slump at Aloha for a couple of years, things have really picked up, and we're growing quickly. It looks like I'm finally going to get to upgrade to captain before this airline goes out of business. This will be a first in my six-airline-old career. The captain's seat is where the real money is, and it's that elusive command I've yearned for since, well, Wiesbaden.

By the end of 2004, Aloha has bid on a newly opened slot at Washington's Reagan National Airport, DCA. There's almost fren-zied excitement among all the employees, and rumors fly that Hawaii senator Daniel Inouye can influence the award. We have high hopes of getting this prestigious award. The bid even suggests that "New Entrants" to the east coast would be given higher con-sideration in an effort to increase competition. It would be Aloha's first flight to the east and is envisioned as a major steppingstone to a vastly expanded route structure.

Just before the award decision is made, newspapers across the country have a new front-page headline. "Drunk Aloha Airlines Pilot arrested trying to operate flight out of Oakland." It's plastered in the news for days and demolishes the chances of Aloha getting the award. This one drunk pilot doesn't just scuttle a major expansion, but seems to have sunk the whole airline. The wind is utterly knocked from Aloha's sails with the loss of the DCA award, and things immediately started contracting for our growing enterprise. Other factors contribute to Aloha's deepening troubles, but this is doubtless the leak that opens the dike.

As we face bankruptcy, a wealthy investor buys the airline and supports it for a few years. His losses are becoming unbearable, so in early 2008, he meets with another investment group and all of Aloha's unions. The plan is, after they do their due diligence, they'll buy the airline and completely rebuild it. Excitement is again through the roof. A new Pilot's Contract that has been bickered over for two years suddenly passes with every single ask the union wants. We receive a note from management that implores us to spread the word to pilot friends working elsewhere to submit applications here. We're about to open the flood gates on hiring. I bid and am awarded a captain's slot with training to begin in May.

I spend a weekend in late March skiing with one of my brothers at his favorite resort, Snowbasin. There's a big spring sale at one of our favorite ski shops in Ogden, and we're both looking for some new equipment. We walk out of Alpine Sports that Saturday evening having each spent over $1200. I don't care. I'm upgrading to captain. I can easily afford it.

We get up early the next morning and hit the slopes again. Exhausted, we leave at 1 p.m. having had all the fun we can stand. As we're driving down the hill headed to my brother's house, my phone rings. It's a pilot friend from Aloha.

"Hey, bro, looks like the gravy train's over," he says.

I think he's calling to tell me our upgrades have been moved up and we have to go back to training right away. I'm thrilled. I've waited so long. No, he's calling to inform me that Aloha is liquidating, and we're out of a job. There's a very long drop in emotions and economics between what I thought and what I got. I'm stunned. The investment group did their due diligence and decided against the acquisition. They must have had good crystal balls given the incredible economic fall about to jolt the world starting with the Lehman Brothers bankruptcy. I say Aloha to airline number six.

CHAPTER 18
THE WORLD YEARS
2008 ~ 2012

Once more the vagaries of life demote me from well-paid airline pilot to scrounging for dollars with my carpentry skills.

Right on the heels of Aloha's demise, another airline company called ATA also bites the dust. ATA is one of a trilogy of airline companies recently bought by Global Aviation Holdings. Its other holdings, not yet bankrupted by this asset-stripping, cash-stashing, company wrecker are World Airways and North American Airlines.

World has been operating since 1948 and has operating certificates that allow it to haul every form of cargo authorized for air transportation into every corner of the earth. Unlike most other businesses and enterprises, it begins growing in the summer of 2008, thanks to some good contracts they've just procured. Given their corporate relationship, ATA pilots get first crack at any new jobs.

I have a close friend, Harry, who's been flying at World for sixteen years. He's well liked throughout the ranks and has a few close friendships with some management people. He learns I'm back on the street and offers to hand carry a résumé into the chief pilot for me. In late June, among a class composed entirely of ATA pilots, I alone the exception, I start ground school in Atlanta, Georgia, the company's headquarters.

CHAPTER 19

THEY GOT 'EM, SO I FLY 'EM.

O n May 25th, 1979, American Airlines captain Walter Lux expertly lines up flight 191, a McDonnell Douglas DC-10, on runway 32 Right at Chicago O'Hare International Airport. Two hundred and fifty-eight passengers have made their way through the trivialities of life—showering, makeup, hair, dressing, and logistics—to get to the airport and board this jumbo jet. Business or pleasure await them in Los Angeles where their worlds will continue in the ebbs and flows of their daily creation.

This ORD to LAX leg is First Officer Dillard's to fly. Captain Lux will be working the radios and performing other, non-flying pilot duties. At 3:02:46, under ocean-blue skies, FO Dillard pushes the thrust levers forward to takeoff power, and all three CF6-6D engines roar together producing 124,000 pounds of thrust propelling the 379,000-pound aircraft majestically down the runway. Ten flight attendants, seated at emergency exits, are charged with ensuring the safety of the passengers throughout the flight.

Fifty seconds after the application of takeoff power, at 183 miles per hour, FO Dillard lifts the nose of flight 191 off the runway. In the same moment the No. 1, left engine, begins to shake violently and separates from the wing. Along with the pylon, the whole 13,477-pound assembly rockets up and away from the wing, taking three feet of its leading edge with it. After flying over the wing, it then drops below the tailplane crashing onto the runway below.

Following rigorously trained flying techniques developed to mitigate the dangers inherent in engine failures, First Officer Dillard keeps the pitch attitude at precisely 14 degrees and maintains heading and level wings with judicious inputs of rudder and aileron. Unbeknownst to the pilots, tremendous damage has occurred to the left wing. Among the most catastrophic is the uncommanded retraction of the leading-edge slats and the loss of the "stick shaker." This safety feature, common to all transport category jets, gives an unmistakable tactile warning, through vigorous shaking of the steering yoke, that the aircraft is about to stall. With airspeed of 198 miles per hour, there's still enough control authority with ailerons and rudder to counter the asymmetric lift induced by the retracted leading-edge slats on the left, but not the right wing. Airspeed bleeds off with FO Dillard's textbook perfect frozen pitch held steady at 14 degrees. This is done deliberately to reduce to a specific speed the pilot targets after an engine failure. As speed diminishes, more and more control surface deflection is needed to counter the rolling tendency of the airplane. At 182 miles per hour, the control surfaces reach their limits of travel. Due to damage neither pilot can see or detect from the cockpit, this target speed doesn't impart enough force on the fully deflected ailerons and rudder to arrest the increasing bank angle of the rolling airplane. At the apex of their flight, 325 feet above the ground, they roll through 90 degrees of left bank, and the nose drops precipitously below the horizon. As passengers and flight attendants watch through small windows in abject horror, no time for prayers or goodbyes, the earth rushes mercilessly from below to swallow every life in the blink of an eye as the airplane disintegrates. In addition to the 271 people aboard, two more on the ground die from flying debris. This is the fourth major crash of a DC-10, and soon after, shrinking orders close out its production.

My new employer assigns me to this airplane as first officer. During six weeks of simulator training in Memphis, TN, I master hundreds of dances partnered with this old, complex three-engine workhorse. Entertaining swing dances and onerous headbangers are all learned to high standards. Even steps, choreographed long ago, have been practiced with a promise of taming the fatal recipe that led to the disastrous DC-10 crash in Chicago thirty years prior. Training drags on for four months. The rigorous simulator syllabus combines with great difficulties scheduling an airplane with an instructor on routing that will get me the hours and line operating experience they demand. I'm finally flying revenue trips by early October 2008.

Six months of colossal life changes have lit my path since returning home from this grueling DC-10 training program. I've met and married Marcia, and in fate's seeming fixation on sixes, six weeks later I bury my mother.

Dust then slowly begins to settle on this turbulent phase of my life, and smooth sailing seems imminent on the horizon.

CHAPTER 20
THE MD-11

In 1991, the DC-10's successor, the MD-11, is certified by the FAA. Astronomical certification cost savings are realized by keeping the DC-10's wing, adding only small winglets to reduce drag. The rest of the airplane is significantly redesigned with larger engines, a longer fuselage that now accommodates 298 passengers, and massive technological advances. The new aircraft is deliberately named "MD" instead of "DC" in hopes it will not be recognized by a jaded public as a sibling of the demonic DC-10.

There are several performance problems with the airplane, and it's not proving to be the fuel-efficient jumbo jet customer airlines had ordered. The tail is subsequently shrunk to reduce drag. This creates its own set of control problems that are addressed with automatic, computer directed inputs to control surfaces that sometimes effect a fight between man and machine.

In August the following summer, 2009, I'm awarded a first officer bid to fly this airplane. It pays more than the DC-10 and returns me to the modern era with electronic flight instrumentation. We jokingly refer to the old, "round dial" cockpits like the DC-10 as "steam powered." This time training drags on for over six months. My first revenue flight isn't until early February 2010.

My primary assignments are transporting United States service personnel from military bases scattered throughout all fifty of the

United States. A typical pattern starts stateside where 280 troops are enplaned and flown to Bangor, Maine. There they transfer to another plane with a fresh crew and fly onto Leipzig, Germany. Up to twenty hours into their travel day, they then board yet another World Airways airplane, again with a newly rested flight crew, bound for Kuwait. It's not unusual for soldiers disembarking in Kuwait to have been sitting in airplanes for thirty hours, but still their travel isn't over. They board military aircraft, usually four-engine C-130s, and fly on to front line locations in Iraq or Afghanistan to engage the enemy.

Several of our MD-11s are configured as freighters, and in late March, I begin flying a lot of cargo in and out of Africa. This is a whole new world for me. I never realized the depth of hardship everyday life offers in much of Africa, and I soon come to realize, if there's a *Universal Force* out there steering me toward lessons I need, my *Guide* is clearly aiming me to realize the truth about real suffering.

PART 2
AFRICA

It is from numberless diverse acts of courage such as these that the belief that human history is thus shaped. Each time a man stands up for an ideal, or acts to improve the lot of others, or strikes out against injustice, he sends forth a tiny ripple of hope, and crossing each other from a million different centers of energy and daring, those ripples build a current which can sweep down the mightiest walls of oppression and resistance.

—Robert F. Kennedy

CHAPTER 1
A KING'S COLONY

In 1885, Belgium's King Leopold II privately owns The Congo Free state. For twenty-three years he sends a colonial military force to his country, one quarter the size of the United States, to enslave the indigenous population. Using conscripted labor, he strips the country of its most valuable commodities including rubber and ivory. His henchmen indiscriminately kill, maim, and torture the terrorized citizenry to keep production of his industry frantically high. One overseer erects a fence around his garden "decorating" its sharpened posts with the severed heads of slaves whose performance annoys him. Little changes after Belgium annexes the colony away from the king in 1908. Millions continue to die in the ongoing holocaust.

In 1965, an army chief of staff named Mobutu takes control of the country and renames it Zaire. The region destabilizes as Rwandan intertribal turmoil leads to a first, then second Congo war.

1997 brings with it a Tutsi president who changes the country's name to the Democratic Republic of the Congo, otherwise known as DRC. On its western border, 320 miles inland from the Atlantic Ocean, is DRC's capital, Kinshasa. It's a sprawling megacity with a population of over sixteen million. Continuous warring within and around the country leaves Kinshasa with more than twenty thousand children living on the streets.

CHAPTER 2
OSTEND, BELGIUM
MAY 6, 2010

Cobblestone streets weave the city center in Ostend, Belgium, in tangled patterns common throughout old European cities. Roads and alleys are tightly bound by a variegated mix of apartments, grocery stores, repair shops, travel agencies, and assorted other small industries. Buildings abut each other even while centuries separate many of their births.

Except for the occasional rhythmic voice of streetcar wheels rolling atop steel tracks, and natural gas-powered buses' straining brakes, it's silent at 6:00 this Thursday morning.

Air rushes past me as I exit the hotel's front door. It feels cold against my face and bare legs. Humid air blows gently from the English Channel just two blocks northwest, lowering my defense against cool temperatures. I shiver unexpectedly, so quickly bolt to a fast gait, coaxing the warmth from my core to the surface. In five minutes, the cold is forgotten, and I marvel at the eclectic theater of European architecture playing to the faint, echoing staccato of my ASICS running shoes against stone.

I'm rejuvenated upon my return to the Leopold Hotel. Hot water massages my back and legs as I linger in the shower's enticing warmth for a few extra minutes. Six miles of sweat and windborne dust washes down the drain to hidden caverns below the city. I dress casually, enjoying the sounds of the awakening city through my open, street-facing window. I take a single flight of stairs down to the café on the main floor. Bulging from wooden shelves are bread loaves, baguettes, and rolls of every imaginable shape and texture. Butter pads, jellies and jams of strawberry, cherry, blackberry, and currant berry, as well as peanut butter tubettes overflow half-extended wooden drawers in the hutch-like contrivance someone carefully crafted specifically for this shallow nook. Cereals, raisins, cranberries, nuts and seeds, yogurt, and half a dozen varieties of milk occupy a large table also stacked with Corelle dishware. Four hot, deep-black aromatic coffee blends soldier side by side in glass carafes. Another station teems with skillets of patty and link sausage, scrambled eggs, waffles, and mounds of steaming hash brown potatoes.

Willpower whimpers against powerful savory scents that activate my hunger. My mouth waters in Pavlovian response to the spread before me, and the battle is lost. In minutes I've piled thousands of calories' worth onto my plate and go back to load another with breads, rolls, and jelly. Finally, conceding to skip the juice bar, I bring half a liter of steaming black coffee to my table.

An hour later, I retreat to my room guilt-ridden for my gluttony. My MacBook computer screen lights upon opening, and I idly browse my email. Checking my company's website confirms there are no recent changes to my schedule. I have all morning to explore Ostend and look forward to a somewhat wider reconnaissance than my morning run afforded.

I have to force myself to leave the hotel. I'm so full all I want to do is lie down and sleep. But that would wreck my rest plan which must be carefully executed. Between now and 8 p.m. I need to get something resembling a full night's sleep.

I straggle out to the street and make my way a little farther afield of the city center this time. I find a huge grassy park complete with copper sleeping Goddess statues lying atop marble islands in ponds, and a clock laid out on a hillside whose face is at least twenty feet across. Dark green grass starkly borders chocolate-brown earth to define its circumference. Hands are crafted of huge wooden paddles harvested from an old windmill. One of my favorite perks of this job is all the exploring and sightseeing it affords me. I've yet to visit a city where I don't find something breathtaking or uniquely creative. Gigantic bathing Goddesses in ponds and the wonder of a defunct old wooden windmill becoming a clock sculpted from earth helps me treasure the artistic diversity that animates humanity. I'm so grateful to George Eastman and subsequent engineers for simplifying cameras, now so advanced and straightforward it's child's play to save and share endless memories. Returning to The Leopold, I run across a 12th century Gothic cathedral that's as magnificent as any I've ever seen. Twenty minutes to circle and gawk gets me back to my hotel at 1 p.m.

I iron my uniform shirt and affix epaulets, then lay out the rest of my attire to make sure it's all ready. A heartfelt email, complete with pictures of my morning sightseeing, gets the full measure of my thoughts for fifteen minutes, and then off it goes at the speed of light to my wife, five thousand miles west. I can hardly wait to hear back from her. She loves this part of my job too, and with the Internet, always "comes along" for the ride. Her reflections are half the fun, adding a whole new dimension to what I see and experience.

I'm in bed by 2:30 p.m. It's little wonder why international pilots have such famously debilitating fatigue. A rare dispensation for sleep endows me with a life-enhancing gift custom-made for my profession. Whatever time zone I'm in becomes mine with little if any adjustment. It's like a magic trick except when it doesn't work. Once asleep, if someone slams a door nearby, or partiers saunter down the hall in reckless cheer, or construction somewhere locally, especially with hammer-drills, assaults an unshielded ear and I wake, I'm stuck. Those hazards, more common in daylight, which is often when I need to sleep, wreck my grand trick, and now I'm trapped in the same drama that haunts so many insomniacs. I've spent a few flights in my career powered primarily by coffee.

As usual, I wake a few seconds before my 8 p.m. alarm. I throw the covers back, exposing myself to the cold air in my room. I shut off all three alarms I've set and roll onto the floor, goose bumps suffusing my arms, to brave fifty pushups. As unappealing as this "morning" ritual always seems, by the time I manage the first two or three, my body races through the rest affably.

Senses recharged, I take a quick shower and shave. Uniform donned, I find an acceptable reflection in my full-length bathroom mirror. I feel confident I embody the time-honored image of a professional airline pilot.

It's 9:00 p.m. A limo will be waiting out front in fifteen minutes to take my crew and me to the airport. With my suitcase and flight bag, I descend by elevator to the lobby and check out.

Captain Hahn and First Officer Leluc settle into the back of the black Mercedes while I board the front passenger's seat. In style befitting kings, we're chauffeured three miles southwest to Ostend-Burges International airport, OST. Waning twilight reveals a few dark-pink summer clouds dim on the western horizon. We ride in silence watching whitecaps surf into shore on the English Channel's restless surface. Dim lights from cities on the eastern shores of England, sixty miles west, can barely be seen across the channel. Practically no other traffic accompanies us on Highway N34. We arrive at the airport's vacant curbs in ten minutes.

We're met by dispatcher Van de Berg who escorts us into the World Airways operations center and briefing room. Mr. Van de Berg is well prepared with a briefing that gives us detailed weather and other pertinent aeronautical information for our route and African destinations to which we'll be flying tonight. With fluent command of five languages, it's captivating to hear Mr. Van de Berg's interspersed phone conversations and discussions with fellow airport workers in so many tongues.

We're carrying 188,544 pounds of cargo today. Our first stop, Lagos, Nigeria, is 3,085 miles due south and will consume six hours and twenty-six minutes of the night. In passenger operations, the 4,000-mile flight from OST to Kinshasa would be well within the nonstop range of the MD-11. But our heavy cargo limits the amount of fuel we can load without exceeding the maximum operating weight of the airplane. A fuel stop is necessary, and Lagos is the dispatcher's choice.

Our flight, number 2614, departs straight out on runway 26 at 10:49 p.m. Central European time. Our westerly heading puts us over the English Channel seconds after takeoff, where we gain altitude with little noise impact on people below. Soon we're directed to turn south and intercept a complex European airway network. We reach our initial cruise altitude of 32,000' in twenty-one minutes and watch Paris, the City of Light, drift by out to the left thirty-nine minutes later.

Only a blurred jagged line on the horizon hints at the French Alps ahead. A short while later the pointed tip of a rising half-moon, blood red at this low angle, begins its ascent into the sky ahead. Its miserly hoarded rays barely illuminate the steel-gray surface of the Mediterranean Sea floating in the windshield ahead. Fifty minutes more brings us to white beaches over Algeria's northern shores as the moon trumpets light onto our world tour. Rick's Casablanca sits not far to our right. Ninety minutes later we begin our descent into Lagos.

The name of the time zone changes to "West Africa" but there's no change from Central European. Captain Hahn lands our behemoth MD-11 at 5:15 a.m. and taxis to the cargo ramp where two huge fuel bowsers await.

Eleven thousand gallons of jet fuel are added to our fuel tanks in just under half an hour. With taxi in and out times added, we're on the ground only fifty-two minutes. It's my turn at the controls which we alternate throughout the trip. At 6:07 a.m. I gently coax the nose of the jumbo jet from runway 18R skyward.

CHAPTER 3

KINSHASA, DEMOCRATIC REPUBLIC OF THE CONGO SAME DAY

The Gulf of Guinea, tracing the crook where west Africa's coastline changes from east/west to north/south, slides under our nose soon after liftoff. Two hours and fifty-five minutes after takeoff, overflying hundreds of miles of dense jungle teaming with pygmy hippopotamuses and western lowland gorillas, I begin a descent to Kinshasa's N'Djili airport, FIH. At 9:29 a.m., still in the West Africa time zone, all ten tires of my main landing gear grab the rough asphalt of Runway 24. Rubber boils as our tires are compelled by our 444,000-pound mass from 0 to 170 miles per hour, instantaneously streaming clouds of blue smoke. After smoothly setting the tandem nose wheels down, I brake cautiously, careful not to overheat our brakes. Not only are we quite heavy, the black asphalt is absorbing heat quickly under the full savanna tropical sun. Eight thousand feet of runway passes twenty-one feet below eye level by the time we've reached a safe speed in which to turn the airplane around. There are no parallel taxiways at FIH, so to reach the parking ramp, we must make a 180-degree turn on the runway. The single runway at FIH is two hundred feet wide, an easy turn diameter for us without danger of scrubbing tires.

Once we've reversed course, I spot a lone soldier standing in mowed grass under a tent canopy about two hundred feet to our right. He's leaning casually on a tall rifle, as if it's a crutch, perhaps to support his tall, lanky stature in the day's already oppressive heat.

From my right-hand seat in the cockpit, I'm closest to him. FO Leluc removes his seat belts and crosses the cockpit to lean over my shoulder and witness this novel spectacle. We all wave from our two-and-a-half-story platform, and he waves back more enthusiastically than I'd expected. Maybe he's rarely acknowledged. To me, he seems equivalent to a "first responder," ready to fight off tyranny the moment it brings threat. Kinshasa, after all, has been the focal point of wars for decades.

CHAPTER 4

A CHALLENGING START

Though we're not scheduled to take off for nine and a half more hours, the tower insists we have a flight plan on file for our evening flight before we're allowed to leave the airplane. I immediately call dispatch on the satellite phone that hangs from a hook on the back, right-hand cockpit wall, and get them working on it. Just as I finish the call, an airport representative enters the cockpit and hands Captain Hahn triplicate flight plan forms along with two pieces of carbon paper. I'm trying to remember the last time I saw carbon paper. I'm at a loss. The form is printed in French.

By sheer luck, FO Leluc is French. The only Frenchman at World Airways who, fourteen years earlier, won a green card in a lottery, allowing unlimited work and residence in the United States. His presence as our third pilot allows us to legally fly more than eight hours during a twenty-four-hour period.

World dispatch sends back a flight plan, but the "dots" don't perfectly connect along the entire route. After scrutinizing the possibilities, we suggest a better one, but apparently, our client doesn't have "overfly authority" for Tanzania which falls beneath the most direct routing we mapped. Some discussion ensues whereupon our dispatcher agrees to submit a new route, of our design, that connects all points seamlessly. Thirty minutes later the new plan spits—tick, tick, tick—from the thin mouth of our printing machine. It's exactly the same flight plan that had been denied half an hour ago. Our French companion settles to the tedious task of hand-printing the proffered triplicate flight plan using data we know Kinshasan authorities will accept. We figure we can negotiate an agreeable compromise with our dispatcher later. Right now, this fourteen-and-a-half-hour day has all of us groggy with fast-growing fatigue.

While waiting for all the planets to align so we can get on with our short layover, I witness remarkable choreography on the ramp next to us. A Boeing 727 had been sitting isolated and completely closed up when we braked to a stop. Now a line of porters snakes their way across the ramp from the passenger terminal. They're carrying long, folding tables, chrome-colored stanchions, coils of rope, and several large boxes. They swarm the 727 from tail to nose. An airstair truck pulls up to the front passenger door, and the flight engineer jogs to the top and opens it. Others set stanchions on the tarmac that are immediately strung with rope to form a line-maze extending two hundred feet toward the terminal. Leg sets unfold and tables spring from the hot asphalt at a gap in the rope near the bottom of the airstair. Box loads of ticketing and office paraphernalia are arranged on the tables, and in the span of three minutes, the plane is ready for boarding. Passengers from the terminal file into the maze seconds after two pilots ascend to the cockpit, flight bags and suitcases carried in each hand, oblivious to the weight or hot sun's efforts to slow them. I see a puff of smoke from the wheel well area as the APU, a small jet engine mounted in the right wheel well, lights off to power and cool the 180-passenger airplane. Two large semitrucks back up to its right-hand cargo bins, forward and aft. In seconds, lines of men and women form bucket brigade type lines, and bags, crates, boxes, and bundles all but fly from hand to hand faster than any motorized conveyor belt I've ever seen and disappear into the baggage holds. The belly is loaded in minutes and the semitrucks drive away, belching black smoke. I'd guess forty people mustered to prepare the plane in a dazzling ballet of efficiency. People power is cheap and in plentiful supply. Such competent craft engaged by so many moving parts is highly impressive. It's taken eight or nine minutes to set up and board bags and cargo. Another ten sees the last passenger vanish into the sleek Boeing, and the boarding door shuts behind him. The engines start one by one and the airplane taxis away, all traces of support staff vanished. In all, a second hand has spun the clock's face less than twenty times to close the curtain on this entire pageant. It's a show I'd pay to watch again.

The new flight plan is accepted by air traffic control, and we're released from the confines of our 202-foot aluminum tube. Carrying bags that didn't seem nearly as heavy half a day ago, we slog down two stories of stairs to the busy ramp below. A Chevy Suburban, wrapped in various shades of red and brown dirt, pulls up, and the driver signals us to load our bags in the back, offering no assistance. After complying, we seat ourselves in the vehicle. An official in the front passenger's seat collects our passports, and the driver motors toward a small, rectangular shack a few hundred feet away. Reaching it, he turns the vehicle around and backs in. The shelter is made from rust-tarnished, corrugated-metal siding and includes two sash windows. One is opened about six inches, the other closer to ten. I assume their apertures are limited by corroded window casing hardware. They're certainly not stuck by too many layers of paint. No air-conditioning is evident.

We're instructed to wait in the Suburban while our passport-snatching emissary climbs out and enters the small, hot-looking hut through a red-dust impregnated screen door.

As we wait, our attention is drawn to a cloud-raising tractor approaching along the dirt road we're facing. The old tractor has five or six men dressed in filthy long-sleeved shirts and equally unwashed long pants holding onto various anchor points like firemen on a hook-and-ladder truck. Most wear sandals whose color, and that of the contained feet, are identical shades of umber brown. In tow is a trailer piled six feet high with caged chickens squawking frantically, heads bobbing like pistons. Another squad of men standing on the trailer's wood planking hang onto the lashed mountain of cages. With three or four chickens per cage, a quick guess leads me to believe there are at least a thousand terrified hens and roosters along for the bumpy ride. They arrived here via my World Airways flight.

As the Keystone Cops collection gets abeam of us, it suddenly shrieks to a stop with the engine coughing smoke and quitting in protest. A small army of men approach from both front and behind, yelling in Swahili. Their anger seems so acute that I can see swollen veins looking ready to explode in their necks. They're clearly indicating, in sign language more than words, that the chicken brigade is going the wrong way. The clear leader of the tractor team is the driver, and he begins yelling with equal ferociousness that they are most certainly going the right way. Understanding of Swahili is unnecessary to follow this exchange. Clearer body language has never been spoken. Veins rise from his neck in equal measure to the other team's captain. In seconds, a yelling match begins among the opposing teams accompanied by the increasingly horrified cackle of a thousand chickens.

Verbal assaults continue until the tractor driver tires of the circus. He starts the stubborn engine to pops, bangs, and puffs of gray smoke, releases the clutch, lurching forward, and seems intent on running over anyone in his path. Men jump clear in the nick of time, and down the little dirt road the dusty chicken brigade chugs.

Several relatively quiet minutes pass as we muse on the hilarity of the altercation from our point of view. But then the familiar uproar begins anew, crescendoing to thunderous magnitude, this time going the opposite direction. All the same characters ride the tractor and trailer, and the riotous din—including chickens screaming wildly—melts away into the distance.

On Apron 2, where we're parked, I notice four airplanes painted white with large, bold black "UN" letters stenciled on their tails. Ironically, given our presence as a "trade instrument" from Belgium, the United Nations initially found a presence in the

Congo as a military force to administer the withdrawal of a Belgian militia that was slow to abide peace accords in 1960. They've been enmeshed to greater and lesser degrees in peacekeeping in the DRC ever since.

Our dour passport snatcher exits the shack's dirty screen door after about fifteen minutes. It's now 10:35 a.m. Weariness deepens proportional to our disappearing liberty. The agent gives us each a stamped "Crew Declaration" which will allow us back onto the airport later this evening. Our passports will remain in the possession of the customs officials until our return.

With this part of officialdom complete, we're ordered off the Suburban and into a Ford Econoline van. It has apparently lived through the same dust storms and rowdy dirt road escapades as the Suburban. Fine brownish dust films the plastic seats to a degree nearly equal to the exterior coating. We retrieve our bags from the Suburban and transfer them to our new carriage, then settle in for the drive to the hotel.

CHAPTER 5

THE ROAD

O ur union, Teamsters Chapter 1108, has negotiated with the company that we pilots will not lay over in Kinshasa. It's too dangerous. It's not unusual for our company to negotiate exceptions on the fly. Our journey continues onto Entebbe next, and there's no way to legally continue today's duty without a fourth pilot. A full double crew, two captains and two first officers, gives us generous flexibility with flight and duty time limitations. With just an "augmented" crew of one captain and two first officers, restrictions preclude us flying on from Kinshasa. Why this schedule was allowed in the first place is beyond my understanding, but then, so much in this operation is.

To mitigate the dangers of driving into the heart of this city, the company has agreed to have our transport include both a driver and an armed escort officer. The Econoliner we're in has five rows of seats including the driver's. Our baggage is piled on the seat immediately behind the driver and escort officer. I seat myself in the back row, and Hahn and Leluc sit in the remaining two rows. There are large windows giving unobstructed views into and out of the van from every angle.

The men in front look tough and capable. Our escort officer carries a holstered pistol on his belt. Lying on the floor between the two front seats is a sawed-off shotgun. Apparently, everyone takes the "armed" business seriously. I'm alarmed. Is this really necessary?

I've been with World Airways for twenty-one months, and my first trip to Africa was only three months ago. That was to Nairobi, Kenya, which hasn't seen the kind of revolution and war that DRC has lived with for decades. This region of Africa is a whole new experience on the stage of fear and anxiety. Luckily, I'm well anesthetized by sleep deprivation.

With all aboard, the driver urges the van onto a dirt road, and we begin an unforgettable ride to the heart of Kinshasa. Just getting out of the airport is surreal. Roads sometimes seem more like trails. Sparely placed cardboard and corrugated-metal huts appear right and left, divulging something between a ghost town and run-down shanty town. Piggy-back type cargo containers, common on flatbed train cars, are haphazardly planted aside the road. Some are arranged facing each other, separated by twelve or thirteen feet. Filthy, raggedy tarps stretch between some, providing slivers of shade during the heat of the day. In some shady nooks, skinny, bare-chested men sit in plastic chairs, vacant stares directed seemingly down, though at what, I can't imagine. My heart aches for the bleakness they seem to endure. Maybe they work here at the airport and are on break. Maybe they're here because it's the one place they presently fit.

We follow this dilapidated road several hundred yards. Sprigs of weeds jut from the dry, cracked earth, and random stalks of maize sprout from other dirt patches not occupied by a shack, tent, or beat-up old trailer. To our right, a football field away, are airplane carcasses appearing like huge dead dinosaurs rolled on their backs. They're the remains of wrecks and old aircraft pilfered to the last usable screw and bulldozed out of the way. I'm guessing there's not a lot of scrap metal recycling around here. Useless waste is just pushed out of the way to be dealt with, maybe, someday.

We slow to a few miles per hour and make a sharp left turn. A hundred feet ahead is a gate made of thin steel tubing welded together in rectangles. It looks like its red-and-white striping were painted decades ago, faded and bleached to indistinction. A rag-tag dusty man guards it and, seeing the Econoline, swings it open, allowing us passage.

In another hundred feet we cross train tracks almost buried by windblown dirt and debris. Their bedraggled condition leaves little doubt they haven't felt the rumble of a train in years. People begin to appear roadside, breathing the heavy clouds of dust we raise even at our sluggish speed. With few exceptions, they carry large payloads, often in wide woven baskets, balanced on their heads.

It's now ten minutes since departing the customs shack, and we're finally approaching a paved road. It's the main artery lead-ing into Kinshasa stretching a straight line, both left and right, as far as I can see. The dirt road we just left appears utterly indistinct from any other crossroad intersecting this thoroughfare.

Immediately we plunge into dense neighborhoods bordering the road and surrounding the airport. Noise buffering to afford people any pretense of protection from the hellish roar of big jets taking off doesn't appear to have been considered in anyone's master plan.

The density of pedestrian traffic is growing steadily. In another mile, the streaming crowd leads me to an internal oath—I'll never again complain about going to the DMV. Speaking of motor vehi-cles, their numbers are growing rapidly as well, and road condi-tions are deteriorating at an alarming rate.

A relatively safe top speed on the good parts of this boulevard is about 40 mph, and our driver probably hits 50 from time to time. Fast reflexes and good brakes are admirably showcased for us over and over as our pilot bobs and weaves and jams brakes often enough to strongly encourage the use of seatbelts. None can be found.

Wild braking usually precedes half-foot drops to washboard dirt in pits that sometimes continue descending until we're two feet below where the road surface should be. Sometimes we zigzag snail-slow, in large arcs, to skirt craters that could swallow us. As far as I'm concerned, this road should be a big part of the danger everyone's talking about, but clearly, it's not the part that prompted a squad's worth of guns and ammo aboard our conveyance.

Long intermissions obviously separate road repair projects here, but then, wars tend to slow that kind of infrastructural improvement. That...and extreme poverty.

Within half an hour the sea of pedestrian traffic has grown denser than any I've observed. It now looks like pictures in National Geographic exploring crowds in India, Pakistan, or China splashing across centerfolds in feature articles.

Simultaneously scared and curious, I'm trying to puzzle out what they're doing. Without exception, they're all pigmented in darker skin tones than any humans my travels have ever offered. Distinct facial features like cheekbones, foreheads, and darkness of skin differentiate them so strongly that it's obvious many tribes and nationalities coexist along this pilgrimage.

Many look fierce, others blank, and some even look content. I see only a tiny handful that I think might ever have known cheer. This isn't like life I've seen in my own passage. I don't think these folks are just having a bad day. There's so much desperation expressed in bent backs, concentration camp-like malnourishment, sagging shoulders, and far away looks of defeat. Probably lungs able to take the next breath is about as much celebration as many have known in years. I wonder if they have any reason to expect better in the future.

Revolutions, power struggles, assassinations of political leaders, and a war that left over five million dead, have all transpired here within the last decade. Surrounding countries have experienced equal or worse, and refugees continue flooding into this region in search of safety and subsistence.

With poverty rampant and a fast-growing population exacerbating it, there's no means by which to fix whatever infrastructure and organization once served this region. Psychological and physical maladies are common as are disease and hunger. Each fuels insufferable torment.

The population is seventy percent Christian, and with so much desperation, Kinshasa is prime real estate for crazed evangelicals to ply their dementia. Followers are easily led to poisoned ideas. One that has gained a lot of traction in recent years says something like, "HIV and AIDS are bad, but condoms are worse." Crushing crowds attest to the millions who subscribe.

Forty-five minutes into this sojourn immerses us in throngs rivaling Woodstock or pilgrimages attending a hajj in Mecca. These teaming masses, however, include berserk motor traffic more unruly than any I've seen circling within the twelve lanes surrounding the Arc de Triomphe or any Middle Eastern traffic frenzies. Mixed into the fray are also hand-pulled carts, donkeys, and hundreds of small darting motorbikes. People crossing the now hundred-foot-wide roadway do so at great risk, though hundreds rise to the challenge.

Our caretakers are becoming agitated. We three in their care are the only Caucasians in this medley and, as such, are prime targets for kidnapping or worse. Robbers will pounce in a second given the slightest opportunity. Knowing this, our driver stops for nothing. His palm is now married to the Ford's horn, trying to give fair warning to any foolish enough to step in his path. It appears time after time that he will run down anyone that doesn't heed his repeated admonishments. People are so used to this dance with death that they literally bounce off vehicles in hard enough impacts to cause bruising. I've yet to see anyone squished or injured to debilitation.

URRRRRT! I think he's jammed on the brakes to avoid killing someone, but he's just preparing to maneuver another sink hole. We crawl through it, our shooter constantly scanning all directions, ready to do battle. Back on pavement, I notice other cars merging from left and right. Our driver pays no heed and dares them to try to take his space. He'll simply allow a sideswipe if necessary. In every case the other driver backs down. Our guy wins a hundred games of chicken during our drive. He's paid to get us through this mass of people, many who surely hate us for being white, fed, rich, and riding in a car with entire bench seats all to our single selves.

Growing stress yields imaginary scenes of us, three bloody white guys, sprawled aside the road, hordes parading by, leering down, amused. The way our driver speeds makes me think he envisions the sequel. He knows this is a dangerous game and willingly participates. I wonder what he's paid.

I ask aloud, "What if we're in an accident?" Shotgun replies that they have a radio and can call in backup transportation immediately. That seems about as comforting as telling a boat passenger transiting piranha-infested waters that a backup boat can be quickly dispatched in the event this one sinks. We're all speechless now, cocooned in awe and shock as our perilous expedition disturbingly unfurls.

CHAPTER 6
CONVEYANCE

The VW Microbus was first introduced in 1950. It's changed little in the following decades if one discounts the evolution of camper van derivatives. At its maximum capacity, it can hold twelve people, and an industry-wide joke postulates half of them must get out and push whenever it comes to a hill. When such a contrivance replaces your large transport bus fleet in a decimated economy that can no longer afford repairs to the big rigs, necessity naturally rewrites specifications.

The now riotous menagerie includes incalculable numbers of VW buses painted in DRC national colors of blue and yellow. The back windows are broken out to accommodate an additional row of passengers who sit only half inside the vehicle. Over and over, I count twenty-five people per bus. There are five rows of five passengers each. The front row includes the driver so there are really only twenty-four passengers. There seem to be no overweight people among this demographic, so at least that helps. People sit half on one another's laps, and many lean forward to allow room for the nose of the passenger behind. Doors are removed to allow passengers to stand on thresholds hanging onto tiny rain gutters. Others sit on framework once fitted with windows. It's a cooperative endeavor. The more amazing part is, everyone seems oblivious to their impossibly cramped confines. It's just what is. If you're born and raised never seeing sunshine, you can't miss it. They have no different vision for comparison. This is simply life in massively overcrowded Kinshasa.

They look uncomfortable but even more obviously bored. The overloading is apparent in the squashed suspension, but no one seems to notice as they barrel along, riders bouncing along inside like comic bobblehead dolls. This seems neither adventure nor novel to these commuters. Repeated games of chicken and dodge 'em lapse unremarkably. I watch fascinated as they dart off and onto the road, disgorging and loading charges they somehow discerned among the thousands along the teeming roadway.

Calling it a road lends an impression of a paved surface with clear delineations of what's for motor vehicles and what's not. It's not nearly so clear-cut in Kinshasa. It all blends together with only hard buildings being the absolute edge of acceptable rights of way for automobiles. The riotous parade includes scores of people pushing two-wheeled carts loaded with massive cargos. From the air they must look like gophers with the rest of the mass a huge snake swallowing them—lumps ingesting within an endless, undulating stream.

There are no Ace Hardware or Napa Auto Parts stores. All goods and services, at least to the millions of street dwellers, must be found along the main thoroughfare winding through fields, hills, and dales. Daily scavenger hunts for needed food and supplies likely define the lives of all these wanderers. Sunrise to sunset finds them seeking what can be found, either to eat, barter, or sleep under.

We narrowly miss carts, donkeys, pedestrians, and other vehicles by inches a thousand times in the course of our odyssey. Often, we pull out to pass traffic our driver considers inconvenient. He forces oncoming traffic into streams of pedestrians hugging their side of the maelstrom. Horns blare and people scramble whichever way to avoid falling beneath wheels that will surely crush them. Several times I see we're in the middle of one of these suicide contests and suddenly, there's someone passing us ten mph superior, headed right for the same oncoming assault. I watch as twenty-five people crammed aboard, heads bobbing under the sway and rocking of long dead suspension, appear utterly oblivious to the high-stakes games in which they're enmeshed. As often as not, there's another similarly laden rig ten feet behind them burdened with another full cargo, using the first as a battering ram I suppose. Where do they hide the squished bodies? There must be hundreds, but I haven't seen a single one.

A morbid thought strikes me that, if a thousand of these people are wiped out every day, it will be years before anyone notices. It keeps circling in my head over and over. Absent hyperbole, it seems like there are a thousand times more people than this city and its infrastructure can possibly support. I can't imagine how they're all fed each meal and feel equally dubious about their bathroom business. There must be tens of thousands of people for every available outhouse. They can't live on more than a few hundred calories a day, and it certainly isn't junk food. There's no money for crap processed food. They eat, I suspect, what can be grown in the fields that pepper the city. The yield from these harvests could be sizably larger if not for the layers of trash, junk, and filth that cover everything. It's not deep, not like people are wading through trash up to their ankles. But it's pervasive, covering nearly every square inch. A garbage truck chugs along a mile back with rubbish hanging off every aspect. I think that must be the surest job in town.

It looks like if everyone vanished into thin air, a certainty if only Dorothy would teach the "click your heels three times" trick, garbage trucks would need years to dispense with the thick blanket of rubble. Kansas, however, would doubtless file a quick injunction against Dorothy and Glinda.

Remnants of cars, trucks, and buses that have broken down litter the landscape. There are no tow trucks on call, at least none that will risk this perilous stretch. You fix your rig on the spot or abandon it. The results of abandonment are swift and highly visible. Scads of used car parts are for sale along the road. No one erects a showroom or stocks warehouses. When parts are needed to fix something, luck, wit, and the resourcefulness of MacGyver are necessary to win the day. Exploration of roadside enterprises begins a scavenger hunt. Once the thing, or something resembling it, is found, bartering completes the transaction. No Black Friday sales or Blue Light specials. Just simple transactions to lubricate the sticky process of life. Here stands a makeshift expo consisting of thick planks perched on stacked bricks displaying an array of motor oil and fan belts. There a capable entrepreneur shovels dirt into two-foot piles, then plunges car windshields deep into them. Glass sticking up like gravestones nets an instant showroom— voilà! used windshields for sale.

Vendors wander among vehicles stuck in increasingly common choke points, selling an endless assortment of wares. One young teenage boy hawks black plastic flutes that look just like the ones Mrs. Huff found for my third-grade class in 1963. Another has individually wrapped waffles. Dozens peddle pint-sized plastic bags of water stored in baskets on their heads. These cargos nearly outweigh some of the children selling them. I marvel to watch a youngster retrieve a bag so fast I can barely follow the "draw." One man stands at the edge of traffic, as much as "edge" can be delineated, close enough to touch each passing vehicle. With his hands outstretched and his long slender fingers undulating like Medusa's hair, he begs for anything that might be offered. As we pass, I see only four inches of leg remaining below each kneecap.

Our driver seems more and more uncomfortable in these bottlenecks. Me too. Shotgun thumbs his pistol grip and keeps looking at the big gun on the floor.

Our eyes and throats burn from clouds of exhaust spewing from thousands of vehicles, most needing new rings and valves to curb oil burning in cylinders. I want, need, to close my eyes to wash away a film of crud and to slow the onslaught of half-burned oil coating my eyes. I can't. The spectacle is too frightening. Something, I suppose, like needing to keep your eyes open during a harrowing scene in a horror movie.

If the World Health Organization bore witness to this, they'd probably mandate scuba gear for every person. It would be the only adequate defense against the poisonous onslaught to lungs in this hellish environment. It's no wonder I haven't seen anyone close to middle age among the hundreds of thousands. For the foreseeable future, any effort to advertise improved lifespans here could probably be established only by counting in doggy years.

After an hour in this dark, swirling abyss highlighting such suffering and strife, there comes a "Y" intersection as the city grows tall around us. Our driver bears right. Shotgun seems to relax. Approaching less primitive real estate does not necessarily eliminate the jungle survival standard. A VW bus straddles a ravine, midroad, obviously broken down. The back tires are blocked with rocks, the one commodity in seeming endless supply. The front is lifted and set on other rocks. A man lying on his back struggles in the dirt below working to fix whatever is broken. His fares have abandoned him to catch other rides. Traffic flows around the impediment like streams of ants diverging and converging around an obstacle in their path. We swim in the right-hand stream.

Mercedes, Audis, and other high-priced cars replace VW buses as we gain entrance to the high-rent district of Kinshasa, though I've yet to see one that doesn't need the services of a paint and body shop. Multi-story billboards swarm every unoccupied inch of space as the city center approaches, advertising items only the wealthy can afford—Sterling watches, Bacio Immortale perfume, Dalmore Single Malt whiskey, and other novelties to pamper the super-rich.

We slow in the rightmost lane and begin turning into a high fence structure. The ten-foot edifice constructed of corrugated metal slides inward, revealing an opening large enough to allow us entry. Three armed guards monitor our arrival but leave us unmolested. We apparently belong. The Econoline van pulls forward to what appears to be a side entrance to a big warehouse.

CHAPTER 7
A NEW RABBIT HOLE

I'm still shell-shocked from the unsettling ride from the airport but recover enough to disembark and grab my bags. My companions accompany. I skip the typical two-dollar driver's tip, opting instead to offer each five. The driver exits his giant van to open the door for us. Shotgun stays put.

From outside I have the impression we're entering a shabby corridor through which we can make a back entrance jaunt to the check-in lobby. The awaiting interior wins the "never assume" award of the century.

The hall is twelve feet high with bright chandeliers along its length. It's all of twenty-five feet wide accentuating its architectural imperative of opulence. We traipse five hundred feet, astonished by the interminable display of unthinkable wealth. Storefront after storefront entices those of the megawealthy class. We gawk, awestruck, especially as irresistible mental gymnastics juxtapose this and what we've just experienced for the last hour. Who comes here, I wonder? Kings, Saudi princes, Russian oligarchs? Probably all of the above, though surely they make their way by helicopter. Certainly, none in those classes would endure a trial by pedestrian such as we just did.

This soul-battering exposure finally brings us into the hotel's lobby. It's crowned with thirty-foot chandeliered ceilings complete with crisscrossed arches, marble sheathing, hand jointed Rosewood trim, and lavish balustrades. Men, including staff, wear silk suits, and women are adorned in floor-length gowns. There are no women behind the counter.

The paradigm shift from the pitiful masses suffusing the streets for the last twenty-five miles, to here, imparts shock similar, I'm guessing, to that of a returning soldier going from killing fields to San Francisco's Fisherman's Wharf inside of forty hours.

Checking in is painless, and though we're of a lowly, working class, we're made to feel appreciated and welcome. We're escorted to elegant, spacious, modern rooms though heavily perfumed with recent applications of bug poison. I take Captain Hahn's joking command to heart and sleep fast.

The sheets and pillows on my bed are smooth and unwrinkled, so I'm puzzled when I hear the soft bell of my room's phone. Is it possible it's time to get up? Did I already sleep? Apparently, I did, and fast, as instructed. Four and a half hours have passed during which my exhausted body stirred not an inch.

Fifty pushups and a quick shower to wash the dust and oil from my skin bring me to readiness for another day. We rally in the lobby at 5 p.m. The staff has specially prepared hot coffee and some danish rolls for our breakfast. For the rest of the guests, cocktail hour is just beginning.

We reverse course, and I find myself rubbernecking again at the ostentatious trappings that pave all backdrops. Then suddenly, the curtain hiding the scarcity side of this unforgettable Twilight Zone opens onto the more familiar stage of rampant desperation.

The same Ford Econoliner waits, staffed with the same guards that brought us here a few hours ago. At least we know the plot this time, so the shock, hopefully, won't be quite as jarring.

We're now traveling at dinnertime. Evening dims the stage as we watch tens of thousands of people crowd the eternal number of shacks and makeshift stores to find meals. Most "stores" consist of blankets unfurled on bare dirt, swept clear of the universal layer of litter. Broken concrete provides most anchorage for these wraps, weighing the corners to allow a taut surface. Quilts of colorful vegetables cover the veneer. I assume most were in the ground only hours ago, picked by armies preparing for the evening meal, probably the only meal for many.

I try to identify what might feed these many tribes of aboriginals. Most contain at least one huge pot of rice. I see tubers, probably cassava, maize or corn, and plantains. Surely there's more to the feasts but I can't identify it. Small fires burn in every direction to heat the rice and plantains. From the smell, which is more that of a burning house than of wood, it at least partially answers the riddle of where they get the fuel.

Traffic is even more frenetic now as people make haste to get somewhere safe before night overtakes them. It's hard to imagine this dance ever stopping. There's too much want, too many distended stomachs, too many mouths to feed. It feels endless, maybe even hopeless. But compared to an active war zone where genocide takes all lives on one side—scenes not uncommon here in recent history—through that lens maybe all this constitutes a marvel. It's life. It's millions of lungs drawing oxygen that fuels animation. It's as many eyes as visible stars in the night sky, stoically blinking away smoke, revealing their world, a world to be improved, maybe even worshipped.

I feel a terrible sense of guilt, escaping in the safety of a big Econoline van. What irony. I exercise daily to keep my weight in check, realizing I often choke down enough food in a single sitting to feed ten of these people for a day.

I turn my focus to my job. I'll be back next week, but that trip has been scheduled with a full double crew so it can operate in compliance with our contract and avoid laying over here. Then we'll drop our hundred-ton cargo, load a few thousand gallons of fuel, and fly on to Entebbe.

CHAPTER 8

FAREWELL

Tonight, we taxi our gigantic MD-11 down the runway and do another 180-degree turn at the end. I spend considerable effort ensuring the soldier standing guard off the side of the runway knows I'm singling him out with a salute bestowing all the honor I can muster.

It's FO Leluc's turn to fly. This sets me mostly free as a backup set of eyeballs in the cockpit. Little requires my attention since this airplane is designed as a two-pilot cockpit. I'll ensure we're within the certified weight and balance envelope before takeoff and take care of other necessary paperwork as we go. In my world, it's universally mused that paperwork must outweigh the airplane before it can legally fly.

Though the sun set an hour ago, I rise from my seat after liftoff to look down from our lofty perch and send a blessing of hope to the masses below. In under five minutes we make the twenty-five-mile journey from the end of the runway to pass over the city. If such a thing can be done, I aspire to send good tidings and love to every light I see. I wonder if miracles, as proclaimed through the ages, can really affect the physical world when enough fervor is pumped directly at specific targets. I hope so.

This ten-hour dip into such a deep ocean of hardship and struggle has changed me. Sobered me. Shaken me. I've borne witness to a dire snapshot that frames a world of which I'm terrified. Survivors of this torn culture make their way through gaping wounds that were once a better place, more easily identifiable as "home."

How blessed am I to know so much about the right to pursue happiness. The tapestry of my busy life, filled to the brim with news and distraction, will likely grind away at my superficial thoughts, effecting a quick recovery from the guilt I feel for having enough to eat, knowing always from where my next meal is coming, and having almost certain protection from the ill wishes of others that might yearn to harm me. I might even forgive the immodest wealth decorating my life with prosperity that now seems out of balance in this struggling world.

Even though I know I'll recover and these memories will fade, I hope to never forget those souls traveling that road to God knows where, in their endless toil and struggle in Kinshasa, Democratic Republic of the Congo.

CHAPTER 9
GHANA

Departing Salt Lake City on March 15, 2010, Delta carries me to Atlanta, Georgia, then on to Amsterdam. There I transfer to Turkish Airlines and continue to Nairobi, Kenya. I meet the rest of my crew at the Stanley Hotel. Henry Morton Stanley's successful feat in finding Dr. Livingstone seems to have levied on him honor after honor throughout much of Africa, hence our hotel's namesake.

While it's a nice hotel, it's subject to daily, sometimes hourly, power outages as I soon learn is the norm on much of the African continent. It takes only one instance of my treadmill suddenly stopping for me to realize imprinting the machine's controls on my belly isn't an experience I want again. I switch to a stationary bike.

We're scheduled for pickup from the hotel at 6 a.m. on March 20th. We're embarking on a cargo flight to Accra, the capital of Ghana. Captain Jenks, First Officer Baum, and I meet in the lobby at 5:40 where complimentary coffee awaits us in Styrofoam cups. We'll have breakfast on the airplane in a couple of hours. At 6:05 we begin fearing that something in the schedule has gone amiss as our transport has not arrived. In ten more minutes we agree it's time to get to work ironing out a solution. When Captain Jenks finally gets a World Airways dispatcher on the phone, he's informed that indeed, errors were made, and we're instructed to pay for a taxi to take us to the airport. It will be an expensive ride, and the taxi services here do not accept credit cards. Too much fraud so it's a cash only enterprise. Between all of us, we're woefully short. A brightly lit sign advertising an ATM machine is in view only a block away. Tom, the captain, has a lot of experience in Africa and says flat-out that he will not go, nor will he allow either of us first officers to approach the money machine. He assures us there are robbers competing for who gets to roll the next uninitiated white man foolish enough to withdraw cash money from a street vending machine at this time of day. We're stuck.

At 6:30, a large, olive-green, fifteen-seat van pulls into the portico. Before anyone shows up to board, I climb into the opened doors and query the driver about his business. He's here to pick up a Kenya Airways crew for transportation to the airport. I ask if he has room for the three of us World pilots and he says he does, if it's okay with the Kenyan crew. It is. We're saved.

We arrive at Jomo Kenyatta International airport half an hour late, at 7:15. We're informed of no special or hazardous cargo for our flight. After inspecting the cargo pallets to ensure all are properly secured to the floor tracks in our 170-foot cargo cave, I report to Captain Jenks that all are well fixed. Each pallet is loaded with identical small wooden boxes stacked about six feet high. It seems an unusually heavy weight for such low stacks that might normally be more like eight or nine feet tall.

We depart Runway 24 with our 165,000-pound load westbound for Accra's Kotoka International airport. Save for the transportation issues getting to the airport, the trip goes uneventfully. Stable, almost static air offers smooth flying the entire 2600-mile distance, and ATC communications for this part of the world are refreshingly clear. After five hours and twenty-seven minutes, FO Baum flairs our heavy, 14-wheeled behemoth onto Runway 21 and brakes cautiously down to taxi speed. Tower instructs us to take the second highspeed exit to our right, a taxiway branching off the runway at a shallow angle allowing safe exit speeds up to 60 miles per hour. Immediately fronting the end of the highspeed taxiway is an expansive parking ramp, empty except for one marshaler and what appears to be a large contingent of Ghana's military and police force.

It's disconcerting that four armed military vehicles form up with us immediately as we enter the parking ramp. They have roof-mounted, large caliber machine guns and flashing red and blue lights over the driver's cab. There are two on each side of us spaced closely abeam our nose and wing tips. The marshaler stands with military bearing, guiding us precisely to our parking spot. Once stopped, another six armed military vehicles form a half circle perimeter around us. Several armored trucks begin to move toward us as soon as we shut down our engines.

Unbeknownst to us, we've just transported one hundred million dollars' worth of Ghanaian Cedi. The paper currency of Ghana is printed on presses in Nairobi, Kenya. It's cheaper to contract businesses in Nairobi to print their money than make it themselves.

World Airways' African flying operations continue to astonish me. Power outages, logistical lapses made of carelessness, streets so unsafe—even in a city of over four million people—it's too dangerous to extract money from ATMs, and heavy cargo valuable enough to entice a huge military presence to greet us with menacing armor while we're kept in the dark. What's next, I wonder.

CHAPTER 10

THE SCOURGE OF COLONIZATION

Inevitably, colonizing occupations end. Occupiers might depart quickly if resources being plundered are exhausted. Or they might take decades when politics is the linchpin over which conflicts persist. Vietnam had to endure both French and American dwellers for decades, suffering casualties in the millions for their trouble.

Usually, time washes away the blood and terror, and the countries often become trading partners like The Democratic Republic of the Congo and Belgium, or popular tourist destinations like Vietnam.

Withdrawal of the foreign presence rarely leaves the "possession" recognizable to the original tenants. While wealthy interests upgrade cities to bustling economic bastions with huge demographics living western types of lifestyles, there's often a much larger social order writhing in poverty. In Nairobi, that struggling group exists in staggering numbers and in plain sight.

The remnants of English colonization has left in its wake modern Nairobi with her massive overcrowding, chaotic city streets, and people divided into terribly lopsided economies. Most westerners understand scales of poverty and suffering in sanitized versions compared to many in the third world. In the USA, where hunger and suffering are very real problems in some demographics, most homeless can get sufficient nourishment from the food wastes we throw away—a staggering two hundred and thirty million pounds every day. In the third world, such bounty simply doesn't exist. Millions go hungry suffering a hopeless quest.

CHAPTER 11
DEAR MARCIA

May 17, 2010
Dear Marcia,

I'm so sorry I didn't tell you about this earlier. I couldn't find words without the time to reflect, and write, and rewrite, and edit, that would even come close to describing what happened. I also couldn't bear to leave you despairing, alone. After reflection, I can now share this with you. I hope by reliving this painful night, I can begin to shed the melancholy about which you've so tenderly inquired.

Last year I vowed to take you as my lawfully wedded wife and to care for you in sickness and in health. I did then, and I still do.

Your loving husband,
Andy
Nairobi, Kenya

On May 9, 2010, my ride to the Stanley Hotel illuminates a picture for me of life among those left out of the banquet.

After my Kenya Airways flight lands at Jomo Kenyatta International Airport in Nairobi, I find my driver just outside the arrivals gate. He offers to carry my bags which roll effortlessly on a trolley. I refuse his kind offer but am impressed, as always, with the genuine kindness that I have experienced in Africa.

Walking from the terminal to the parking garage in the evening light is hazardous given the zealous parade of traffic hurrying to pick up or drop off passengers. There are still long lines of people queued up to enter the terminal. Common in many African and Middle Eastern countries, metal detectors and baggage X-ray machines are set up immediately inside entrance ways creating a stop-and-go flow. Those still outside skirmish with burdensome baggage, squeezing against walls as cars zip by heedless of roadway boundaries. The smell of hot asphalt and car exhaust eclipses any aromas the light breeze offers.

Arriving at the Toyota Signature minivan after a few minutes, I seat myself in the front passenger seat, and my driver, Kioko, which means born in the morning, sinks into the right-hand driver's seat. He pulls from the parking stall reserved for hotel taxis and merges into moderate traffic departing the airport.

A few minutes later, we join Mombasa Road, a main artery from the airport. This three-lane highway fronts the Nairobi National Park on our left for several miles. Free to roam anywhere they choose in the park's refuge are giraffes, lions, leopards, zebra, cheetah, wildebeest, black rhinoceros, and a host of other imperial Kenyan animals. Acacia trees stand as sentinels not three hundred feet from the roadway, and like a scene from Jurassic Park, I see giraffes ambling along near them. Closer yet are a few zebras and impalas wandering casually on the grassy plain, as common here as antelope in Wyoming. I'm spellbound, seeing these majestic animals in real life.

On our right squats the quintessential ingredients of cultural destruction. A flood of one- and two-story commercial buildings pepper the landscape. An occasional scraggly tree breaks through asphalt, but otherwise, it's an ocean of warehouses and industry.

People along the crumbling sidewalks are gathering trash and whatever will burn to start cooking fires. The farther east, toward downtown Nairobi, the more profuse their ranks become. Fires mature. Some flames shimmy chest high among the growing throngs. The fragrant scent of trees and grass near the wildlife preserve has been robbed by the stench of burning trash. The tastes of burnt rubber and plastic coat the inside of my mouth and throat.

Small groups gather around the numberless fires to warm themselves in the cooling twilight. Some are wrapped in torn and tattered sleeping bags. I can't imagine what they have to prepare for an evening meal, but judging by their gaunt statures, it certainly won't be much. The trappings in a dumpster outside any big city McDonald's would boost the calories available for these folks considerably. James Taylor's soulful "Millworker" loops the deepening melancholy in the halls of my mind where the lowest in the corporation never meet the man whose name is on the label. Lives once filled with possibility now crushed by entrepreneurial gorging.

A pleasant, unmobbed night seems nearly surreal in its absence of frantic automobile traffic and street vendors. It's 4 a.m. on May 11, our scheduled pickup time from the Stanley Hotel. Tropical breezes of the Kenyan night are refreshing on my face. The scent of gardenias fills the air with perfume strong enough to wipe away foul odors the vastly overpopulated city contributes. I'm excited to climb aboard our minivan whose driver will have us at Nairobi's airport in thirty minutes. With our mighty MD-11 freighter, Captain Tracy Hahn, First Officer Ramon Leluc, and I will transport just over 180,000 pounds of fragrant, fresh flowers to Ostend, Belgium. By evening, people throughout northern Europe will be arranging them in vibrant bouquets on fireplace hearths, nooks in church chancels, and in vases on street café tables.

The white Toyota minivan is splashed with red "Signature" logos across its sides and back. It's just ample enough for baggage in the back, two passengers in mid seats, and the driver and myself in the front.

Our driver, Alhaadi, aptly meaning guide, begins our journey on vacant streets. Even at red-light traffic signals, there are no other cars in sight. I recognize the sidewalks where huge assemblies of people congregated around fires earlier. A few lay dozing in sleeping bags. Ribs ripple the torso skin of famished dogs sniffing for any morsel of food that might have escaped human consumption.

Within five minutes we're once again on Mombasa Road, whose route will take us past the game preserve and to the airport.

Our way is dimly lit under streetlamps fitted with filthy lens caps. Several of them are burned out, turning dim to dark. Alhaadi nonetheless drives with confidence. He knows the route well having driven it many times in the dark. Few other vehicles share our road, and I see only two or three people walking trails alongside.

A group of three bicyclists materialize a couple of hundred feet ahead in our headlight beams. I'm astounded by the cargos they carry. Barnum & Bailey's scouts must have missed this crack team or surely they'd have gainful employment in the Big Ring.

Plastic crates, like those dairy companies use to transport fifty school lunch-sized cartons of milk, are lashed five stories high on back fenders. As we approach, it's obvious the bikes themselves are heavy, steel bikes, probably of WWII vintage. The crates appear to be overflowing. Poles and hose-like protrusions stick out at odd angles. I suspect these are the FedEx equivalent of express shipping in this territory. Villages or camps too small to warrant truck or van deliveries are supplied by bicycles, and the drivers, like pony express riders, learn the perfect balance points and limits of their conveyance to deliver their effects. Needy hands in nearby villages will have their requisitioned goods by daybreak.

Only ten or fifteen minutes from our destination, I'm feeling my morning caffeine diminish. The anxious energy that propelled me into my morning is fading quickly. My eyelids are heavy. I try to find interest in the highway and surroundings rather than allow sleep to take me. I've seen this road enough now to know it could use several more lanes. Presently, it's hard to imagine it's too narrow, traffic being so light. But daylight hours bring dangerous choking and flaring tempers. The shoehorned masses would feel less tormented if they had another lane or two to ease congestion.

In this predawn hour we're nearly alone. A few hundred yards ahead, a large, flatbed truck canopied with canvas over hoop staves begins a long merge onto the road from a right-hand entrance. His own lights seem muted and dim, as if not to disturb the night. At nearly the same location, a car merges in from the left. After a long absence of neighbors, it looks like we'll soon be sharing our deserted road with two other vehicles. I'm perturbed by the arrival of them intruding on our solitude. Had it been a single vehicle, even a large transport truck, followed a few minutes later by another, that would've been okay. But after such sedate transit, adding two vehicles at once offends my sense of calm, and I'm unwittingly harassed into a higher level of alertness.

Soon we become hemmed into our three-lane highway by vehicles nearly abeam us both right and left. A few hundred feet ahead, I see something in the road. I think it's in our lane.

Forty years of driving automobiles has always borne out the same results when something shows up in the road. It's always a cardboard box or a plastic garbage bag. Never anything more.

I'm sure that's all this is, but its shape begins to rouse my curiosity. My flight crew is sound asleep in the bench seat behind. Alhaadi seems too quiet. At the very top of his spinal cord, a pea-sized gland attaches to its backside and, at sunset, as light dims to dark, a drop of melatonin hormone jets into Alhaadi's blood beginning a biological preference to sleep. That's how it works for diurnal creatures great and small on this green earth. Sheer willpower, especially combined with a stimulant like coffee, can temper the compulsion, but the signal is tenacious and usually wins in the long run. I think Alhaadi's surrender flag is rising.

Our speed is sixty miles per hour. Eighty-eight feet of pavement disappear beneath our tires every second.

The garbage bag is only about two hundred feet ahead now. The "form-matching" software wired into my brain traverses from dubious concern to adrenaline pounding shock. I lean forward as if six inches closer will bring more clarity to the lumpy shape.

My eyes are riveted straight ahead, and I feel paralyzed. I want to look at Alhaadi to see if he recognizes what I'm now certain I'm seeing, but I can't look away. My head aches as I strain my eyes rightward in their sockets. My head refuses to move. There's no time. I can't tell if Alhaadi is digesting the fast-clarifying object ahead. I want to yell or scream but that seems as stifled as the rest of my motor functions. It's like a nightmare where movement is retarded by unseen forces to extreme slow motion.

One hundred feet. Implausibly, Alhaadi drives straight ahead. A guttural yell to STOP wrenches from my larynx. Alhaadi sees the body just as my scream materializes, and he pulls the steering wheel hard right, barely missing the back of the canvas-covered truck.

The strongest image burning into my mind, the one removing all doubt about the identity of this "lump," is the pink color of the bottoms of the feet. It's a man. He lies on his left side, his head a ball of darkness craning toward the left side of our lane; his skinny bare legs huddle side by side, limp against the road, knees slightly bent, spilling pathetically across the dark asphalt. Alhaadi's lurching is too late to miss the young man entirely. *Thump thump* jars the van with gut-wrenching resonance as we run over his legs.

While it happens too fast, and below the insulated floor of our vehicle, in my mind I hear, almost feel, the bones in his legs shattering under our weight. I bend my body down and to the left to see in the rearview mirror on my side. All visibility through the back window is blocked by our luggage. I barely see his carcass bounce and then lie perfectly still. He's naked from the waist down with only a T-shirt tangled around his torso.

Tracy and Ramon startle awake from our hard swerve and the twin bumps. I'm recoiling in shock and gloom but find enough tongue to offer in a thin voice, "We ran over a dead guy." It's all I can spit out for now.

I realize I'm nauseous and my nose is suddenly runny. I've never even seen a dead person outside of a casket. I might be surprised at the emotional toll I'm tasting, but I don't have enough discretionary logic right now to guide me. Tears swell on my lower lids, slowly building in mass until they fall onto my cheeks, and for a moment, not for the first time, I hate the unfairness of life.

I've read numerous accounts about the dangers of being involved in accidents in third world countries, especially if you're white. No matter the degree of separation between the victim and your involvement, sometimes mobs form and take out their anger on the most visible enemy which can easily be a white guy if he's unlucky enough to happen onto the scene. I've even read US Department of State advisories admonishing US citizens not to stop in or near any accident, demonstrations, or any kind of civil unrest. We're even advised to seek refuge at a US consulate in the event we've been in an accident and let our representatives deal with the fallout.

Alhaadi needs no counsel on this. He knows better than I that distance between himself and any death is his most certain sanctuary. He makes no attempt to slow and drives on, recovered in our lane, bound for the airport at sixty miles per hour.

Now, however, his somnolent bearing has transformed to excitedness. He speaks so rapidly I can hardly distinguish a single word. He's obviously unsettled and uses the only tool at his disposal to seek stability. He excitedly relays, mostly in babble, that something happened just last night around this same place and time. "Here!" he declares pointing to the left shoulder. "Here last night, three were down!" What the hell, I think. Is he telling me he saw three dead people off the side of the road here last night? I'm stunned. Are dead bodies on the road common around here? I can hardly believe this, but his terrified countenance is persuasive. I wish I could inquire about the details of what he's talking about, but with his excited state and my understanding of his words, it's a certain recipe for misunderstanding and frustration. I let it drop, hoping his temper will soon burn out.

I'm trying to puzzle out the scene I've just witnessed. Did this John Doe make a failed attempt to cross the wide road and get hit by a car? Unless the offending car was traveling with its headlights off, no matter how dirty or pitted its lenses, it seems hard to imagine he couldn't see him coming in plenty of time to hustle out of an injurious, in this case, fatal path. Why on earth was he naked below the waist?

The sickening movie plays repeatedly in my head. I see his carcass bounce and resettle after we run over his legs, his exposed penis, and short curly hair adding repulsive details I don't want to think about.

Only a mile or so farther down the road, we pass a police car creeping along in the far-left lane. What are these police doing rolling along so slowly on this highway in the middle of the night? This is the only police car I've seen in Kenya and here, merely a mile from a dead body. Hadn't they seen this dead youth in the road?

Bad, unjust things happen all over the world, and whenever I get too shocked by them, I resort to irrational fault finding trying to stick someone with the black hat. I begin to wonder, is life such a cheap commodity here? Do the masses of poor and hapless Kenyans annoy corrupt kingpins into murder so easily? Hitler, Stalin, Tojo, Pol Pot, Kim Il-Sung, Idi Amin, Pinochet, not to mention rampant hate crimes perpetrators who cause endless death and suffering on my own country's soil. I simply can't find a corner of the earth, or a skin tone, immune from tyranny. The blame game stops.

I've watched my share of crime and drama movies, so maybe my imagination is getting the best of me. But that crawling police car so close to a dead body seems to stretch disassociation to the breaking point. It's said that if you go to bed and your yard consists of green grass, and you wake up to a few inches of snow covering it, that your proof it snowed overnight is merely circumstantial. Sometimes, circumstantial is more than enough. The more I play it out, the more I think that police car deposited the deceased.

I never speak to Tracy or Ramon about this. They've both been around the block enough to know when to let sleeping dogs lie.

Alhaadi, too, knows that if one's objective is to extend life, periodically it's best not to see and not to ask. Wounds occasionally need to be taken to our souls with motion forward commenced in silence.

So it ends?

In the span of five days, I've borne witness to calamity twice. Twenty-three hundred and seventy miles west, by roadways transiting Kenya, Tanzania, Burundi, and DRC, sixty-three hours of driving will bring one lucky enough to survive it to Kinshasa, the capital of DRC. There I observed hundreds of thousands of suffering souls struggling along a twenty-five-mile path to perdition. Here in Nairobi, I've just faced the loss of a single life, extinguished nearly before my eyes, doubtless still warm when we mangled his legs.

These nightmares tear at my soul, fraying what only days ago seemed smooth edged.

On Thursday, May 13th, with more than half the circumference of the earth behind, I finally end my duty in Salt Lake City, my home. Marcia collects me at the airport, soon detecting my diminished spark. I'm guarded with what I tell her. I have to do it with great forethought and honesty, careful not to diminish either ordeal. The populations I've encountered deserve the best I can marshal. But I need to push the distance farther away from my bruising. I trust time to drain some of the lament I'm feeling.

Ten days after my homecoming, I'm happily back with our choir. We've rehearsed for months preparing for our Memorial Sunday requiem. This year, it's The Ellingboe Requiem. Not only do we get to sing it to our congregation, but we've also been invited to join several other choirs and sing it June 9th in Carnegie Hall. It's a stunning composition.

This singing business is exactly the medicine I need to boost my dwindling flame back to blazing. Dazzling harmonies reached among rich voices touch some magical place in most people, eliciting something close to transcendental rapture. It's certain Marcia and I are among this lucky demographic.

Having swam in deeper pools the wide world has offered, I feel the depth I bring to my tenor part is vastly more vibrant than I could have achieved before swimming in Africa's.

Our church is the Unitarian Universalist church. In it there's an extraordinarily wide swath of belief structures, so my humanist views are embraced and appreciated just as much as anyone else's. I can't claim a pious nature, but as we conclude the finale in the last movement, Elegy, I decide to speak to God in private. I ask Him to watch over the millions of people facing so much hardship in Africa and over the face of all the earth. I also beseech Him, Please God, I think I've received Your message. I will do my utmost to offer love unconditionally as widely as I'm able. Meanwhile, would it be okay to pause the lesson? It's been all I can bear. For now, please let it be enough.

Elegy
Lux aeterna luceat eis, Domine:
Cum sanctis tuis in aeterna:
Quia pius es,
Requiem aeternam dona eis, Domine:
Et lux perpetua luceat eis.

Light eternal shine on them, Lord,
With your saints for eternity;
For you are merciful.
Grant them peace eternal, Lord
And light perpetual shine on them.

CHAPTER 12

DAKAR

So often three seems to be the magic number that ends, at least for a time, a series of misfortunes. I think my *Universal Guide* gave me a brief respite after my prayers, but *She* must feel like I'm now ready for more. Almost exactly one year after the hurt and shock of running over a dead man's legs near Jomo Kenyatta Airport in Nairobi, a third apocalypse visits my consciousness, shaking another generous helping of awareness into my root cellar.

On May 1st, 2011, the Airbus 321 in which I'm riding flares gracefully onto the concrete of Léopold Sédar Senghor International Airport's runway 36. The Iberia Airline pilot at the controls shows off his mastery, bringing a praiseworthy conclusion to my Dakar flight. It's been a thirty-eight-hour trek from Salt Lake City with a layover in JFK and a short overnight stay in Munich, Germany. Fatigue claws at my brain and creaky body, but I dutifully follow the loudspeaker instructions from the flight attendants to remain seated. I massage my neck muscles, plagued with tension as I try to imagine the next few days. This is my first trip to Dakar, the capitol city of Senegal. I have more than two dozen trips to Africa under my belt now with multiple-day stays in eight African countries. Senegal makes number nine and the first on the west coast of the continent. Each trip brings surprise and suspense and greater and lesser degrees of danger. My African experiences to date have caused me to psychologically prepare for a gauntlet of self-reflection and a little self-recrimination. I can't get through a visit to these struggling countries, so steeped in hardship, without coming away with a portion of my free-flowing mirthful disposition cauterized. Now begins another episode. I don't yet know whether to shudder or celebrate the new wonders that lie ahead.

My itinerary had already transited rough turbulence when the ticket agent at the Iberia ticket counter in Munich informed me that, while my ticket to Dakar was valid, it hadn't been paid for. Typical Sunday morning office hours, imperfect linguistic translations, and the idiosyncratic nature of international telecommunications conspired to end all efforts to contact the operations people at my company back in Peachtree City, GA. After nearly an hour exhausting every possible avenue, the sales agent and I contrived a plan that got me on my way. Rebooking from scratch, as if I'd just that moment chosen to fly, ended up doing the trick. Money is not an issue. World Airways issues each pilot an American Express credit card that has no limit. Use of it is left to our discretion, but monthly expense reports must legitimize all expenses. She typed at what seemed a frantic staccato tempo and soon produced a ticket. I boarded the flight bound for Africa's westernmost city. It seems I'm off to a messy start.

Three buses arrive planeside to transport us five hundred feet to the International Arrivals building. Once full, the bus doors hiss shut, entombing us in hot, depressing humidity that exaggerates scents of West Africa and itinerant wanderers. After the bus jerks to a stop, we slowly traverse the ramp, arriving at customs. Uniformed officials wearing ostentatious brimmed caps common among communist militaries impatiently guide us to assemble. We're herded into a well-lit passport-processing hall. No signs welcome us or tell us to segregate by nationality or other status which feels strange. The eagerness displayed by the pretentiously uniformed authorities showcases a familiar air of self-importance. I've grown wise in third world ways and know it's best to move along in subdued compliance. I'm guided into one of four lines that seem to move quickly. I'm acutely aware that I'm the only white man in the entire hall, so I lay on the respect and courtesy. I hand my passport to the officer caged in a phone booth-sized plywood kiosk. He scrutinizes it for a long time, and I begin to worry something's wrong. I'm tired, but more importantly, I'm the odd man out. I catch myself falling too easily into unnecessary alarm. He finally stamps my passport and sends me on.

The next man is stationed behind a long counter topped with well-worn, gray laminate. Without a word he slips my Disembarkation form out of my passport. After a cursory glance, he nods toward a temporary door that's nothing more than a slit in some plastic nailed up over an opening in the wall. There's construction in progress, and the suspended plastic sheeting covers what will obviously be a doorway sometime in the future. Emerging through the slit brings me to the baggage claim room. Before I can hesitate, I'm sucked into a horde massed around a single, large, conveyor belt. People are vying for position with the impatience of stock traders.

From my perspective, this melee teeters on the edge of pandemonium. Crying children, the incessant yapping of a small dog in a woman's oversized purse, and an endless stream of porters anxious for tips fill the sweltering air with frenetic energy. My eyes sting from a combination of sleeplessness and a not very well masked ammonia smell I fear stems from latent urine. My two bags chug along the belt toward me, and I snatch them as they come within my reach. Piggybacking them and my carry-on into a single heavy trolley, I'm struck realizing I have the unusual distinction of ferrying luggage that doesn't outweigh me. Wherever my fellow travelers have come from, apparently they've found groceries cheaper there than here and have stocked up like Costco shoppers.

Two more bustling lines form at X-ray machines whose purpose is to safeguard Senegal from incoming contraband and levy duties on items deemed to present unfair competition to local retailers. While practiced in all countries I've visited, I can't detect any serious interest in the screeners' manner. Baggage moves through these checkpoints faster than valid scrutiny can possibly follow. They're disgorged from the belts at a rate guards can't keep up with, so they pile up and spill haphazardly across the dirty floor. Retrieving mine, I hastily merge into the thinning crowds that approach the building's exits.

I ask a uniformed guard if he can tell me where I might find the shuttle to the Pullman Hotel. He distractedly motions me toward a rough, plywood wall in a makeshift waiting area, also under construction. A short while later a large man in casual, light brown summer wear, who I'm guessing had little trouble spotting me in the crowd, arrives to usher me through this Sunday evening crowd. The mass and movement of people make me feel like I'm approaching the starting line of the Boston Marathon, and the predominant odor probably approaches what awaits finishers. I feel unnerved by the incessant honking of horns, squeaking brakes, slamming doors, police whistles, and the hustle of thousands of excited travelers being welcomed home.

My passage through this turbulent throng reminds me of stories of Moses parting the Red Sea and seems no less miraculous. Cars, trolleys, carts, and people alter their courses, diverging to allow my gentle giant unhindered passage. I follow close behind. The two dollars I tip him seems miserly for the service he's rendered, but he accepts it with the kind of gratitude I might expect had I handed him a hundred. I later learn that in the local economy, hidden to foreigners, two American dollars easily buys what twenty would buy me back home.

I climb aboard a small, white van with "Pullman Hotel" stenciled in black lettering on its front giving encouragement I'm not being kidnapped. It's packed with Australian businessmen, boys really, bound for another hotel along the shuttle's route. There's one seat left, and I scrunch into it as unobtrusively as I can, not wanting to interrupt the Australian party. Our eleven-mile journey begins negotiating a sea of pedestrians, yellow taxis, and dilapidated buses, reminding me of an anxious ride I'd survived a year ago into the city of Kinshasa. To my western eyes and heart, even with a year of African travel under my belt, this immersion still shocks me.

Along the way, I puzzle trying to imagine a time when the sights appearing out my window might have been new and pristine. The age and totality of damage and disrepair tricks me into believing the sidewalks and streets have always looked like refugees of a 7.0 magnitude earthquake. Could it ever have existed when weeds weren't exaggerating all the cracks and rubble and litter hadn't adorned every inch of real estate? People sit cross-legged along the way with woven baskets of fruits and vegetables beside them. Some enjoy larger pantries by partnering with burros harnessed to tiny wooden carts. They look comfortable and content.

Buildings are in various states of disrepair. I wonder if there's money anywhere that could lure businessmen or industrious renovators to take a stab at rehabbing. I feel bad riding through the middle of such poverty completely insulated from it, as if I should either not look or actually try to do something, but not just gawk. For now, I guess my gut will just have to stew in its juices.

Omnipresent taxis swarm the streets in two guises, solid yellow and their competitors, also yellow but checkered with black quarter panels front and back. Both companies must have found the same sale as they're all aging Renault sedans. An Internet search reveals they date back to the 1970s. They all show their age. Still, I marvel at the resourcefulness of a people that, with little money, can keep old cars running for decades. There are also scores of blue and yellow minibuses, plastered with Muslim slogans, darting side to side along the roadways, picking up and discharging passengers.

A code of conduct seems evident on roadways in both African and Middle Eastern countries that displays a shocking degree of apathy regarding collisions. Dakar fits seamlessly into this class with testimony in the prevalent form of dented side panels, scraped doors, and bashed-in back ends. Apparently, sideswiping and rear-ending are common forms of queuing here in narrow, potholed streets, appearing to be as common as neglected turn signals in the west. While body shops would seem to be likely candidates for large profits, there's little evidence of them. Sellers of Bondo, on the other hand, must make a fortune. Whether economic or cultural, surface beauty seems trivial here. Practical application of duct tape and other resources readily available to the local population appears widely and expertly showcased.

Multistory buildings line nearly every inch of frontage beyond the decrepit sidewalks. Fully half of them are in some phase of construction, but the work seems to have been paused an eon ago. On the ravaged earth surrounding these hulking, abandoned projects, camps abound that house many of the city's residents. In this part of the world these people aren't considered "homeless." Their makeshift dwellings appear to constitute legitimate intercity living judging from their sheer numbers. Neighborly gatherings casually front many huts along the promenade. Their lodging seems to be made primarily from tree branches, cinderblocks, discarded rugs and carpets, old bathroom shower curtains, and cardboard. Those sheathed with corrugated steel are the castles on the block. Several burning fires shed light on evening festivities, and families and friends appear to engage in the rituals of living without any evidence of stigma for this lifestyle.

Walking appears to be the primary means of getting around. It's free, and haste isn't an essential ingredient to many in this population. When distance or time become relevant, buses appear to be the first choice. There's a large collection of old vans, fifteen-seat artifacts, most likely pre-World War II, whose aesthetic qualities elicit little attention. They're as bashed and bruised as their yellow taxi brethren, and few survive with an entire set of windows. At first glance I think the back doors on these rigs have been wrenched so far open that they're permanently stuck. Upon closer inspection, too frequently available at alarmingly close range, I come to realize they're tied open with bungee cords or lengths of rope. I can't tell if the intent is for "air-conditioning" or rapid ingress and egress of their charges, but I'm fairly sure it's the latter. Most are jam-packed. If designed for fifteen, thirty can fit.

At the Pullman Hotel, I'm immediately surrounded with help-ful hands. My driver gratefully accepts my two-dollar tip with appreciation that, again, seems unbalanced against the offering. He motors off into the crowded night with his happy cargo of Australians.

At the front desk, I'm handed forms whose blanks exceed some employment applications I've completed. After I submit them, the receptionist produces a calculator whose screen is as big as a small TV. His meticulous button tapping displays results he confidently shares. My American Express slips from my wallet, and the charge is duly advanced. The entire transaction, check in and out, is concluded on the spot. I've never seen this before. What if I order room service?

I make my way to elevators through a crowded lobby peopled with wealthy foreigners whose night festivities are just beginning. A door whooshes open, producing an entrance just wide enough for my rolling suitcase trailing behind me. One more person would exceed the space afforded in this tiny car. Ascension to the eighth floor gives me just enough time to realize how weary I am. I long for a bed. Nothing else infringes against that narrow yearning.

In the twenty hours since my arrival, I've seen and successfully swat-ted only one mosquito. A strong scent of bug toxin demystifies the lack of infestation, but I can't help but wonder which is the more dangerous adversary. I believe there's only a slight possibility that malaria threatens me from the local mosquito population. I'm much more suspicious about the integrity of whatever chemical company concocted the poison. I've become jaded by too much evidence of corporations' focus on profits above the health and safety of humans. Taking a wider view jogs me to a rosier outlook. Daily life is fraught with risk. I commit to not getting bogged down in bleak skirmishes with fate over which I have no control.

The breakfast buffet on the lobby level occupies a huge expanse on the south side of the hotel. Its ten-foot windows offer breathtaking views overlooking the Atlantic Ocean. This high-ceilinged dining hall adjoins a large outdoor patio, providing another bevy of tables to satisfy the outdoorsy among us. The ample spread consists of at least ten steaming serving dishes wafting irresistible aromas. Several islands offer colorful salad, generous varieties of fresh fruit, rolls, baguettes, and sliced, rich textured breads. Also in evidence are jellies by the dozen and gallons of exotic juices, coffee, and teas of every description. Outdoors, a chef expertly creates beautiful custom egg dishes at his omelet station. My willpower to stay healthy, as usual, collapses abruptly in the presence of such bounty. Three hundred feet south, beyond tall, iron fences, the city's permanent residents survive daily on scraps. Repetition of this dismal paradigm endures predictably.

Stuffed to a level of uncomfortableness, I plod back to my room and find irresistible allure waiting at a south facing window. The absorbing and stunning panorama is ceilinged by cerulean-blue skies entirely virgin of clouds. My focus naturally draws from distant horizons south and east to real estate more immediately in the foreground. Countless tall buildings pepper the city's skyline. I'm encompassed by a civilization that presently consists of more than three million residents. The geography used to consist of several distinct boroughs, but urban sprawl seems to have obliterated all division.

Originally, when the Senegalese Lebou people settled this far western peninsula, they divided it into four villages: Ngor, Yoff, Quaqam, and Hann. Those communities, to this day, still hold predominately Lebou descendants. These were, naturally, fishing peoples. Portuguese slavers showed up mid-fifteenth century, followed by French, Dutch, and English pilgrims who traded occupying troops and citizenry in continuing and perverse reiteration. They brought with them the worst of mankind just as they did everywhere they could find anchorage. Our European ancestors long ago perfected "Manifest Destiny," a philosophy I thought endemic only to early habitation in the United States.

Looking east I realize I'm peering at Goree Island, just a mile offshore in the Dakar Bay. One of the oldest buildings on the small island is The House of Slaves, a rock edifice built by Afro-French colonists in the late eighteenth century. It was a major "distribution center" built expressly for the furtherance of industrial slave trading. I stare for several minutes, shaken and depressed by the insuppressible images of terror and sorrow that suffused that building's interior for centuries. I can't seem to wrap my head around kidnapping happy, healthy people living their lives as richly deserved as any sentient being, torn from families, friends, and traditions, beaten repeatedly, often to death, to claim ownership over another's sacred being. To serve a cruel master for life, while he exercises Godlike powers over you, runs counter to any imaginable strand in the fabric of empathy or decency. Heart-wrenching darkness washes the canvas of humanity, not from African skin tones, but from charcoal-black hearts beating in alabaster-white chests.

Torment still rends the souls of the masses here with poverty being its primary weapon. Senegal achieved independence from French colonial forces in 1960, but class distinctions are deeply honed and stubbornly persist. It's everywhere I look.

From my eighth-floor window, I see the hotel is surrounded by a picket fence identical, I think, to the one Tom Sawyer whitewashed using free labor. In fact, Tom's conscripts gave their most prized valuables for the privilege of painting. Tom's entrepreneurial skills doubtless mirror the kind of trickery that leaves the wealthy and poor on opposite sides of a deep chasm. In Mark Twain's masterful telling of *Tom Sawyer*, this accounting is highly entertaining. In the real world, it's anything but.

The hotel's fence allies with a few scrubby bushes but mostly dry, hard dirt. A guard stationed in a shack, who carefully screens all approaching vehicles, watches the Pullman's small parking lot. Several other guards patrol the hotel's grounds. This level of security is hard to breach and puts a wanderer on notice that the "unwelcomed" must stay out.

Young men shuffle outside the hotel's border, resolutely intercepting all guests bold enough to venture off the grounds. They're selling brightly colored "Post-it" note pads. It strikes me as curious that these enterprising people imagine this merchandise might appeal to the kind of wealthy clientele most likely to be in residence here. To be fair, they're quite exotic Post-it notes. Multiple packs hang from tall sticks like brightly colored leaves decorating a branch. I get the feeling some shyster found himself burdened with these trinkets and convinced these desperate merchants that if they wave them excitedly enough in the faces of their prey, surely many will bite. For several minutes I watch, rooting for the vending team consisting of no less than twenty, but see only endless defeat. Struggling to puzzle out the rout my team suffers, I stumble onto the answer. It's a game whose rules mandate penetrating the Post-it Note forest while pretending it doesn't exist. I recognize this behavior in myself. It's exactly how I respond every time I see someone with a cardboard sign at a freeway entrance in my own hometown. They want a dollar. I pretend they're not there. I find myself in an angry internal dialogue whenever I see one about how bad they make me feel. My internal voice praises my ungrudging willingness to pay taxes, much of which is supposed to go toward social programs to feed and house everybody. Sometimes I disparage them in my mind for not getting a job. I had menial, minimum-wage jobs in my youth. Why can't they? I try to hide from my shame by ignoring my white, wealthy worldview which voids most of my logic. I have a lot; they have none. The walls we build to shut out the poor and wretched stand ridged and ugly and are daily whitewashed with justification. Such callous indignity torments me.

I lie on my bed, allowing minutes to tick by. My multi-thousand calorie meal is digesting noisily, punctuating the silence with unflattering groans that would embarrass me were I not alone. Now I feel too guilty to continue just lying down. There's another window facing east I can explore. Maybe its "movie" will launch a happier plot.

Across the street is a two-story, private home, shoehorned between two apartment buildings. It has Spanish terra cotta roofing and chiffon-white stucco walls. Trim, fascia, and soffits are all painted rusty brown. Two "LG" air conditioners huddle in coves on its balcony. The adjacent apartment buildings are in various states of deterioration. This part of the world cannot yet wrangle arbitrary building codes into existence. There's too little wealth in the hands of the many.

One element adorns every roof in view—TV antennae. No matter the economic prominence revealed by the building's state, there's a dish, aimed skyward, identically coordinated with its neighbors like soldier's heads angled in perfect unison.

The rich gain wealth in proportion to how broadly they beam their promotions. With most of the citizenry tuned in, slaves are remade by insatiable desire promulgated through advertising. Once convinced life's pleasures, even its worthiness, are measured against new possessions, the battle for West African francs is won.

Government leaders similarly homogenize thinking among the country's masses when messaging finds eyes fixated at TVs in every residence. Economically and politically speaking, it's a no-brainer to subsidize TVs and antennae throughout the country.

To the right of the private residence with the Spanish tiled roof is a six-story, run-down apartment building whose uppermost residents enjoy a rooftop patio. If my windows opened, I could play catch with people on that open court. I watch a sturdy woman washing clothing in a large plastic tub, rinsing them in another, and finally hanging them from one of several clotheslines spanning the width of the patio. Under warm, sunny skies and light breezes, her laundry surely dries more quickly than mine at home where I pay a gas company to power my dryer. Her pace is unhurried, and she takes occasional rests in a faded blue plastic chair that abuts a sturdy railing. She sips casually from something like a 7-Eleven Big Gulp plastic cup, seeming to enjoy her repose. Watching her is refreshing. She's far from wealthy but lives casually on seemingly gentle terms with the hand that's been dealt her. I think it might be wise for me to take a lesson from this productive, easygoing woman. There's much to relish in my world that I too frequently miss for my habitual bustling.

CHAPTER 13

THE FAMILY

Adjacent to the laundry lady's apartment building is a small field, about a quarter of a city block. A ten-foot, gray-blue metal fence borders two sides connecting at right angles. One runs about eighty feet along the street, set back only inches. The other juts into the block about forty feet. It's like security fencing that commonly surrounds construction sights, but here, it seems overzealous just to secure a field. The lot's remaining two sides are hemmed by apartment buildings, one of which houses the laundry lady.

The lot features a colossal baobab tree that is at least forty feet tall judging from its reach to the fourth story of the apartment building. Known as "the tree of life," this giant with its cork-like bark has a trunk the size of a house. It looks like an old boiler type furnace with proportionally small ducting reaching away in wide circumference, offering generous shade. Several smaller bushwillows barely survive, deprived of sunshine robbed by large buildings and fences. The rest of the land is covered in weeds and small, tangled bushes.

Bisecting the plot is a rambling, well-trodden footpath whose origins are soon revealed. At its head, near the six-story apartment building, a lodge is fashioned from scavenged assets found on or near the property. Another byway branches off the main trail leading to a water source near my hotel. A small pipe pricks from the apartment building's side and drip, drip, drips into a make-shift trough.

The lodge is fashioned from thick tree branches sunk into the earth at four corners. Its roof is only about six feet high with old boards, plywood, and a couple of slivers of corrugated metal sheathing it. Old, tattered blankets, tree branches, and tires hold the medley in place against whirling dust devils. Another shanty stands about fifteen feet away, similarly constructed. Its walls each measure about eight feet producing about sixty-four square feet of living space *indoors*. An opening just big enough for a small man faces me. A "door" consisting of a heavy, faded blanket covers the access. Just to the side of these two quarters spring two six-foot wooden masts lashed with cross beams that anchor clothes lines. The twenty-five-foot cords suspend gently waving shirts and shorts sized to fit children and adults. The homestead would probably take radically different form if only someone would offer these folks a box of 16-penny nails and a hammer. But what occupies a jar or old dusty box in every garage in America is simply unavailable to those here left impoverished.

Commanding the compound is a tall thin woman wrapped in a long burgundy swatch covering her from head to shoeless toes. Running helter-skelter along the trails are two children, a little boy four or five years old, and another about two or three. Their bare feet ply the trails among rubble and bramble bushes with reckless abandon and unerring finesse.

They wear short pants with colors so muted by time and sun that it's impossible to deduce what hues they were when other kids wore them in years past. Green and red T-shirts hang loose on them so maybe they'll last half a year before they're outgrown. Their rambunctious natures attest to joyous curiosity and boundless energy no different than Rockefeller kids might enjoy romping around Park Avenue.

I can't know the whereabouts of their father, or if they have one, but suspect he's roving the streets in search of French francs or other forms of livelihood for his family. He might even be out front selling brightly colored Post-it notes.

It occurs to me that pleasures available to adults hemmed into such confines, making do with what there is strewn about the ground or petitioned from reluctant tourists, must be few. Before the grind of life and poverty erase whatever passion still rides randy within, that which produced the miracle of those two kids running wild, it's not difficult to imagine them finding solace at day's end, under a ragged roof of earth and stone, engaging age-old rituals, creating more mouths to feed and bodies to clothe.

Once again Africa delivers a gut punch that leaves me achy, pondering the injustices visited upon my fellow human beings whose crime is being born of irrepressible passion welled from the human heart. Chains of steel no longer bind slaves as private property, but bondage just as sure rends freedom from millions with tools of oppression, fear, greed, and poverty. There's a fix, and most people agree that basic education is the starting place. Astronomical growth in populations least able to care for themselves—and the new lives they bring forth—could easily be stemmed. What if the word of unimpeachable science was supported over irrational drivel shouted by kooks who seem to find such delight, and self-import, pretending to know things that are just nonsense?

Most corporate entities, with their enormous powers of the purse, long ago outgrew humane reasoning and empathy. Stockholders demand the largest possible return on investments, and long-term outlooks are distant considerations at best. That mentality tends to keep the status quo in place even while many individuals can see a bigger picture. Sadly, chief executives must abide the will of their investors and directors, and no switch can just be thrown to change course. Other CEOs hidden in the cracks of indifference will happily take the reins from anyone who stumbles along and discovers his heart.

A few years ago, someone told me that the "Information Superhighway" was merely a dirt road in terms of massive information caches and avenues available to efficiently tap it. That its forthcoming reach and volume would stun me if I had any inkling of the colossal behemoth soon to appear with technology's exponential advances. That behemoth is here now, even beyond the imaginings of my clairvoyant friend, easily accessible to most of the world's population. With it, concentrations of more universal truth, unscrubbed by corporate boards, find wide-ranging audiences weary of lies and half-truths.

Maybe, as our Superhighway adds lanes and ever faster speeds, the wealth and power of corporations will find their influence overtaken by massive grassroots groups seeking changes most people agree need making. Maybe the elevated visions of luminaries that see with the aid of compassionate hearts and strive for the long-term health of the world and all its precious life will begin to overtake the greed-based model so deeply engrained in the human condition.

CHAPTER 14

AFRICA, AFRICA, AFRICA

Between June 2008 and now, October 2010, I've gone through two full training courses at World—one on the DC-10 and another on the MD-11. Because of the unconventional training programs here, those two airplanes ate up ten months in classrooms, simulators, and line training. I'm now starting my third. If it was on any airplane other than the Boeing 747-400, I'd be disheartened. But in my eyes, this is the King of Airplanes, and I've ached to fly it since it came out. Adding to the tremendous exhilaration of receiving this assignment, all the ground and simulator training is in Denver, a mountain paradise similar to my hometown of Salt Lake City.

Our hotel is located only a short walk from a long trail network fronting Cherry Creek which is more of a river than a creek. I put in ten miles a day on these trails melting away most of the stresses of school. I know the 747's systems inside and out from eleven years on the Classic. I literally wrote the book on the airplane at America West and taught engineers to operate it. While the flight engineer has been eliminated from the -400 cockpit, and the job they did is taken over by computers, we still must know the systems intimately. This is familiar territory for me, and ground school, for once, is delightful.

Our -400 fleet is composed of four freighters. I'll be flying only cargo from now on. Training is complete in early March 2011, and I'm released to the line with a fourth type rating added to my collection—Airline Transport Pilot B747-400. For six months I'm flying mostly out of Hong Kong, Luxembourg, and Anchorage. I also get to visit some new destinations located in what was the Soviet Union—Azerbaijan and Bishkek in Kyrgyzstan. The airplane is as awesome as I'd hoped, and the destinations I'm flying to are fascinating.

By August that year, the occasional trips I fly to Africa are becoming common. I'm still fairly new to the company so don't have a very good "big-picture" view, but colleagues are worried this means we're losing good contracts and replacing them with less lucrative flying. The folks in the contract division have changed under Global Air Holdings. Strong rumors circulate that the new guys are connected more broadly in Africa than Europe or elsewhere and that this could be costly. I notice pilots tend to be pessimists, so I choose to just hear this as hearsay that will return to the dusty cupboards from which it came. The *rumor mill* is rarely accurate.

This job ranks in the top five on my list of favorites. The -400 is wonderful to fly and the trips are incredible. I've had junkets where I circle the entire planet twice in the span of twenty days. The adventure is tempered by jetlag that comes with circling the globe, but World typically schedules trips with several days off at each destination. Care in sleeping and a rigorous exercise plan mitigate most of the problem, at least for me. I hope for once the airline lasts. I'll be so happy to do this for the rest of my career.

By spring 2012, the rumors of financial difficulty begin to grow teeth. Jeddah, Riyadh, and even Lagos in Nigeria no longer allow us to charge fuel on World's account. We're forced to pay by AmEx or, in some cases, with cash. On these long-haul trips where we spend weeks on the other side of the earth, it was long ago realized that a big cash stash sometimes saves the day. The captain has access to wads of it. Filling the tanks of an airplane that holds over

53,000 gallons can cost well into six-digit dollar territory. Maybe my comrades weren't just being skeptics. World has been a strong player in the aviation contract business for sixty-four years. Is it possible this is really happening?

In April 2013, I get heartbreaking news that I'll be furloughed within weeks. On June 2nd, I fly my final flight with World and am once again jobless. I'm not fired. If a miracle happens and the airline returns to profitability, I'll be recalled. But that doesn't seem to be the MO of the holding company at our helm. They have a reputation for squeezing the pennies out of their charges until they die. I've learned for instance that they charge World a *management fee*. The fee—however much is left in the cash register at the end of each month. I've had the misfortune of coming on board once again with crooks like Paul in Farmingdale and the reigning champ of greed, Frank Lorenzo. My 747-400 *career* lasted two years. I'm fifty-eight years old. For forty-eight years the mandatory retirement age for US airline pilots was sixty. It was raised to sixty-five just over five years ago, in late 2007.

PART 3
HAJJ

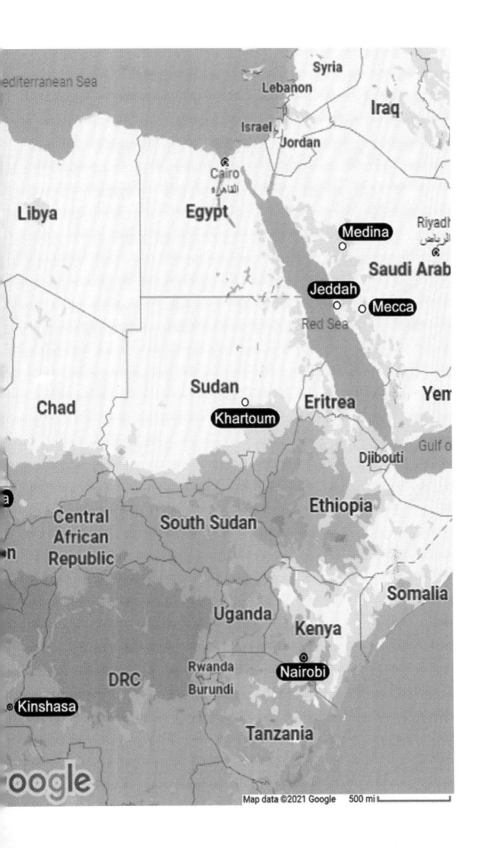

CHAPTER 1

ISLAM

Deep in the earth in southwestern Germany, artesian well water percolates through ancient rock seeking the surface. Along this continental divide in the Black Forest, some water flows west, feeding the Rhine River. Other springs not a hundred yards distant, find flow-ways along terrain folds oriented east. Trickling capillaries fresh from caverns within the earth's crust offer life-sustaining hydration through channels so petite, even the forest's tiniest newborns cross them with ease. Three hundred twenty-five miles east, in Lower Bavaria, the village of Passau perches at a junction of rivers adjoining this growing tributary from both north and south. Here the Danube River's capacity to the Black Sea, a thousand miles east, confers upon any entrepreneur or army means to dominate much of Europe. Vienna, a strategically important city of the Holy Roman Empire, is another one hundred seventy-five miles east.

For three centuries, armies of the Ottoman Empire advanced, eventually across the Turkish Straits into the Balkans. In sweeping, bloody campaigns, they spread Islam widely into southeastern Europe. In the seventeenth century, for the third time in a hundred fifty years, Muslim forces attempt to conquer Vienna but are soundly vanquished. The Danube will never serve their empire-building aspirations. That contest, championed by King Leopold

I of Poland in alliance with The Holy Roman Empire, began on September 11, 1683, and ends Muhammad's Islamic assault into Europe. Christian forces ultimately regain dominance throughout the region.

In 1998, Khalid Sheikh Mohammed approaches al-Qaeda answering fatwas—binding religious edicts—issued by bin Laden to jihad against enemies of his version of Islam. His plan is to use airliners as missiles to destroy important buildings in the USA. Once the plot matures, bin Laden chooses 9/11 as the date for the attack to reverse the tide against Islam achieved in Vienna three hundred and eighteen years ago.

Islam, like Christianity, has an extremist faction. If a body of Christians decides to return to teachings of The Old Testament and enforce its decrees, death will be prescribed for persistent rebelliousness on the part of children and for any child who hits or curses his or her parents. Working on the Sabbath and premarital sexual intercourse add to the list of capital offenses, and should a priest find his daughter guilty of harlotry, he must burn her alive.

Such a sect actually exists in Islam, al-Qaeda at its helm, practicing a radical interpretation of the Koran. In their enforcement of Sharia Law, bloody retribution is widely dispensed to any that stray from their strict version. Included in that category, in rigid supplication to their monotheistic embrace of Allah, are all people of any race, creed, or belief that do not fully adhere to their tenets. Presently, that suggests about 7.6 billion of earth's human inhabitants should be killed by loyal jihadists.

One of those people is me.

CHAPTER 2

HAJJ
FALL 2013

Hajj is a religious pilgrimage dating back to the seventh century, and all Muslims physically and fiscally able must attend the rite at least once in their lifetime. The gathering takes place in Mecca, Saudi Arabia, fifty miles inland from the ancient seaport city of Jeddah. Costs to each pilgrim vary greatly. In wealthy countries, the cost can easily exceed $10,000. In poorer Muslim countries from whence the vast majority of non-Saudi participants hail, costs might bottom out under a thousand dollars. Long-term, interest generating funds, similar to 529 plans for college, have been established in many countries to subsidize the cost for people who otherwise couldn't afford it. Lotteries determine who gets a ticket. With 1.7 billion Muslims worldwide, the logistical and fiscal machinations to present this each year are epic. The monetary rewards to the Saudi Kingdom, however, are remarkable, falling only slightly under those realized by their fossil fuel industry.

Centered in the Great Mosque of Mecca stands the Kaaba, House of God, around which the multiday promenade circulates. The mandate to participate and its cleansing and renewing popularity bring annual participants numbering in millions. Special air terminals in both Jeddah and Medina accommodate the colossal crowds who are traveling by air into and away from the ten-day ceremony.

CHAPTER 3
DELIVERANCE
AUGUST 2013

After my furlough from World Airways, my fifth career loss in a depressing succession, Marcia and I decide maybe it's time to give up on this flying business and venture elsewhere for livelihood. During the previous two years, I've partnered with a contractor to pursue a patent for an invention of his that seems promising. I like woodworking and carpentry anyway and have a professional grade woodshop. My contracting partner, Mike, is a good friend by now, and he welcomes me into a full-time alliance.

Fifteen months of industry seem to indicate the entrepreneurial shoes I'm trying on might be a couple of sizes too big. We're running out of money, and our future looks bleak. Even if the patent goes through, it'll be years and tens of thousands of dollars to get to that side of the rainbow. We don't have the money—or faith—to see this risky enterprise through.

My furlough status at World affords me full access to the pilots' electronic bulletin board. I check it daily searching for a new aviation opportunity. One day a notice appears advertising for an airline called Max Air. They're looking for Boeing 747 pilots to fly a hajj contract out of Nigeria. I'd seen this ad a few days earlier but had discounted it as too dangerous.

Max Air is based in northern Nigeria, in the megacity of Kano. That would be the primary base from which flying missions would dispatch. A Google search of Kano and my prospective employer, Max Air, paints a grizzly picture I'm not very keen to add to my bucket list. The first headline in the news available for Kano is "25 Killed in Explosions in The Christian Sector." Terrorist factions Hezbollah and Boko Haram are active in this city, and throughout Nigeria, with stated objectives of killing or kidnapping anyone white or non-Muslim, including Muslims outside of their extremist sect. They seem to have a particular disdain for girls in educational institutions, insisting a girl's future is bound up in baby-making starting at age sixteen. They'd rather see them dead than educated. In fact, I learn that Boko Haram translates loosely to "Western education is prohibited."

I see the hotel used for Max Air's pilot base in Kano is the Tahir Guest Palace Hotel, owned by a Lebanese gentleman by the name of Mr. Tahir Fadlallah. By the time I understand Boko Haram's feverish desire to kill and kidnap westerners, my *DANGER* flag shoots high up my stress scale. It doesn't take much research to learn this property probably has the highest concentration of white and western clients in all of Kano, yet I can find no reports of any terrorists' threats or attacks. While comforting, I still feel unnerved bunking with Kano's most concentrated mix of Boko Haram's arch enemies.

"Hits" in pilot chat sites also state emphatically that Max Air can't be trusted to pay contract pilots. Even if that turns out to be erroneous hearsay, I feel like while this avenue could end my financial issues, it could also end me.

The aviation industry worldwide is in decline right now which is partly why I'm on furlough. Hoodlums at Global Air Holdings make up the balance of my circumstance. Still, I dismiss the ad and move on down the page. I find nothing.

I go back to the Max Air ad and read it again looking for anything I might have missed. There is something. I hadn't noticed a note at the very end stating that this job isn't as bad as its reputation infers, and if I'd like more information, contact the author.

I do.

The posting pilot is a fellow World Airways captain. He informs me that he has a close friend, Reid, who's going to fly this year's hajj for Max Air and that Reid is an exceptional pilot I should contact for details. A phone call later, I'm confident Reid is someone with vast knowledge of this underbelly world of nonscheduled flying in third world countries.

My hunch bears out over the course of the next few days while trading several emails and engaging telephone conversations. Reid lives near São Paulo, Brazil with his soon-to-be second wife and their young child. He's going to fly this contract and, at the very last minute, gets authorization from the director of operations in Kano to recruit me to fly with him. Reid has dispelled much of the media-induced fear about the location of our base but hasn't tried to paint an entirely rose-colored picture.

"Do you have any idea why the Tahir is never attacked?" I ask.

"I've always heard," Reid says, "that Max Air wields Godfather-like power and influence in Kano, maybe throughout Nigeria. So much so that even the baddest of bad guys know to stay away from their pilots."

I'm intrigued. Am I going to work for someone who's secretly more feared than the terrorists themselves?

Reid goes on to explain that together, we'll navigate the potholes of Nigerian politics, religion, and her terrorists with great caution, and feels our chances of survival are about what they'd be in any big city. This turns out to be a bit of a salesman's pitch with its exaggerated claim. Reid desperately wants another pilot in the cockpit with him who is highly trained and competent, and speaks English as a first language. The money will be good. In less than three months I'll make enough to get us back on our feet and will pick up premium qualifications, making me infinitely more employable back in the airline world after I return.

I have one week to prepare for an accelerated ground and simulator course in Miami. I sit in my office all day every day studying the airplane from which I've been absent for more than a year. It seems an impossible task to coax lazy neurons, dendrites, and axons into firing again with specialized, technical information long dormant. But it comes back quickly. With the aid of my imagination and a B747-400 cockpit hung on my wall, I rehearse the various operational dances required of pilots until they begin to feel familiar again.

Preparations to leave my home, wife, family, friends, and choir, and to button up the financial necessities that will fall to Marcia during my absence, take every spare minute. With his gracious consent, I leave my contracting partner midstream in a project that's trickier than most where another set of hands is often necessary.

Marcia is used to long periods of my absence from a five-year marriage, most of which found me gainfully employed as a long-distance international pilot gone for weeks at a time. She assures me I'll be missed, but she'll be fine on her own. Friends volunteer to take on my responsibilities and encourage me to take advantage of this unique opportunity.

CHAPTER 4

WEATHER DELAYS, DELTA DELAYS

I meet Reid at the boarding gate in Atlanta. I've come from Salt Lake City and he, from São Paulo, Brazil via Seattle. It turns out Reid has an ex-wife in the *Emerald City* who's raising their twin sons. He's been there for a few days visiting his kids. We form an instant bond that feels safe, assuring, good. We fly to Miami and participate in a week-long training program designed to get us quickly up to command mastery. Having instructed on this aircraft for the last year, Reid is already there. His skillful tutoring spools me back up to speed in giant strides. We complete the program and say goodbye to our instructors at Pan Am's International Flight Academy and proceed to the airport to begin our long migration to Kano.

An oversight in some office somewhere has us booked on separate flights from Miami to JFK. Reid's American Airlines flight departs at 11:25 a.m. while mine on Delta will depart at 12:16 p.m. Both flights leave over three hours at Kennedy to reunite and connect to our flight on Egyptair to Cairo, Egypt.

I move along unhindered in the nearly vacant Delta terminal on Labor Day morning with a casual check-in and easy passage through TSA's security checkpoint. While reading in a quiet, virtually deserted end of the concourse, my cell phone rings. It's an automated call from Delta informing me that my flight is delayed with a new estimated departure at 12:50 p.m. This still allows me at least two and a half hours to connect in Kennedy, so unconcerned, I return to my book.

The completely full flight is boarded on time, and as departure time nears, the captain's voice fills the cabin with what I expect to be a "welcome aboard" announcement. "Ladies and gentlemen, this is your captain speaking. ATC has just informed us of weather in the New York area, and a ground stop has been issued for all New York flights not already airborne. They've informed us to expect an *Advise Time* at 1:30 p.m. That's when they expect more information on our delay. I'll keep you posted as I learn more. Meanwhile, please remain seated so we can get underway quickly in case we're released earlier."

My clock sense tells me I'll still make my connection albeit not with the degree of comfort I prefer. This assumes our "advise time" and "go time" remain close together. I text Reid that things are beginning to go south for me. He's airborne and can't receive or respond to my message.

A few minutes later the captain informs us that our "advise time" has moved forward to 2:30 p.m. and he's decided to deplane. We're all given cards with telephone numbers we may call to rebook connections we'll likely miss in New York. My booking has been done by an agency in Nigeria, and they're the only entity that can change it. It's about 6:30 p.m. in Nigeria, and the offices are long closed. My California Max Air connection, Charmaine, doesn't answer her phone. Delta agents inform me that this is the only flight that will get me to JFK today as everything for the rest of the day is oversold, and no flights are scheduled to depart earlier than mine.

A new public address message booms from the terminal speakers informing us that thunderstorms in the New York area have finally dissipated and Kennedy has reopened. A large thunderstorm has, however, centered itself overhead, and now the Miami airport is closed.

At 2:00 p.m. my phone rings and the screen lights with "Reid." I answer.

"Hey buddy, what's happening with your flight delay?"

I explain what I know.

"Okay, listen, I'll talk to the Egyptair agents and see if I can get them to hold the flight a few minutes for you. I've sent emails to Shyam and Charmaine so they know what's going on."

"Thanks, Reid. There's still a possibility of me making the flight if we actually get outta here by 2:30. I'll keep you posted."

"Okay, buddy. Good luck!" he says and we hang up.

At 2:05, Delta announces the re-boarding of our flight. Slowly, American style, we saunter aboard our one hundred-sixty-seat Boeing 737-800 with a large number of travelers unaware or uncaring that they jam the boarding process as they fiddle with their carry-on luggage. Incredulously, they stand firmly in mid-aisle, oblivious to the repeated pleas of flight attendants to stand clear, anxious to board all passengers. From nine years of flying for Japan Airlines I know that disciplined Japanese passengers board a 556 seat Boeing 747 in about twenty minutes. We of more careless western sensibilities are unlikely ever to adopt such courteous efficiency.

Finally, fully loaded, we should be ready to push back from the gate. There's still an outside possibility I'll make my Cairo flight if it's just slightly delayed. The PA crackles back to life, and the boarding agent announces the names of ten "pass riders," airline employees riding for free, who must collect their belongings and deplane. As part of the security enhancements after 9/11, whenever a passenger deplanes, his or her baggage must also be removed from the cargo holds. This helps ensure would-be bombers don't get away scot-free in villainous plots. The captain explains that the deplanement is due to the additional fuel that's been boarded due to the questionable weather in the New York area. The additional fuel has made our aircraft overweight, so people must be removed.

Surely a decision to board extra fuel for inclement weather was made long ago, and the overweight status of the aircraft had to be obvious to dispatchers and pilots. Those airline employees should never have reboarded, and their bags should have been pulled before the new fuel was pumped into our tanks. This sloppy mistake will cost us thirty more minutes on the ground.

The only possibility of making my connection has vanished, and of course, a significant number of the other passengers share my plight. I text Reid, "Situation hopeless. See you in Kano." Reid texts back, "I've made a reservation for you in a NY hotel. Check email upon arrival." We initiate our takeoff roll at 3:40 p.m.

We fly uneventfully to New York and descend in brilliant blue skies to Kennedy's runway 4L. A feather-soft landing occurs at 6:14 p.m. As we taxi toward our gate on Terminal 2, I notice the Egyptair Boeing 777 sitting regally on a gate at Terminal 4. Out the other side of the plane, I can see our parking marshaler standing at our drooping gate holding his wands crossed meaning "STOP." We stop. We're about three hours and forty minutes late, but no one in operations has thought to send an operator to adjust our jet bridge elevation and meet the flight.

A flight attendant makes an announcement apologizing for our unavoidable delay, including some required boilerplate about seat belts, cell phones, and laptop computers, and thanks us for flying Delta. The second we stop, dozens of passengers jump up, open the overhead bins to collect their belongings, and plug up the aisle trying to rush to the front door hoping to be the first off the plane. Not a word is spoken over the PA. I know we can't move with anyone standing in the aisles, yet I'm looking at the marshaler two hundred feet away with the crossed wands.

Because of this FAA rule, in the seven airlines for which I've flown, an announcement is always made from the cockpit stating something like, "This is the captain speaking. We must stop short of our parking spot, and I want to remind you to remain seated with your seat belt fastened, blah blah blah." We know people don't listen to the boilerplate, and they're conditioned to jump up when the plane stops. Not many passengers pay attention to the little, usually dimly lit, iconic seat belt signs above their seats, but almost everyone listens to the captain. Neither pilot bothers with the announcement, and the flight attendants seem oblivious. A full minute of calamity matures before a flight attendant announces that we cannot proceed to the gate until all passengers return their luggage to the overhead bins and go back to their seats and fasten their seat belts.

After deplaning, I find the shuttle bus that connects Terminals 2 and 4 and board it with a glimmer of hope that my Egyptair flight is delayed. As we snake across the ramp, I watch as the jumbo Egyptair B777 taxis toward the runway ahead. I'm not going to Egypt today.

I enter Terminal 4 in search of Egyptair gate agents. Somebody tells me they always depart from the A gates. No luck. In fact, I can't find anyone with any idea what gate the Egyptair flight departed from. Hard as it seems to imagine covertly boarding three hundred fifty people onto a two hundred fifty-foot-long airplane in the middle of JFK, they seem to have pulled it off. Had Alexander the Great had this kind of trouble finding Egypt, the port city of Alexandria might instead be called Hannibal.

At Egyptair ticket counters I find CLOSED signs.

I call the 800-number displayed on the sign—"We're closed; leave a message."

Defeated on all fronts, I settle down with my computer to see what information Reid has sent. Just then my phone rings. It's Charmaine. She's finally received my phone messages and emails. Like me, she'd hoped for a miraculous delay of the Cairo flight. We're equally disappointed. She's already tried to call the travel agency in Nigeria, but they're closed. It's 1:00 a.m. there. The office will open at 8:00 a.m. Charmaine says she'll do what she can, and we hang up. I try to check email, but hackers have hijacked my email password, and I'm locked out of my account. This is shaping up into one of the most turbulent days I've had in years. I call Marcia and am thrilled when she answers her phone, at home, where she's able to access her computer. She finds a notice from Google informing that my account has indeed been hacked and is locked until my password is reset. We dutifully follow the instructions until my computer is safely mine again.

Marcia lets me go to sort out the fragments of my dilemma. I find an email from Reid with the hotel's name and phone number. I call, and they assure me my room awaits. I tell them I'll call again after I find my bags.

While Delta and Egyptair are not affiliated, they do have a baggage interline agreement. An intermediary called Swissport facilitates the transfer of checked bags between them. I go to Delta's Lost Baggage Office and they send me straight to Swissport, which is only fifty feet away. A cheerful agent takes all my information and does a quick search. No luck. She tells me she'll send a "runner" to find them but warns it could take as long as an hour. I call Marcia, taking advantage of the downtime, and catch her up on the clunky day I'm experiencing. Her patience and loving assurances pull me from my funk, and I hang up back on my game. I check in with the cheerful agent after an hour and a half, and again at the end of two. My bags remain unfound. I call the hotel for a ride.

I check into the Five Towns Motor Inn, finding it a lovely hotel with a quiet, comfortable room. Taking stock of the situation, I realize that my uniforms are in my lost luggage. Uniforms are not optional in hajj flying. The Saudis simply won't allow a non-uniformed pilot access to the airplane. Period. I must get my bags before departing, knowing I possess little hope of finding suitable replacements in Kano. I don't know when or how I'm going, but I know I'm stuck 'til they find my bags.

The next morning, I call Swissport and Maria answers. She knows nothing of my misfortune. Having taken today's reins, it seems she's been left uninformed about crises in progress from yesterday. I give her all the pertinent information, and she assures me she'll get right on it. I go to breakfast.

An hour later Maria calls to report that my bags have been located and are sitting safely in Swissport's office. Charmaine calls to include me in a three-way call to Nigeria which is incomprehensible to me. It turns out Egyptair had automatically rebooked me when I missed their flight, but their Kennedy agents took that information home with them without so much as leaving a message in a bottle at their closed ticket counters. Subsequently, when I didn't show up for that secret flight, Max Air agents picked up the ball and rebooked me on the same flight I'd missed the day before, nonstop to Cairo. To my delight, it's an uncrowded flight that departs on time.

CHAPTER 5
CAIRO AND KANO OR BUST

Penetrating an early-season jet stream meandering across the Atlantic, the sleek B777 jumbo jet makes the ten hour and twenty-minute flight in just nine and a half. With boarding and taxi times, it's still ten and a half hours crammed into my seat. Egyptair is accommodating, even to coach passengers, on their long-haul flights, so the comfort is okay, and the service is excellent. The buzz from stress and uncertainty during the last thirty hours leaves me with a tall order for sleep. Our truncated night's darkness, shrunk to only four hours, compliments of flying against the earth's direction of rotation, adds to the challenge. I know a meal will help so I ask for dinner. It's a meager salad, a sesame seed-encrusted hard roll, and a box of apple juice. There's an unidentifiable piece of meat on my plate about which I'm certain only that it's Halal. That designation ensures it's Muslim approved and must, by Allah's decree, exclude any hind quarters, dog, cat, monkey, or pork. I skip the meat and ask for another roll. As the cabin warms and my stomach steals blood from my arteries for digestion, I finally manage a couple of hours of restless sleep. Our twin GE90-115B engines can produce 110,000 horsepower each, more than twice the horsepower of all the Titanic's steam engines combined. When pulled to idle, they still need to tap air from the high-pressure compressor sections of the engines to maintain controlled cabin pressure, and the valve synchronization is just imperfect enough to bump the atmosphere in the cabin. That's all the jolt I need to tell me we're about thirty minutes from touch-down, and I wake to face my continuing adventure.

I have eight hours on the ground in Cairo and am intercepted after customs and immigration by a gentleman who wonders if he can lend me any assistance. Highly suspicious and nearly certain this is the beginning of a con in which I'll be relieved of what little money I have, I accompany him. He seems very kind and turns me over to his colleague in the middle of the main terminal floor. They try to talk me into a bus ride to the Pyramids, finding it difficult to believe that I'm choosing to sleep over such a once-in-a-lifetime experience. But sleep is the only thing on my mind, and I insist on going to the airport Novotel, an aircrew favorite hotel, of which Reid has informed me. They check a computer to see if I have a reservation and find I don't. If I reserve through them, I can get a room and a taxi for $140 total. If I elect to go to the hotel without booking through them, it'll be closer to $250. I bite. They set it up and escort me outside to a line of taxis.

The air-conditioning in the terminal building is chilling. I've got goose bumps. But once the large glass doors slide open, the outdoors assaults me with shocking heat. It's ninety-seven degrees here on the northern edge of the Sahara Desert, but through the middle of Cairo runs the Nile River, and its flowing mass adds staggering humidity to the environment. I immediately wilt in the lambasting furnace. Jet exhaust fills the inferno so pungently I'm queasy. I'm lucky to be ensconced in a cab in minutes, rescued from the oppressing outdoors, heading to the Novotel—almost. We're stopped by a security guard inside of ten feet after we begin rolling, and I'm certain this is the sting I've been expecting. The guard talks to my driver for a couple of minutes and then takes something from him—his license, maybe? As we drive away, what sounds like Arabian disco music rends the air. I'm annoyed, too tired to tolerate loud music. I think my driver has turned on his radio, but it's not the radio, it's my driver's cell phone. He engages in a lengthy, Arabic conversation and then turns the taxi around just before leaving the airport and returns to the starting point. This must be where I get rolled. My heart pounds, and I chastise myself for being so stupid. But it turns out he just forgot his license, and soon, we're on our way. I've heard so much derisive talk about Cairo I'm continually expecting terror. I'm the only Caucasian I've seen and feel practically fluorescent in my western dress. I'm in a constant state of fearful stress, much as I don't want to admit it.

Arriving at the Novotel, my driver wheels my bags in and stays to ensure everything's okay with my check-in. It is and he leaves. I note the "Standard Room" rate posted on a marquee on the wall behind the front desk says 192 Euros per night. That's $253 so I realize these guys have been on the up and up from the start. I feel ashamed I'm so mistrusting. And anyway, the company is reimbursing me.

My room has a bed, and that's all I care about. It's as beautiful a thing in that moment as watching a sunset over a high mountain lake. One last time I check my email and find a note from Reid explaining details of my continuing trip and some good information and tips about arrival procedures in Kano. I fall asleep instantly and wake up three minutes before my alarm intones a familiar melody, three hours later. I shower and notice no towels. Had sleep not taken the edge off my shriveling temper I would have been quite perturbed. But I grant my unusual check-in time probably upset the cleaner's normal routine so pass it off as an honest oversight. Gobs of Kleenex work in a pinch. I make my way down to the Novotel shuttle bus, and I'm off to the Egyptair terminal.

I'm again intercepted the moment I get off the bus and have just tipped the driver with the last of my small bills. I have nothing left but seven American $20 bills, much too large for tipping. I tell the porter I have no money and am happy to take care of myself. He insists and says, "No problem on the tipping."

Score for everyone but me since arriving in Egypt: 100

Score for my trusting nature: 0

I find my way through all their security and make it to my gate an hour and a half before departure time. There are a dozen or so others in the area, and we all take seats in the concourse hallway awaiting the gate's opening. These people and the rest that trickle in for the next hour are very dark-skinned and all are dressed in traditional kaftans and taqiyah caps. I'm the outlier. After the boarding area opens and we all pass through a final security check, I notice many assemble for evening prayers on their prayer rugs. I hope they're appealing to Allah for an eventless flight and arrival into Kano. I reflect for at least the millionth time in my life how convenient it would be to believe a heavenly father listens to the wishes of us here on earth, or slightly above it. But I see too much evidence to contradict this notion. Not that I don't believe in some kind of Universal intelligence. I see miracles in everything—a blooming hibiscus, snow falling from the sky, and the billions of interconnected wonders that animate life. While I revere *It*, I don't imbue *It* with human emotions or a grand plan for earth and its inhabitants.

When it comes time to board, they mob the gate entrance, making the boarding of passengers in even the most aggressive European cities—famously pugnacious where queues are concerned—seem tame. I'm squeezed to nearly the back because I didn't spring from my seat like Wile E. Coyote after the Road Runner when the signal was given.

Upon entering the plane and proceeding to my seat, about halfway back in the plane, it becomes clear that there's no room left anywhere in the overhead bins for my bag. Also, there's a man in the seat I'd just been assigned half an hour earlier when I requested an aisle seat. I pass my seat in search of overhead space farther back but am met by a flight attendant who assures me there is none. I settle into a completely vacant emergency exit row on the left side of the plane and wait for boarding to be complete. No one has come to sit in any of the seats in my adopted row. When the flight attendant comes by again, I query, "Hello, my friend. I'm a pilot on my way to Kano to fly the hajj. I'm two days into a very long journey and wonder if it would be okay with you if I sit here in the emergency exit row. My assigned seat seems to be taken."

He says, "You're welcome to this entire row, and is there anything else I can get or do for you?"

I'm startled but shouldn't be. Anyone flying the hajj is doing God's work as far as any Muslim is concerned and is accorded deep reverence. I bow with praying hands to chin, returning his veneration. Stashing my bag under the aisle seat, I take the middle for myself. In flight I fold up both armrests and lie down across all three seats for a good snooze. It feels as if the fates are being overly kind for my small exercise of patience, but I'm hopeful it's a preview of the luck to follow throughout my Nigerian engagement.

As we start down, the idled engines once again jar my eustachian tubes, nudging me slowly to consciousness. Gradually, I realize where I am and on what adventure I'm embarking. I slide over to the window seat to get my first views of "home" for the next few months. I'm hoping to see a sprawling city in which I'll be inconspicuous. There are widely scattered, dim, orangish lights peppering the landscape, and my hopes for anonymity vanish for the moment. Touchdown is smooth, and taxiing into the gate is in pitch blackness. Only the taxi light mounted on the nose wheel strut is lighting the way for our pilots. When we come to a stop, everyone rushes to the exit door as if a fire has broken out in the passenger cabin. Five minutes later, when everything outside is ready, the boarding door is opened. I make my way out of the airplane into the dark night and am slammed with tropical humidity infused with heavy diesel fumes. Add copious body odor from dozens of unwashed people, me included, and my olfactory system has its unique imprint, forever embedded in inalterable memory chambers. My introduction to Kano, Nigeria begins.

CHAPTER 6
KANO, MENAGERIE OF FEAR, STRESS, AND SURPRISE

own on the tarmac are two ancient buses waiting to transport us the five or six hundred feet to the customs terminal. We're to load only one bus at a time, and the one I'm presently queued up for has only a forward and rear door to accept us. Both the front and back of this bus are cram-packed full by the time I get near the front of the herd. No one moves to the middle. I can see five or six rows of empty seats, but everyone insists on being near the doors to expedite their egress into customs. Selfishness and inconsideration transcend race, creed, and color and may be among the highest-ranking universal attributes humans share. Slowly, some people pop through the membrane of insistent door hogs and make their way toward the center but soon I give up and turn toward the other bus. I'm stopped short because that carriage must pull up to the official passenger loading spot. Only after the first bus roars off with its deep growl and heavy exhaust cloud are we allowed to begin boarding the second. Maybe this spot is under video surveillance, and the field of view is narrow. Whatever it is, choreography requiring conformity must be adhered. The second bus has three doors, the perfect solution to the "me first" rule, and we board quickly and are off in billowing puffs of half-burned diesel fuel.

We disgorge into the terminal where a man, reminiscent of my school years where one lucky kid picks teams for dodgeball, is charged with sorting us. I'm an easy "sort." I stick out—bad. Everyone sees a lone white man in the crowd with no affiliation to any brotherhood with which they're familiar.

In this simple rectangular room about the size of a soccer field, I make my way to the first checkpoint. Four stations, each staffed with a control officer, process the four lines into which we've been divided. Our progress is tortoise slow. In the twenty-five minutes it's taken to shuffle to the first official, I've been asked to show my passport twice. My sarcastic voice mumbles in silence, "Gotta be careful. You never know how many Americans might be trying to sneak into Nigeria at two o'clock in the morning." The officer looks at my passport and checks my visa and sends me forward to the next desk, which takes another ten minutes. This official looks mean. It seems like he's X-raying me with a look of utter fury. As he examines my passport, he continues to look up at me too frequently. It's clear he's looking for confrontation, and I'm not going to make it easy. I'm intimidated knowing his power over me. Doubtless, he can shoot me dead if he wants to with complete impunity, making the lamest excuse. I choose not to test him and just look at all the interesting people around me, avoiding his stare with great intention. He finally motions me to his colleague two feet ahead, who seems genuinely friendly and even shakes my hand, welcoming me with enthusiasm. My mind, deeply fatigued, believes I'm hearing the voice of James Earl Jones. "What are you doing here and how long will you be with us?"

I'm tempted to call him Mr. Jones but doubt he'll get it, much less appreciate the humor. I check my impulse and say, "I'm a pilot flying the hajj for Max Air, based here in Kano. My contract is for three months. I'll be leaving the country in mid-November, I think."

He seems to process this information and writes something in my passport next to my Nigerian visa. "I have given you two months, until November 3rd," he says, pointing to the 3/November he's written in my passport. I say I think it will be closer to November 15th. He says, "No problem, your company can change it later."

The more time I'm in this building the more susceptible I am to threats, intimidation, and extortion, so I fear he's intentionally set me up to return at least one more time. I've been told that Max Air is like the mafia in Northern Nigeria and has great power to make things happen in alignment with their choosing. I'm hopeful they can handle this slip of the pen with little difficulty.

I'm pointed to the next checkpoint which is a simple table behind which are five female officers. On the table are signs that read, "Currency declaration." I declare $140 dollars. Verbal response is good enough. They're giggly, seeing my apprehension, and I tell them I doubt I can buy much of Nigeria for that amount but will try to make more now that I'm here. They giggle even more and send me along to the baggage claim. This is a gigantic conveyor belt, about three feet wide, that runs in a straight line from the tarmac, through a large opening in the wall, to about fifty feet into the building. No baggage has arrived yet though it's been more than forty-five minutes since we arrived.

My driver, wearing a fluorescent vest with "Max Air" emblazoned across its back in large black letters, greets me. For him to identify me in the crowd offers him little challenge. To my surprise, it turns out there's another Max Air pilot in the terminal, a Jordanian named Qeis—pronounced "Keez"—with a fashionable stubbled black beard and olive-colored skin. A porter arrives with a trolley to help us. We don't want the help, but he wants to help more than we don't want it. His tenacity wins the round. The belt begins a tortured roll to bring our bags from a newly arrived cart, easily twelve feet wide and piled ten feet high with mostly huge canvas bundles that look like they might bulge with two hundred pounds of cotton each. The sixth item on the belt is my first bag.

Retrieving it, I reach into the zippered top pocket for the strap whose purpose allows a second bag to be piggybacked aboard, allowing one-handed trolleying of two bags at a time. The baggage handlers here long ago learned about this strap, its purpose, and

its likely location. The strong advice I'd received prior to embarking on this journey—to buy mini padlocks for my suitcase's zip-
pers—would have made the trip to the hardware store well worth
it. But it's one of the last-minute checklist items I neglected, and
now I'm sorry. The hour between parking the aircraft and the first
sight of a baggage cart lends credence to the stories of pilfering of
bags that is common knowledge among most people whose travels take them into the third world. My missing strap evinces this
practice, and now I have no way to hook my bags together. Since I
have three large bags, it's no longer possible for me to move them
together, single-handedly, and a porter becomes necessary. These
people aren't stupid. Maybe a little dishonest but when you have
practically no opportunity for income, you learn all the possible
tricks to get into the pockets of those with cash. It's a fair bet my
thief and my tenacious porter are one and the same. I'm guessing this cadre of baggage handlers and porters show off their col-
lections of baggage straps like Olympic athletes showing off their
medals.

James Earl, who had welcomed me warmly a few minutes earlier, appears with a wide smile welcoming me and shaking my
hand—again. A fellow officer, not nearly so engaging, stands near
me straight-faced. The smiling Mr. Jones moves off to other duties,
leaving me with "straight-face" who leans in close and says around
the cacophony of ambient noise "they like you and don't want to
see you dead." Then he adds that he would like to protect me, but I
must "find something for them." This is blatant extortion to which
I don't respond. I realize my best bet is to keep a distance from
everyone, realizing their primary mission is to get money from this
westerner. He repeats, "Find something for us," and walks away.

My porter, who has witnessed the exchange, informs me, "That
man in uniform is a crook. Don't give him one naira! I will take
care of you." I'm much more comfortable with my porter's meth-
ods of fleecing me and conclude that staying close to him might
be wise, at least for the time being. There's the problem of prior
fleecing, however, that's left me without tipping capital. I explain

that all my tipping money is in the pockets of Egyptians back at the edge of the Red Sea. A $15 entry visa fee, levied upon me as I was leaving the Cairo airport en route to the Novotel, has cleaned me out of small bills. If only I'd overpaid that official with a $20 bill, I'd still have my five-dollar bill and ten ones. Being punch-drunk from little real sleep and my circadian rhythms grasping for meaningful reference, I didn't think that action through very well. The porter says not to worry, there are "changers" outside that can handle any denomination in any amount. I'm not feeling particularly trusting of anyone right now so don't know what to think, but "changers, any denomination, and any amount" sounds ripe for crime.

The third gigantic cart brings my second bag, and the very last bag on the fourth and final cart is my Jordanian comrade's. Finally, we can progress to the last checkpoint. Halfway across the divide, buried in a thriving sea of people, the power goes out. It's suddenly pitch dark. Our escort, like a starling in a murmuration, stops along with the flock, bored indifference in his voice as he explains this is very common. Still, I strain to see, half certain cat vision would reveal a throng of pickpockets being loosed upon us.

Several bright light beams activated from cell phones begin slashing the humid air, and moments later, the lights come back on. Common as these may be, my suspicious mood wonders if valuables didn't just surreptitiously change ownership.

At the baggage check station, they thoroughly inspect nearly every bag. Mine lie beneath Qeis's. Our porter pushes along in lockstep with the throng and, arriving at the inspection table, heaves Qeis's bag onto it. The security guards check it earnestly, and then our porter throws it back atop our cart, mine buried beneath, and aggressively shoves us along through the crowd. His quick, assertive actions save us several minutes of additional studious bag exploration, and we're home free—almost.

Outside it's a dark night, and the crowds are thinner than I'd expected. I surmise that meeting inbound friends and relatives in the middle of the night at Kano International Airport is probably not a particularly safe way to spend an evening. I'm relieved by the sparse crowd, until suddenly we find ourselves mobbed by the aforementioned "changers." They swirl around us like locusts with huge wads of 1000 naira notes. Nigeria, like so much of Africa, was once a British colony, and surprisingly, many here still refer to the currency as "pounds" even though, since independence more than five decades ago, they've been printing their own naira. They never succumbed to the "wrong side of the road," right-hand steering wheel, a frequent British hand-me-down, unlike Kenya and many other African countries. I'm grateful for one less thing to which I need to adapt.

They yell, "CHANGE, CHANGE, CHANGE," and I wonder where they got all that money. A reasonable exchange rate, allowing a little for the changer, is three thousand naira to twenty US dollars. I didn't know this until I got to the hotel and checked the Internet, another pre-departure checklist item I neglected, and I didn't trust them, even though my strap-stealing, death-threat thwarting, customs-crashing porter agrees it's a fair exchange rate. Reluctant to do any business with the "changers," we scurry to the van completely unprepared for tipping. When we get there, I ask our driver if he has any tipping money, and he promptly declares, "No!"

Qeis is searching his wallet and finds a single one-dollar bill. He offers it to a chorus of loud protests from the porter and a few changers that have tagged along with us to the van. Qeis wants to slam the door on them and drive away, but that seems too harsh a treatment to me, so I bite the bullet and take three one thousand Naira notes for twenty dollars and give one back to the porter. In real exchange terms that gives him $6.10, a respectable tip for moving a few bags. Then another hand flings into the vehicle with a demand for his.

"Who the heck are you?" I ask before we slam the door and take off.

CHAPTER 7

FIRST NIGHT

Our driver is a bit of a maniac. It's after 2:00 a.m. and this guy seriously hauls. There are barrels arranged at the airport exit, otherwise wholly indistinguishable from the rest of the road, to slow traffic. There is no traffic—we're alone in a sea of darkness. This guy would make a great Le Mans driver, I think. He doesn't slow down or hit any barrels. We beeline right into an area of sheer decay and desolation. There must be a soul or two haunting these streets, but I can't see them. We come upon pack after pack of small dogs, obviously the cleanup crews of Kano, and their status—alive—indicates they've seen our driver before because they scramble out of his way at lightning speed. He will surely run any down that don't make way. He knows with batlike precision exactly where the "hazards" are, consisting of deep holes and trenches in the road where growing damage is left to mature. He jacks on the brakes, and suddenly we're crawling two miles per hour through bumps and troughs that would destroy any speeding vehicle. His suspension feels old and worn-out, and we bounce off our seats even with our slow crawl. Then he comes out of the deep, rotten sections, floors the gas pedal, and away we race, barreling through the lightless city.

Another fifteen minutes of radical accelerating and braking that could be affected just as smoothly with off/on switches as the *finesse-free* approach he utilizes with gas and brake pedals, brings us to something new—a police checkpoint. Three uniformed policemen, two sitting and one holding a dim flashlight, wave us to a stop. I'm sure it's another extortion attempt about to take place, and again, my suspicious beliefs are proven unfounded. The driver rolls down his window, says something to the security officer, and away we go. A sign in English informs us that we've now entered a "restricted area." It looks more intact and livable than the shantytown we've passed through for the last ten miles, but the roads don't improve. We turn into a long, dirt parking area that's pitted and pocked so badly I spend more time in the air than on my seat. He drives several hundred feet, loosening my dental fillings, and finally turns left to intercept a somewhat improved paved street. Soon we come to a gate on our left. He turns and abruptly stops. Invisible men appear from dark shadows and open a double set of steel gates, and we enter the Tahir compound.

Despite the name, the palatial hotel is more like an army barracks or university dorm with quantity in terms of square footage a healthy substitute for quality. The hotel grounds are composed of several large, rectangular, three- and four-story buildings surrounding a parking area that accommodates about fifty cars. There are guards everywhere though none are visibly armed. Their defense strategy seems to consist of fast communications afforded by cell phones and walkie-talkies they all carry. I hope, in an attack, others are armed who can be quickly summoned and that they don't forget to rouse the guests.

I'm relieved and surprised to find Reid waiting at the front door since it's just after 3:00 a.m. Certain restrictions, enforced either by Max Air or the hotel, prohibited him from traveling to the airport to meet us, so he's chosen to wait up in the Tahir's front lobby. He wants to ensure there are no mess-ups during check-in.

We trade stories and a few laughs, and then Reid shows me to my room which is only two doors away from his. We're on the third floor of building G. The fifty-one-minute time period that separated us in Miami has translated to more than twenty-six hours of solo journeying to a foreign and dangerous destination. I'm relieved to be reunited with my mentor who has more third world experience than I do, but am also proud to have stood on my own so far. It's been an experience of hardening the steel inside of me which is a good place to begin if one intends to fly a hajj out of Nigeria.

There are guards stationed at each building entrance I've transited plus one on each floor. It's clear they want the guests to feel safe, and though they're unarmed, their presence does add a feeling of security. As we part at the door to my room, Reid suggests, "Hey buddy"—he almost always starts this way—"I realize this is your first time in Kano, so let me tell you some tips for long life. It's a good idea to locate a removable ceiling tile so you can hide in the space between floors in case we're attacked. Make sure you've got a chair or desk or something that gives you access, something you don't need to move. Also make sure and leave the deadbolt on your door unlocked so attackers might believe you're not hiding inside." It's a cold slap of reality shaking me back to full awareness of where we are and new survival precautions I'd better engrain.

A few hours of sleep are cut short by morning's light flooding through my windows and jarring sounds of steel pounding concrete. I stumble from my bed to find there's a building behind ours being demolished. Their system involves attaching ropes around key structural members and then pulling them with a grader. Some ropes break, zinging like breaking guitar strings. The structure looks just like the rest of the guest buildings but falls in one crashing plunge with dust clouds curling up around it. Maybe it was too old and decrepit to leave standing. It's all concrete construction with lots of rebar. Workers walk into the settling dust cloud and tear into the demo work with small, ten-pound sledgehammers. It looks like back-breaking work, but under their repetitive blows, it fractures quickly into football-sized rubble. Their efforts present a startling display of what can be done by hand. Being an American, I'd forgotten that such a mighty enterprise could be done with sheer human brawn.

We meet for breakfast in the hotel's restaurant. It's a buffet complete with typical Western fare as well as baked beans and several unfamiliar Muslim dishes. The instant coffee comes from packages they supply with pots of hot water. Most guests appear to be drinking tea. Everyone is friendly and helpful. Afterward, I settle in for a nap, hoping to catch up on some badly needed sleep.

CHAPTER 8

SWARMING KANO

The shrill ringing of a seventies-style telephone pulls me from my fog. We've been summoned to a meeting in Max Air's office building downtown. A new driver picks us up at 10 a.m., and now I get to see the real Kano in broad daylight. It bears no resemblance to the ghost town we toured a few hours before. The streets teem with people, bicycles, motor bikes, tuk tuks, cars, and minivans. As in other African cities I've visited, vendors are stationed along roadsides to sell their wares to anyone who will buy. Children in school uniforms walk together, and others of similar age are dressed in rags. They most likely can't afford school. I don't know what cultural distinction separates them—tribe, maybe. I reflect on my mission here lasting only a few months. I realize many of these people will never know any other life. It's a morbidly depressing thought, and nothing has ever made me more genuinely happy to be me. I would choose any fate over this dreamless future of hard manual labor under a boiling sun. The strict fundamentalist lifestyle imposed on nearly all residents from birth must feel so oppressive. Add malaria to the list of difficulties awaiting a huge percentage of the population, and that's even a sadder commentary on their futures. Nigeria and Democratic Republic of Congo together generate forty percent of all malaria cases on earth.

Among the masses in Nigeria, there is abject poverty. There's no such thing as discretionary income; nothing earned can be squandered. The only avenue open for some semblance of fulfillment for most people is the embrace of their religion. While that's free, it isn't necessarily peaceful. The divisions between those practicing Islam and Christianity are stark. Each believe the other to be their enemy, and in extremist teachings, their mortal enemy. While the Koran has wide disparity in its interpretations, as does the Bible, its five Pillars begins with "Declaring that there is only one God, Allah, and that Muhammad is his messenger." Many Christians make exactly the same claim about Jesus Christ and their religious convictions. Much in the two doctrines sows division, and at the extremist ends of both, deadly battle has proved a common arbitrator through the ages.

By the fanatical dictates of Boko Haram, practicing Christianity, being anything but a zealous practitioner of their convictions, or having a western education are all punishable by death. Passageways to survival weave a precarious path between fanaticism and starvation and offer challenges blessedly unfamiliar to most of the civilized world. One other pathway chosen by a sizable percentage of the population is a lifelong contest of wit and cunning to see how much money they can swindle from a foreigner's pockets. By comparison, this seems an innocent and viable path.

I'm now a visitor in this foreign land and will be taking thousands of devout Muslim pilgrims from throughout Nigeria to Jeddah and Medina to begin their sacred journey to Mecca. Max Air is contracted to fly about seventy thousand Nigerians on this pilgrimage over a period of several weeks. Once positioning is complete, pilgrims take ten days for the prescribed rituals, much of which entails circling the Kaaba, also known as "the cube" or "sacred house," and praising Allah. I'll be relieved of all duty during the break and can stay at the hotel or go home. It's entirely up to me. Individual pilots can have considerably longer breaks depending on when they're first back on the flight roster. Once back, we stay and fly until all the hajjis are home. I fly one of five

Boeing 747s Max Air has acquired for all this flying, all retired aircraft from Japan Airlines.

At the high point of a typical Hajj, three to four million pilgrims, from all corners of the Muslim world, will circle the Kaaba in a single day. If no more Muslims added to the present population, at the maximum capacity of the Grand Mosque in Mecca, it would take five hundred and eighty years for all of them to attend. Saudi Arabia imposes quotas on all the major Muslim countries, and the waiting list for those seeking a ticket range from seven to thirty-seven years. The Kingdom is hard at work expanding infrastructure to allow wider attendance. My 587-passenger 747-400 seems like a speck in the mix against the numbers hoping to participate. It humbles me to realize many people I'm carrying have waited decades for this opportunity.

CHAPTER 9

TERROR

Northeastern Nigeria has been a hotbed of terrorist activity for several years. Boko Haram has become increasingly bold since 2011 when al-Qaeda began pipelining lethal weapons into the ranks of this violent extremist group. They struck wildly into even large population centers with al-Qaeda's gifts of weapons causing a massive military retaliatory response that scattered and splintered their members. Unfortunately, much of Boko Haram's membership derives from desperately poor young people who see few prospects for survival but find some kind of hope among this band of terrorists. Until the government faces the fact that it is abject poverty that makes recruiting young men relatively easy, things are unlikely to change very much. The government so far seems unwilling to channel money beyond the privileged class, so things look bleak for any real change in the foreseeable future. Meanwhile hundreds continue to die hideous deaths at the hands of these ruthless killers.

I have signed up with the Nigerian US Consulate's Smart Traveler Enrollment Program, STEP, so the State Department can keep track of me while I'm here and send security notices as they're updated. The two I've received to date are so alarming that I find myself unwilling to leave the compound, and when I do, I go with eyes wide open and head on a continuous swivel. I feel my anxiety skyrocket during the only times I breach this self-imposed quarantine, which occurs only during travel to and from the Kano airport. Visitors to Kano, and Nigeria in general, are advised to exercise extreme caution and make sensible plans for their security. STEP notifications also suggest checking that our wills are current and making plans for our next of kin should we not return. Marcia and I double-checked my will before I departed, and I updated her on what duties are necessary to keep the financial wheels of our lives oiled. I do not share the alarming cautions the State Department has sent. I can't see any profit in deepening her disquiet.

When my partner, Reid, arrived here to fly this same contract five years ago, his drive to the Tahir Palace Hotel encountered many marauding, armed bands of men. They were stopped five or six times at police checkpoints. Things have changed dramatically in the ensuing years, and the terrorist factions have grown more powerful and stealthier. We'll have to be extra cautious at all times and be mindful of where, when, and what we do. Breaking taboos here is a near certain invitation to explore the afterlife. Walk softly and breach no laws is the prescription I intend to follow. In a few weeks, inshAllah, God willing, we'll return home to different and more familiar lands filled with our hopes and dreams and those we love.

CHAPTER 10
THE -400

I'm midway through my first personal experience flying a hajj. Max Air has four "classic" Boeing 747s and one Boeing 747-400. The 400 series aircraft is a significant redesign of the classic, emerging eighteen years after the original. The -400 has an entirely redesigned wing that includes large "winglets" and a horizontal stabilizer on the tail incorporating a fuel tank. Other major changes derive mainly from advances in computer technology that, according to powers that determine such things, eliminate the need for the third pilot, the flight engineer. Now we fly this modern variant as a team of two. I'm one of six pilots hired to crew the -400.

We're grouped in three sets of two pilots and, so far, have managed to keep our partnerships intact. Given the lack of any kind of formal standardization in this flight operation, staying with your companion becomes important so that we all get used to the styles and techniques of our colleague and consequently form de facto "standards."

CHAPTER 11

CONTINUOUSLY DERAILED PLANS THIRD WEEK IN NIGERIA

Captain Reid and I are on a rest break, having arrived at the Tahir Palace Hotel in Kano at about 1:00 a.m. this morning. We've both slept about six hours since checking in. We intend to spend the day awake and active, affording us a restful sleep tonight to be ready for a long day tomorrow, September 25th.

We enjoy a long workout in the hotel's gym followed a few hours later by dinner. Since we've each brought a ton of bulk foods and a rice cooker, we usually make our own meals. Tonight, it's curry lentil soup over Jasmine rice with steamed bok choy. This preplanned strategy gives us the option to eat healthier than if we had to always count on hotel food. We're encouraging each other in fitness and diet and are finding remarkably reduced stress and fatigue for our efforts. Between the Kano airport and the Tahir is a small, local grocery store with fresh fruit, vegetables, and a surprisingly large assortment of beans. Our driver is happy to stop there, allowing us to restock our pantries, but only during daylight hours.

Tomorrow morning's schedule has us flying to Abuja as passengers on Arik Airlines. A company vehicle will pick us up at 7:30

a.m. for a 9:00 a.m. departure from Kano. Once in Abuja, we'll check into the Sheraton Hotel and get a nap in preparation for a proposed afternoon flight to Medina.

We've both settled to our evening rites, Reid turning in early to allow him a 3:00 a.m. local wake-up so he can Skype connect with his young son in São Paulo, and me to a book. At 8:30 p.m. my phone rings. Reid says, "Hey buddy, our airplane's here, and it's being dispatched to Maiduguri. One of the classics just hit a flock of birds on takeoff. It's down with two beat-up engines. The -400 has to go grab the stranded pilgrims and haul them to Jeddah. They can't seem to find Stuart. You and I might need to take it."

"Okay, Reid. I'll head to the front desk to see what I can find out. I'll keep you posted," I vow and hang up. Maiduguri is the capital of the Borno State in northeastern Nigeria and has been a hotbed of violence since Boko Haram infiltrated it in 2012. It's just over three hundred air miles east of here, an hour away. It's supposed to be solely "classic" flying, but when the chips are down, they can assign the -400. I'd hoped to avoid Maiduguri for the whole hajj. It's super infiltrated with terrorists. Maybe they'll find Stuart.

The next pilots in the "pipeline" are Stuart—the only other American flying this hajj contract—and Mark, a retired Australian military pilot. They get along well, having surprisingly similar backgrounds and social inclinations. Their schedule has them taking a trip to Jeddah departing at 2:00 a.m. Stuart sleeps away the afternoon but wakes around 8:00 p.m. Unable to fall back to sleep, he gets up and goes for a walk. Stuart's a lot laxer about leaving the compound than I am. Maybe he hasn't read the State Department warnings or maybe he just doesn't care, feeling the risk is acceptable. He tells the front desk he's going out and will be back in an hour. While English is widely spoken here, full comprehension is rare. Trouble conspires to mess with Stuart's immediate future when he absentmindedly leaves his cell phone in his room.

A driver from Max Air arrives at the hotel moments after Stuart walked through the security gate. He tells the front desk he's here to pick up Stuart and Mark and can he please have their room numbers. It is an odd way to inform pilots of an abrupt schedule change, but it's the way Max Air chooses tonight. Calls to Stuart's room and cell phone go unanswered. No one at the front desk remembers that Stuart just left. Soon he's considered MIA, and Reid and I are called.

My phone rings again at 8:40. It is Reid. "Hey buddy, looks like we're probably going." I tell him I'll go knock on Stuart's door. At the front desk I find the anxious Max Air driver who needs pilots in his van immediately or *he's* in trouble. The front desk tells me Stuart's room number is 140. I charge off to his alleged room and begin knocking loudly. Behind me I hear a shout. It's Stuart's copilot, Mark. The receptionist had Stuart's and Mark's rooms reversed. I'm knocking on the wrong door. Mark has been out knocking on the right door. No Stuart. I backtrack to the front desk where the driver tells me a new schedule has been decided. Reid and I are taking the flight. I tell him I'll be back in ten minutes.

I call Reid. His phone's busy. I run to his room and he's hurrying to get packed. Before I can say a word, he tells me we're going. "That's what I came to tell you." I hustle back to my room and pack and dress with no time for shaving. Minutes later, I'm schlepping my entire stable of bags across the parking lot headed for the office building. I don't know whether we're returning here or to some other city, so all belongings need to come along. I want to kiss whoever invented rolling baggage trolleys. Halfway across the lot, I see Mark. He's in uniform headed the other direction with some people from security. They've decided to open Stuart's door to see if maybe he's incapacitated. Mark claims there's over $1000 in overtime riding on him doing this flight, and he's bound to fly it one way or another. I'm a little dubious as there's no provision for "overtime" in my contract, and Reid and I are determined not to split up. We've grown into a comfortable alliance in the cockpit, and no scheduling mishaps, missing pilots, or wild claims of lost income are going to dissuade us. We both consider it a safety issue in this disorganized place where specific training regarding procedures, the bulk of any airline's training syllabi, are entirely absent. Mark strenuously objects. Neither Reid nor I really care. Management stands firmly behind us.

At the front desk we're assured the changes are final—the night flight is ours. I'm running on adrenaline but know it'll burn off in a few hours when fatigue sets in. Sometimes you've just gotta bite the bullet. There'll be plenty of coffee on the plane.

The driver begins pulling out of the courtyard when we encounter Steve, the -400 chief pilot. He brought the plane in from Jeddah two hours ago and wants nothing more than to go to his room and get some rest. But he's embroiled in this drama and was instrumental in the changes. He wants to be sure we know our new schedule and that Stuart and Mark have been reassigned to our morning commercial flight to Abuja. We assure him it's all understood and wave goodbye. But a hundred feet ahead, white shirts reflecting brightly in our headlight beams, Stuart and Mark rush toward us. They're in full uniform, baggage in tow. "Oh boy," I think, "here we go."

Arriving breathless at the van, Stuart yells, "This is our trip, get out."

Steve, still present, yells, "NO! Reid and Andy are taking the trip. All changes are final."

Stuart shrieks, "NO! It's OUR trip and we're taking it!"

Tensions and tempers escalate between tired and irritated pilots. Silently I hope Stuart wins, but I'm going to stay clear of the slugfest. I know it's going to be a miserably long night with not two, but three flight legs. We'll end up being up for at least thirty hours before it's over and that's starting on an empty tank of rest.

Finally, Stuart changes his tone to something approaching pleading, and Steve eventually relents. He seems upset about it, but I'm not. We trade places and away drives the van. Bullet narrowly dodged.

Resetting to our original assignment is more troublesome than I feared. I'm totally wound up. My head on a pillow brings nothing but frustrating restlessness for the distance separating me from sleep. I'm two full hours lying wide awake before the sandman begins his industry. I think I manage about five hours of sleep. Rest is a thing Max Air is comfortable thinking of as optional. By the end of this hajj, I begin to understand why.

With my alarm, I jump as a soldier awakened in a foxhole with conditioning often reinforced that any breach of silence is cause for dread. I take in a few calming breaths as I recall the day's proposed agenda. I shave and prepare to check out. Reid and I meet in the restaurant at 7:00 a.m. for breakfast. We're enjoying a few minutes of peace before the day's almost certain hysterics of interminable changes begin. Then Reid's phone rings. It's someone from dispatch wondering where we are. Reid tells him we're at breakfast and will be out front in fifteen minutes, at our scheduled pickup time. The voice on the other end says our ride is waiting now and hangs up. Conversations are always minimal between Nigerians and us. So much is lost in translation, especially when it's just phone dialogue. Absent the huge percentage of communication translated through body language, clear messaging usually clocks in at something under fifty percent.

I don't even need to ask what's going on. I can see in Reid's expression that the games have begun. Before he says a word, I'm on my feet taking my half-full plate to the cleaning station. Wordless, but with a thousand words spoken by his eyes, he's right behind me.

I've become so used to this circus of calamitous disorganization that my demeanor is hardly affected. But all of a sudden, I feel agitated. I'm jarred when I realize we're in a country where a huge percentage of the population doesn't get enough to eat. I sit here with more than twice what I need, working hard to stuff down all the associated guilt for later torture, and I'm supposed to toss it? That certainly deepens the guilt in which I normally wade, so I take out my frustration trying to devour what's left as I approach the trash can. Maybe the gods of injustice will find that more forgivable. It's a ridiculous scheme, and now my stomach hurts.

We're now at the pickup curb at 7:20. No ride. At 7:30 Reid calls the mystery number that had hung up on him fifteen minutes ago. No answer. A call to another dispatch number—no answer. A call to the system chief pilot—no answer.

Next, texting to various managers begins. At 7:45 Reid's phone rings. It's the boss of all bosses, Shyam. He says transportation's on the way. We're certain at this point we'll miss our 9:00 a.m. flight. Shyam assures us we'll be driven directly to the terminal where someone will meet us with our tickets. We push the driver to go as fast as he dares, which is twice as fast as prudence would allow.

A ride from the Tahir Palace Hotel to the Kano airport is not without adrenaline-inducing discovery and some sense of danger. It's distressing enough to be in a race with a rapidly expiring clock, but to do so in the confines of Kano is disquieting in additional ways. Being constantly aware of the perilous intent around us by would-be assassins and aggressors, combined with desperation so rampant and pervasive in this extremely poverty-stricken part of the world, makes for uneasy travel. We're sitting ducks in this bus with its big windows. Dozens of machine-gun toting police walk the streets along our route. There are a couple of traffic circles that always find us stationary for a few minutes in impassible traffic jams. When we stop, my heart begins a tumultuous parade in my chest. I sense we're most vulnerable right now, and it unnerves me. I worry my fear is palpable—that I'm telegraphing it and thereby inviting attack, a response often evinced by vicious animals. We become trapped spectators in an unsettling show as beggars mob our bus, and suddenly, a quarter-inch thick piece of glass separates our stage from theirs.

Young children, maybe only five or six years old with bowls for alms, street hawkers, and lame men sitting with their useless leg tucked beneath them on impoverished skateboards, lodge on the street, inches away but light-years when measured by any other scale. Outstretched hands mock our comfort. The disabled men with inert legs dart into the streets at lightning speeds, reaching with Gollum-like, trembling hands. They gaze through despondent, oversized eyes, smiling while begging, praying, and straining for handouts. It's shocking and heartbreaking.

I wonder how many people would be trampled if I reached out through the window with a thousand-naira bill. Would a dozen people with dire needs pull me bodily through the window whereupon I would enter their stage?

I don't dare. Maybe I'll write down the horror movie playing in my head and send it to Stephen King.

People inhabit every nook and cranny. In spaces too small to emplace a small storage shed, there's invariably a thrown-together rusty corrugated shack in which an American wouldn't put their lawn mower. Inside, a family lives on dirt floors. Goats share the streets searching for discarded garbage. What concrete is here for sidewalks is broken and almost completely unwalkable from neglect and age. Streets are so pocked with holes and scars that they lend no better riding surface than dirt though less dust is raised.

Typical Kano street scene. The "canal" behind the young boy flows with all runoff water, including raw sewage.

After half an hour we race past Max Air's office, raising a terrible cloud of lung-stifling soot behind us in our final dash to the airport. The driver's cell phone rings, and he pulls over. "NO, you must stop here at the office and pick up the tickets!" We do a U-turn. They'd seen us fly by. Communication is consistently poor to nil here, and we note ruefully that our airport/ticket rendezvous is voided. We turn around and race back. No chance now of catching our flight. A dispatcher climbs into the back with Reid and me and hands us our tickets. Printed on the ticket, in the lower right-hand corner is *DEPARTURE TIME: 9:40 a.m.* Really? Does anyone in the office understand that there's a difference as big as a 747 between 9:00 and 9:40? Probably not.

Time is among the most baffling elements here, which is demonstrated often and in almost all things. I think back to the first morning we were here. There was a meeting at the downtown office and all of us—contract pilots—were being picked up at 9 a.m. sharp. The bus came at 9:30. By the time everyone was on board, we pulled away from the hotel at 10. Arriving at the office at 10:30, we were escorted to the fourth floor where a hundred and fifty chairs were set up for the meeting. The meeting began at 12:30.

We get to the terminal with that extra forty minutes added to the clock. Circumstances, however, conspire to rob us of any reprieve. At the baggage counter, the agent wants $50 to check our baggage. It's certain this is a spur-of-the-moment, made-up fee. Fifty dollars is serious money to people outside of government's corrupt circles here and would handily fill the pockets of all aspiring frauds. The dispatcher who's guiding us doesn't have $50 so makes a snap decision to avoid the charge by sending us, with all our baggage, straight to the plane. He corrals us to the security checkpoint consisting of a single magnetometer and X-ray machine. We heft our bulky loads onto the conveyor belt, so large they barely fit through the machine, and walk through the magnetometer. The sentries on the other side are incensed that we have three gigantic bags each and begin yelling excitedly about the size of the plane on which we'll be flying—at least I think that's what they're yelling about. We try to explain that it's not our idea, but they don't care. We plod the walk of shame back to the starting point, monster bags in tow, among much excited chatter, none of which we understand. At baggage check-in they still want $50, but the dispatcher, still acting as our Hausa speaking surrogate, tells them he has no money. They say okay and check our bags for free. The miracle of straight talk. Nigerian business practices take some getting used to. Fees and procedures are often malleable, particularly when white foreigners are the subjects of focus. We go back through security and enter the waiting area with twenty minutes to spare.

Reid sees Muslim skullcaps—taqiyahs—for sale and adventurously advances on the proprietor. "How much?" The denominations of US dollars and Nigerian naira are confusing, but Reid thinks he's getting a cap for $10. Heck, for ten bucks I want one too. We each get one. Price: $100. In unison we emphatically say "No! Ten bucks each." The shop owner argues aggressively in words we don't understand but body language we do. He pesters us relentlessly, his shrill voice escalating toward soprano, until we walk out the door to board the flight. A hundred bucks for curious souvenirs? Whether that's combined or each is a moot point, and we don't bother to clarify. Too pricey for us.

It's an uneventful 40-minute flight in the CRJ-90 Arik jet. As we approach Abuja, I press my face against the window, excited to see brightly colored red and blue roofs adorning an ocean of homes. Floating below are divided highways and commercial buildings surrounded by thousands of acres of lush, green agriculture including clusters of tree farms and furrowed fields of crops. It looks richly fertile.

CHAPTER 12

HAIR-RAISING

After landing we're met by the station manager as we walk to baggage claim. He's outwardly friendly and makes a heroic attempt at small talk. He tells us we're flying tonight at 11 p.m. We're both thinking, *Good—plenty of time for a nap.*

After collecting all our bags, the station manager takes us on a long, confused odyssey in an attempt to unite us with our chauffeur. After walking for a quarter of an hour we're finally spotted by a man in a light-blue Toyota Corolla. He rushes to meet us and assist with our baggage. The trunk is much too small for the burden assigned it, so some of our luggage is stacked in the back seat beside Reid. I'm amazed our driver is able to smash the lid down on the overstuffed bin, but with puzzle-master skills and unrestrained confidence, he finally succeeds.

The station manager hands the driver several thousand naira and tells him to take us to the Sheraton. It takes more than twenty minutes to get out of the parking lots because we're stopped twice and forced to pay thugs. It's common practice in this country to take money from others in any way you can, right or wrong, and seems widely accepted. Thug band number one argues with our driver for a few minutes. It seems to be a hostile encounter, and angry tension deepens on all faces. Our driver extracts himself after appropriate tithing and drives to a lower tier parking lot where we're stopped by thug gang number two. A similar exchange takes place, and we're finally free to leave the airport. I'm one part appalled and one part curious about these intercessions. How brutal might these guys get if they aren't satisfied with the bounty offered? Is there such a thing as security or law enforcement nearby? Then it strikes me—these guys are probably the de facto security agency. Will their predatory enterprise migrate to the passengers next, or would that cross some invisible line? Scary tension seems never far from the horizon in this place.

We now begin a gripping ride to the hotel. While roads are infinitely better here than in other parts of Nigeria we've toured, drivers are not. Lanes and queuing seem a mystifying concept here. Traffic organization, at least most drivers' willingness to abide any semblance of it, and heaven forbid, courtesy, is demonstrably absent. We pass on the right a car that is lumbering along twenty miles per hour, straddling the line delineating the left two lanes. Seconds later we're going sixty miles per hour on the right-hand shoulder. All seems fair on Nigerian roadways, and no hardtop is wasted. Shoulders shmoulders. If you have a flat tire, your life is at terrible risk if you assume the side of the roadway is a safe haven for changing it.

Our driver, not an aggressive maniac by any mannerisms he's displayed so far, shows us his preferred scheme of passing other cars he feels are impeding our way. He closes to within a few feet of the offending vehicle's rear bumper and then lays on the horn. If that doesn't produce an immediate right-of-way, he barges into an adjacent lane, even if someone else is in it. He maneuvers left or right—I never can decode his partiality—and pushes hard on the gas and horn. He seems truly ambivalent about sideswiping another vehicle. Each of the dozens of cars we challenge backs down from his bullying. To ice the cake, I notice him repeatedly giving menacing looks to those who dare to be in his way.

Thirty hair-raising minutes later, we arrive at the Sheraton Hotel. Our driver transforms back to the affable Dr. Jekyll, helps unload our baggage, and offers a humble bow before pulling away. I suspect his menacing Mr. Hyde will soon be terrorizing those unlucky enough to share "his" highway back to the airport.

CHAPTER 13

ABUJA

The Sheraton is a masterpiece of architecture on lush, tropical acreage. I'm almost tricked into thinking I'm entering a Hawaiian resort hotel. Nice as it is, however, our elation descends to more familiar territory when we're told our rooms aren't ready. We move a few feet away to a comfortable lounge. An hour later, after drinking dark, rich coffee provided by uniformed stewards, they bring our room keys. We take one of three side-by-side glass-fronted elevators to the fifth floor where our rooms await.

The hotel consists of two large rectangular towers soaring ten stories high. Each edifice has rooms arranged around its outer perimeter surrounding ballpark-sized atriums planted with tropical trees and plants and honeycombed with flagstone walkways. Wide promenades access each guestroom with tempered glass and hardwood rails skirting the passageway to protect guests from falling into the atriums. Their transparency encourages me to hug the wall instead of the rail as the breathtaking "high-dive" effect sinks into my stomach. Across from my room's entry door are sliding glass doors that open onto a large balcony. Thick padded cushions married within wicker frameworks adorn it, and potted ferns and a Queen Palm stand sentinel right and left on the balcony. It overlooks a modern and densely forested city below, offering sweeping panoramic views.

We unpack and agree to meet in a few minutes to check out the gym. Unsurprisingly, it's beautifully outfitted. After a long, stress-draining workout, we discover there's both a steam and dry sauna. Lavishing in every delight, we visit both. Back in our rooms, we conspire to make another large dinner and agree to get some sleep to be rested for our 9 p.m. expected wake-up call.

My afternoon nap is the first comfortable sleep I've had in a month. A high-quality mattress and assorted hard, soft, big, and small pillows have made it perfect. Where am I again? My shower has both cold and hot running water, a rarity in Nigeria, with enough pressure to flood dual showerheads. The upgrades and, in fact, the whole city seems fake within the borders of poverty-stricken Nigeria. It's a tremendous step up from our "Palace" in Kano. I keep having to pinch myself.

At 7 p.m. Reid gets a text from Steve—"We're departing Kano for Jeddah at 9:40 p.m. You can expect the plane back in Abuja by midmorning tomorrow. "Our" 11 p.m. flight is for a Classic Boeing 747, not the 747-400. There's only one 747-400 in Max Air's fleet, and it's the only airplane Reid and I fly. Apparently, our station manager mistook us for a Classic crew though such crews consist of three pilots because the old Classics need a flight engineer. The -400 doesn't. Admittedly, we've just completed the outbound transportation needs from Kano, and Abuja flying is just beginning. Maybe the station manager doesn't realize the distinction between the two different aircraft types. Maybe he doesn't even know there are two different airplanes that require uniquely qualified pilots for each. Until Reid got that text from Steve, we had no reason to suspect our -400 wasn't the aircraft on tonight's schedule, and I don't believe the station manager knew any better. Just another hiccup in this multimillion-dollar-per day flight operation. We're now on the hook for a pickup at 10 a.m. and are exuberant about spending the night and having a leisurely morning.

At 7 a.m., after a fairytale comfortable night only a small number of Nigerians will ever experience, we meet for breakfast. The restaurant is amazing. Five stars if not six. Every kind of cuisine imaginable, both Nigerian and western, are artistically arranged in a series of buffets. It's extravagant beyond any hope one could entertain during Nigerian travels, and we stuff ourselves, badly breaching our carefully ordered self-control.

We retreat to our rooms intending to meet at 8:30 for another workout. Bloatedly digesting the excess of my wrecked diet in the comfort of my room, I'm annoyed by the unwelcome ringing of my room telephone. I answer, and unsurprisingly, it's the dispatcher. "We're going to quick-turn the airplane and want you on an 8:30 bus to the airport," he says. Unbidden changes compel a sense of alacrity as usual. I'm beginning to feel like a fireman, expert in hasty, spur-of-the-moment preparations. We meet as if by well-rehearsed choreography on the landing outside our rooms, fully packed, in uniform, charging into another Max Air day.

CHAPTER 14
GET READY, GET SET...

We check out and load into a waiting company bus with fourteen flight attendants already aboard. They'll accommodate our passengers on the first two thousand miles of their hajj pilgrimage. We're bound for Medina, two hundred miles north of Mecca. At the airport, we're funneled through an abbreviated version of security for crewmembers. The dispatcher instructs Reid and me to continue to the VIP section of the terminal while the flight attendants prepare the aircraft cabin for the passengers. We find ourselves in a private room adorned with comfortable couches and a flat screen TV blaring a live soccer game. We've had our fill of adrenaline this morning already so turn off the game and settle in to read for a while. An attendant enters and takes coffee and snack orders. I like how serious they are about VIPs in Abuja. I appropriate a large, gleaming bathroom to shave. Our fireman's egress from the Sheraton hadn't afforded that luxury earlier.

At 10:30 a.m. we decide to go to the airplane to enjoy an unhurried preflight. We complete all our duties too quickly, and now we're stuck in this hot and muggy grotto. Memories of the cool, comfortable VIP lounge grow distant, and I pray for enough sense to stop doing stupid things. The Auxiliary Power Unit, a small jet engine mounted in the tail, powers our air-conditioning units, but the package is tired and old and doesn't perform as it did at birth, twenty-four years ago. It struggles vainly to cool our vast cabin in these tropical climes.

Fueling seems painfully slow, and regulations prohibit boarding passengers while the volatile fluid is flowing into our tanks. An hour crawls by before we're finally able to emplane our guests. When the signal is given, a dozen sets of double doors fly open, and out stream hundreds of Muslims. The two-hundred-foot charge is led by men dressed in loose-fitting, full-length robes. Women follow wearing matching, colorful hijabs and voluminous, full-length gowns blossoming like sails in the wind. Men and women typically carry their personal belongings balanced on their heads. Groups of fifty to a hundred are attired in identical colors. The first group approaches like a huge azure blue wave. Next comes a tsunami of canary yellow followed by a regiment of orchid pink. The distinctions are stark and indubitably facilitate distinguishing the various groups and tribes for their own congregating and to speed clearing customs as they enter the Kingdom of Saudi Arabia.

With about a hundred people on board, the crowding on the airstairs begins to get dangerously aggressive. In a perilous act, the loadmaster commands the trucks bearing the giant stairways to back away from the aircraft. He fears the gross overloading of the stair structures might collapse or topple them. It's an admirable demonstration of the capability of the boarding agents and flight attendants that no one falls to the ground, more than twenty feet below, as the airstairs are moved.

As envoys try to thin their ranks and reorganize the pilgrims into some semblance of order, a pervasive shadow from the northeast darkens the ramp as it moves overhead and begins riveting the airport with large bullets of water. Then there's a blinding flash of lightning accompanied by a loud clap of thunder as if Allah Himself is commanding order. Hundreds of colorful plumages, now soaked and wilted, melt together in continuous tides, cartoonishly fleeing for shelter inside the terminal. A downpour ensues with so much force the tarmac looks like the surface of a lake, with an endless series of waves driven by gusty winds. Fifteen minutes later, the storm subsides, but most of our waterlogged passengers have to dry off. It's all time-consuming. More than an hour crawls by as they trickle back to the airplane a few at a time. The soaking storm and still damp passengers make it nearly unbearable aboard as the cabin's humidity closes on 100%. Water separators in the plane's belly are like kitchen sponges to Niagara Falls, so weak are they against the challenge.

Finally, a group of men dressed in long white robes and a lone, blue-gowned woman meet a hundred feet in front of the airplane in what appears to be an animated discussion. What tempest decision is being weighed I don't know, but it's an agonizingly long delay as we and our five hundred and fifty passengers wait aboard in this gigantic steam sauna. After twenty minutes, they finally break ranks, and the female pilgrim in blue dashes to the airplane. An annunciator panel in the cockpit shows all boarding doors are now closed, ensuring we're safe to get underway. Our "quick-turn" has contorted into five hours. We'll never leave comfort for cockpit again until forced.

CHAPTER 15

...GO!

We take off on runway 22 at 1:36 in the afternoon with five hundred and fifty-three pilgrims on board and begin our journey with a series of long sweeping left turns that soon bring us to a northeast heading. During the next five and a half hours, we'll cross out of Nigeria into Chad and then Sudan. The longest river on earth begins its journey northward from Lake Victoria in Uganda. It's the mighty Nile, 4132 miles in length. This trunk of the river is called The White Nile. Beginning far to the northeast in Ethiopia is the Blue Nile, and the place where these two great rivers meet is the ancient commerce center of Khartoum, which falls directly under our nose when we are two-thirds of the way across Sudan. Half an hour later we approach Port Sudan, marking the eastern edge of the African continent and the beginning of the Red Sea. Across this two-hundred-mile-wide waterway separating Africa from Asia is the Saudi Arabian port city of Jeddah. Our flight plan routing over Jeddah is cut short by a Saudi air traffic controller directing us toward our final destination of Medina. A few minutes after turning onto our new course, we begin a one hundred thirty-mile descent from 39,000 feet.

Jeddah is a central navigation point for airplanes transiting to and from dozens of airports blanketing Africa to the south and west, Europe and Mediterranean resorts to the north, the Stans east of Iran, as well as India to the east across the Arabian Sea.

Native tongues spoken by the aircrews piloting these many aircraft number in the hundreds. But by international convention, English is the official language of pilot and air traffic communications throughout the world. The dialects overheard in such an international melting pot are both comical and confusing. The number of times I hear "Please say again" can't be counted and take up the majority of beehive-busy air traffic communications.

Jeddah air traffic controllers are as anxious to cull the air traffic herd in their region as are the pilots flying above. Whenever Jeddah isn't the destination of an overflying airplane, local controllers will do all they can to turn them away. Within five minutes of our northbound turn toward Medina, we're switched to a new air traffic control sector, and our radios suddenly become blessedly quiet.

Reid and I look at each other realizing these are the first moments of peace we've enjoyed in at least half an hour. While descent planning and the final maneuvering of our 600,000 pound 747 takes a lot of concentration to properly manage, in the absence of riotous, mostly incomprehensible radio acrobatics, it seems as sedate as pulling into my driveway at home.

At 5:08 p.m. local time—7:08 Nigerian—sixteen wheels carried on four trucks of four tires each straddle the centerline of Runway 35 and briskly engage its grooved concrete. As the landing gear struts compress, logic sensors relay a touchdown signal to automatically deploy ground spoilers on each wing, firming our adhesion to the runway. I gently fly the nose down the last of its twenty-foot arc to its own landing. I'm honored to welcome our pilgrims to Medina and the beginning of their quest.

We taxi with our eyes nearly thirty feet above the ground from our high-rise perch in this monstrous airplane. Twenty-five miles per hour seems like ten from three stories up. We must continually check a ground speed readout on the instrument panel to avoid throwing our flight attendants on the floor or scrubbing our tires while rounding corners. Nine minutes brings us to our remote hajj parking spot and the beginning of the disembarkation of sore, bent, stiff bodies that have just endured seven hours in tiny seats.

CHAPTER 16
FLOUNDERING BACK TO BASE

N ext to Mecca, the city of Medina ranks second in the hierarchy of most sacred soil in Muslim faith. This is the first excursion for many outside narrow confines that often imprison the poor. A moment of awesome import is upon these pilgrims now wherein the hopes of a lifetime will be realized. The discomfort of a few hours crammed into a small airplane seat probably doesn't even register against all the daily trials in lives filled with such titanic challenges. Sparks of elation joyously brandish their faces, even after such long confinement.

I make my way through a blue-robed parade of passengers on the stairway as I descend to the ramp below. I must inspect the airplane in preparation for our flight back to Kano. Halfway down the stairs, on the only landing of the two-story airstair, I encounter a stooped, elderly woman who doesn't have the strength to carry her bags any farther. She blocks half the path's width grousing at the charge facing her as a stream of her companions accelerate around her, demonstrating Bernoulli's "venturi" effect.

I pick up her bags. They're surprisingly heavy. I hope that my good deed isn't mistakenly construed as theft which would cost my right hand and maybe more under Islamic Sharia law. I set her bags on the tarmac and am relieved when no long knives are wielded. Twenty minutes later, I return to the cockpit for final preparations for our flight "home." One hour and twenty-two minutes after arriving, we're ready to release the parking brake and push back from our spot to begin the journey back to Kano. This flight is a hundred and fifty miles shorter than the one we just accomplished, and the winds are on our tail, so our return will be much quicker. We're airborne at 8:30 p.m. and settle our passengerless airplane at 40,000 feet before reaching the Red Sea. An eventless four hour and twenty-four-minute flight above dark deserts brings us to Kano's runway 24 where a soft touchdown is followed by seven minutes of taxi to complete our day's mission. It takes fifteen minutes to secure the ship and do all the necessary paperwork before we can descend with our heavy baggage to await the bus that will take us to customs.

It's rarely within our purview to know or understand the behind-the-scenes workings of the systems emplaced to move us to and fro on the ground once our aerial ballet is complete. Consistent with a growing body of evidence, our hunch accumulates support that no real expertise exists in this facet of the operation and so we're unsurprised as more than thirty minutes tick by in the middle of this calm and cool Kano night before our transport arrives. Aside from five hundred pilgrims assembled outside the embarkation side of customs preparing to board the aircraft we've just delivered, the airport is utterly deserted. Nineteen hours has elapsed since assembling for departure in Abuja's Sheraton Hotel this morning, but apparently, we alone credit such a long day of service as deserving of timely relief. So we pace under a luminous, waxing gibbous moon, silently waiting. Finally, a bus, headlights dimmed from layers of dust and dirt, penetrates the lonesome night, and we ascend the stairs to board. The aging vehicle takes us to an empty customs area. Not a character from the normal cast occupies the entire hall, implying abandonment of all formalities we normally engage under bored eyes of government shepherds. And why not, I wonder. Does a sole airline crew from the hometown airline, having just returned from a sacred hajj flight to Medina, really pose a threat to national security? Apparently even the security officials agree not.

Exiting the deserted building, we walk to an opening in the fence and file past a few armed guards watching over the anaconda-like line of Mecca-bound pilgrims. Several minutes later our dim lighted bus lumbers to rendezvous with us. We've traipsed a quarter mile through empty halls, walkways, and parking lots with onerous loads to reboard the bus. I don't think anyone knows why.

With all stragglers aboard, we're driven to Max Air's office compound where half a dozen of our ranks disembark. They've made other arrangements to get home. Always wary about the potential for baggage mix-ups, we watch carefully, hoping to stem the calamity that would arise from a lost bag. I notice one of mine being removed and hurry outside to stop its offloading. After retrieving it, I notice some flight attendants still on the bus shouting through open windows. They're frantically signaling me to grab their misdirected bags too. Just as I'm resettling in my seat, the driver decides we must all disembark. Annoyed, I gather my belongings and, among the remaining crew, parade down the aisle to get off the bus. We numbly wait for whatever new transport might approach, but after several minutes, our driver, who has remained aboard throughout the procession, beckons us back. Plans change quickly around here in the middle of the night, but we're used to disorganization. Dimwitted from lack of sleep, no one even questions the apparent folly marking the night's finale. We leave the Max Air compound forty minutes after we should. Along our usual route we're stopped twice at police checkpoints where the midnight shift seems more agitated than normal. Half an hour more brings my bed within walking distance at 2:30 in the morning. Twenty-one hours have swept along since the morning's "you need to hurry" phone call in Abuja, a billion "poverty miles" away.

I check email before bed and see a new alert from the State Department. They have information that terrorist elements are making ready for a renewed wave of attacks in all the usual places, Kano being high on the list. Now I get the heightened police activity. I'm so tired my own sense of doom is unheightened.

CHAPTER 17
WITH NEW EYES

For all the turbulence and struggle I encounter, my woes have no more weight than a dry sponge against granite stones compared to the daily life of the vast majority of the indigenous population. I'll need more aging before I know the net effect of Africa upon my soul. On the surface, I feel a trembling horror at continually witnessing so much human suffering and hardship. Pervasive filth and poverty plant dark shadows inside me. Is there a *right* way to act or feel here, I wonder? Being thrown into the deep end of a world I know so little about, I feel like I stumble too often. I'm confident I know few right ways about much in this land, but I think a broader viewpoint is evolving. I just need to constantly remind myself to be patient and try to check my foreboding.

A few documentaries I've seen make worthy attempts to bring some idea of the shocking depth of torment here. I soon realize, however, it can only really be assimilated by immersing here in the breathed air and ravaged grounds that are the stages of life on this vast continent. I'm encouraged that beneath the surface I continually find gold and diamonds. A smile and wave never go unrewarded no matter how disconsolate the recipient appears when first I offer. Without exception, that simple moment of recognition is returned with unblemished candor and kindness.

Shall I celebrate the inextinguishable spark of the human spirit of which I see abounding evidence, or wallow in despair of the countless lives lived in such insidious plights of want and adversity? Time may be my only real ally to bring clarity to the musings rambling within me as I walk my own pilgrimage upon this amazing earth.

CHAPTER 18

ESCAPE

It's warmer and more humid this morning, especially dressed in full uniform with black slacks that absorb and retain every photon of solar radiation. But a flight home is in my immediate future, and I'm choosing to take my flights in full uniform hoping that will smooth my way through Nigerian officialdom.

It's day four going to Max Air's office building attempting to resolve a pay issue. The company apparently had not received our specific contract. "We" are Stuart, Reid, and me—the only Americans flying this Nigerian hajj. There are several contracts under which the shuttling is being accomplished, but apparently, they've mislaid ours. When several days ago they asked if we agreed with their tabulated pay totals, it was clear their calculations weren't based on our pact. We were assured that the issue would be resolved "tomorrow," but each tomorrow has brought a similar response from our paymasters. Analysis of accounting progresses slowly in Nigeria as it does anywhere when the questioned balance is against the corporation.

Nevertheless, I'm leaving this Friday afternoon whether my pay issue is resolved or not. I have discovered that a way home is available to me with my Delta frequent flier award miles. One hundred and forty-five thousand points and $95 in fees will get me economy class seating all the way from Lagos to my home in Salt Lake City and back. When I clicked "purchase" on Delta's website last night, I set in motion an irrevocable option to travel this October night. A provision of Delta's policy on award travel is that no changes may be made within seventy-two hours of the booking, so I've bet 145,000 points and almost a hundred bucks that I'll be on that flight.

I've also booked a flight on a local carrier called IRS Airlines from Kano to Lagos. That flight is scheduled to depart Kano at 3:45 this afternoon, fly to Abuja and then continue to Lagos with a scheduled arrival time of 5:40 p.m. That gives me three hours and fifty minutes to make my 9:30 p.m. Delta flight. Due to endemic fraud in the Nigerian economy, use of credit cards to purchase things on the Internet is severely restricted. I was able to make my IRS Airlines reservation online, but purchasing the ticket must be done at a local bank or at the airport, with cash. The transaction must be completed at least one hour prior to the scheduled flight, or my reservation will be canceled.

Having concluded the "outbound" portion of this hajj where we take the pilgrims to Jeddah and Medina, we've been waiting for our release so we can engage in the leisure of our choice during the next two weeks. The pilgrims will be engaging their religious rites in the holy city of Mecca during this time. Release came yesterday afternoon, but we're reluctant to leave with our pay issues unresolved. I've decided that what they've paid me is close enough and feel confident the issue can be resolved when I return if today's attempt proves fruitless. That faith is what prompted my "Purchase" selection on Delta's website last night.

CHAPTER 19

DECEIT, INDEPENDENCE DAY, AND PAY

S tuart is sitting in the front, right-hand seat of a car driven by
a Max Air employee who happens to be at our hotel and has
offered us a ride to the office. Stuart is going only to Lagos for the
break and will not depart Kano until this evening. His wife, a pilot
for Arik Airlines based in Lagos, stays there a month at a time in
a rented apartment. Stuart plans to join her there. Reid is sitting
behind Stuart, opposite me, in the back seat. He admits he's in too
much debt to leave town before his compensation is made whole.
Unlike me, he's dressed casually and has made no preparations to
fly home today, though I know he's just as determined as I am to
leave Nigeria for the break.

The traffic is by far the most impenetrable, and proportionally
belligerent, that we've ever seen in Kano. Though normally bad,
this Friday begins Nigeria's "Independence Day" weekend, and
the volume of traffic is enormously dense and drivers doubly impatient. A ride that normally takes twenty-five minutes is stretched to
fifty by endless snarls of pedestrians, bikes, carts, motorbikes, cars,
tuk tuks, and minibuses.

BOOM! A loud, glass-shattering noise accompanied by glass
shards peppering the right side of our car shocks us. I think

Stuart has been shot and look around frantically for the gunman. The "terrorist" is a fellow motorist whose perception of breadth is inadequate for the inch or two of navigational precision he's attempted while trying to squeeze between us and a vehicle next to us. His rearview mirror has crashed into ours, shattering to bits with a recoil that caused a loud bang. Relieved that our plight doesn't include intentional attempts on our lives, our driver buzzes the right passenger's window down and begins a surprisingly tempered discussion with the reckless man next door. They speak in the native Hausa language and make an agreement to meet at a gas station a mile farther down the road. I don't believe there's insurance per se in Kano, at least none in widespread use. It seems instead that an honor system is used where the parties involved in an accident meet, argue liability, and then agree on a price for damages that's paid on the spot. Being in traffic that moves slower than walking speed does not give our antagonist much opportunity to slink off and get away from the agreed rendezvous. Meanwhile a man knocks on Stuart's closed window. He's picked up some parts off the street from our damaged rearview mirror and is attempting to deliver them. Our driver puts down the window, and Stuart accepts the bounty from the Good Samaritan.

After five or six minutes, we approach the gas station where the parley is to begin. We maneuver cautiously through columns of dense traffic on our right, mostly tuk tuks and bicycles, ultimately entering the gas station's lot. I'm watching the offending driver, now ahead and left of us, and report that he's making a gesture that he'll enter the lot through the next entrance. We watch him continue in a thick, serpent-like stream of traffic, Y'ing off to the left around a rotary. I drop my head in embarrassment and simmering anger for the villain. Both Reid and Stuart hurtle some choice words at him, vocabulary with which I possess world-class standing but feel inhibited with our Muslim driver. So much for the "honor" system I felt excited to witness. Deceived and cheated, we pull back into the incessant flow of traffic, our right rearview mirror dangling like a nearly severed hand, knowing we'll never see the rogue again. We press on toward our destination.

The one truly maligned among us, our driver who has every right to be furious, reacts moderately. Our bandit's bold, slow-motion getaway seems to deepen the deception and yet, rather than shake his fist and curse, our benefactor grumbles only an indecipherable word or two under his breath and then recovers his merry disposition. I could take a lesson from him, whether sourced from the Koran, the Bible, or a bottle of pills.

Arriving at Max Air's office building at 11 a.m., we find the chief accountant at his ground-floor desk. He waves us across the dimly lit hall to another accounting clerk who welcomes the three of us into his tiny office, overflowing with files and eclectic ornamentation. It's clear our host has occupied this haunt for years and is comfortably at home in the sprawling disorder surrounding him. His English is difficult to understand, but it seems clear that he's telling us that our pay issue has been resolved and that we can expect our full earnings shortly. We all look at each other in disbelief. Really? They've fixed it? We're jubilant and excited. Then the voluminous paperwork begins so our corrected wages can be paid.

Reid checks his watch and realizes a marginal possibility exists that he might get back to the hotel, pack his belongings, and make the flights on which I'm booked. He's riding on Delta with a "buddy pass" that requires no reservation but is a "space available" ticket offering no assurances of boarding.

The act of being paid here is not like anything I've ever seen, and because of its unique discharge, is quite time-consuming. Once the accountant settles on an exact sum and I agree, he walks to a huge safe whose massive door is swung open. He stoops down to a shelf and withdraws several stacks of brand-new hundred-dollar bills. Because they're straight from a distribution center somewhere and have never been portioned, the crisp bills stick together. It's the accountant's job to count them out precisely. We're each receiving between fifteen and twenty-five thousand dollars. Like a blackjack dealer in Vegas, he sits at his desk and counts out the hundreds one at a time. My stack is about an inch thick, and suddenly, I'm perplexed about how to deal with all this cash. If I bring less than $10,000 into the US, I don't need to declare it. The folks at Max Air have long known the preference most pilots have about the amounts of cash they want to carry so have developed a bank wire courtesy. For a 1% surcharge, they'll wire whatever amount I want directly to my bank. I can send ten grand for only $100. Fair enough. Nigerian rules on what I can leave the country with are ambiguous. I've read anything from five to ten thousand dollars. I take the time to wire some home. Rumors grind away within the pilot ranks about potential penalties for trying to take too much out without declaring it. I'm sure if I declare it, they'll demand a percentage, maybe a big one. If I don't, and they discover it, I'm scared they'll confiscate it, and I might even spend some time in a Nigerian jail. Risk again assaults from dark places where I have very limited power and information. I decide to risk it and endeavor with Houdini-like efforts to find a good place to hide it. I feel confident with my result.

The pay process is complete at 1:05 p.m., and we begin an earnest hunt for rides—me to the airport only ten minutes away, and Reid and Stuart back to the Tahir Palace Hotel. No driver can be found. Reid's window of opportunity is contracting quickly, especially given the terrible traffic. I go to the front gate and ask one of the guards if there's a Max Air driver available for transporting us, and he assures me there is but, "he's praying just around the corner and will be done soon." I look at my watch noting it's 1:15. I ask, "Like two or three minutes soon?"

"No," he laughs, "not that soon." I go back to Reid and Stuart and tell them I think the driver will be done praying at 1:30. We realize there's not time to take me to the airport in the same vehicle with them because that will add at least twenty-five minutes to the skinny time frame for Reid who needs to go in the opposite direction. Minutes pass, and then it looks like deliverance has just shown up in the form of a small Toyota sedan pulling out of a parking space twenty feet away. I run to ask the driver if he can take me to the airport. Without hesitation, he assents, so I bid my companions farewell. I toss my luggage into a back seat already overflowing with paper files and cardboard boxes. His hand signals clarify his spartan English—"Just shove everything out of the way and jump in." With my bags askew in the back and me shoehorned into the front, we race off.

He drops me in front of the domestic terminal ten minutes later, and I slip him a thousand-naira note. He's grateful and wishes me safe travels. September was an unusually dry month here, leaving dust and trash to collect on the airport's hardtop road, baking in the sun. My kind friend, behind in his itinerary because of me, speeds away leaving me hacking in flying soot, disappearing behind the cloud in seconds.

I cross a hundred feet of hot, cracked concrete and dilapidated blacktop to small entry doors into the terminal and notice it's mostly deserted. I'm here at 1:30 for a 3:45 flight and proceed to the IRS check-in counter which is about the size of a card table. Immediately to my left, across a small, four-foot-tall partition, is a passenger security zone staffed by two men and a woman. They're idly chatting among themselves with nothing else to occupy their time. The young man nearest to me, dressed in clean western clothing, smiles and asks if I'm there for the IRS afternoon flight. I attest that I am, and he leaves his post to come and greet me.

He introduces himself as Richard, though I realize most people here with western names have adopted them for the benefit of us non-locals who can't wrap our tongues around their native names. He tells me to leave my bags where I'm standing, at the counter, and follow him. I'm intrigued but suspicious. I look at my bags with a concerned glance. Richard catches my hesitation and assures me they'll be safe. In my small bag is most of what I've earned in exchange for risking my life with terrorists rampaging the country. I've kept arduous schedules so afoul of US regulations the FAA would revoke my licenses if I were home, and have waded through frustration after frustration in logistical support in order to safely fly six hundred people at a time at ten-miles-a-minute, seven miles above Africa. Nope, I'm not leaving my small bag but will wager the other two on Richard's faith.

Once out front and back in the hot sun that I'd been all too happy to flee, Richard begins telling me he's the gate security guard whose job is to "profile" approaching passengers to discern their threat grade. He explains that he reads body and face language fluently and had determined me to be okay from two hundred feet away. Some people approach from across the street, and he gets very attentive, clearly taking his role seriously. He tells me they're all okay, but he still stops one man and asks his business. I get the impression he's genuinely performing his job and not just showing off. I wonder if common life would be different now if Richard had been guarding gates in Boston's Logan Airport on the morning of September 11, 2001. I bet that sneaky clan of rogue terrorists would never have made it past him.

We chat amicably for a while when the subject of our children comes up. I boast that I have a thirty-one-year-old son who's a flight medic, attending to the critically ill or wounded in the confines of a speeding helicopter. It's always hard to stop bragging once I start talking about my heroic son, but Richard interrupts. He has a two-year-old girl and a new infant daughter and, "Oh, my two-year-old is here at the airport with me today, and she's so thirsty and I don't have any money."

It's kind of comical, and usually predictable. At first, it's telegraphed through body language. Reinforcement comes when my *friend* finds no more words to share but stays at my side. Final confirmation is complete when the ruse gives way to a plea for money, sometimes delicately, sometimes bluntly. For many, I'm sure it's a learned form of survival nothing about which is comical. Maybe I say comical because it makes me uncomfortable, and I tend to gravitate toward any form of comedy when at loose ends. Starvation and malnutrition is far too common here because of the massive, top-down corruption that keeps money flowing upward and away from the lower working classes. Acceptance of this reality comes slowly, begrudgingly, to me when it's my own wallet that needs prying open.

Feeling generous with fresh reserves only moments before added to my stores, combined with a highly elevated spirit knowing my time in these unfathomable lands is coming quickly to a temporary end, I find I'm completely unperturbed and ask if a thousand naira will be enough. For my own selfish stock, I recognize that loyal, well...*paid* for, friendship of a senior security guard might serve me well if something unfortunate happens between now and departure time. I cheerfully dig out a thousand-naira bill to offer. He accepts but not before warning me that there's a security camera above pointing toward us. I ask if it's okay for me to give him money to which he hesitantly declares *yes*—and pockets my offer, subduing a smile. I've since learned there's some obscure law that forbids bribes and payoffs in Nigeria, but I think it's regarded with the same kind of conviction as the prohibition against dancing on Sundays in Utah.

To Richard's credit, a while later I find him at the concessions counter buying his youngster a drink. I get to meet this tiny twinkle in her daddy's eyes as she's consuming the prize. She's about two and a half feet tall with a lanky build and radiant bronze skin. Her tight curly locks are tied back with pink ribbons in two short pigtails. Her eyes are as wide as a Margaret Keane painting and sparkle like Tinker Bell's. She sets off some twinkling in my own eyes, and I'm delighted I was able to help Richard. I suspect a big, icy cold soda is a rare treat for her. True or not, it warms my heart to see this cute little girl giggling with delight.

At 2:30, a brother and sister team arrive at the IRS ticket *card* table to complete the business of booking passengers. They explain in heavily accented English that my purchase must take place at "the office," not here at the "ticket counter." The young man offers to take care of it for me, but I want to go with him. He leads me outside through fields and over ditches bridged by ancient dimensional lumber, to a shanty office some quarter mile away.

Inside, a woman—another sister by her looks—is sitting behind a large, metal desk. There are half a dozen people sitting on folding chairs finalizing business with her. When it comes my turn, the sitting sister voices concern about the US currency with which I'm attempting to pay. She's growing somewhat impatient, and I'm not sure if it's because of the difficulty we're having communicating or the dollars she sees me counting. I assumed she'd be happy to accept one hundred and twenty-five US dollars, the price advertised on their web site, but she's acting like my money is some kind of slur. Maybe this is another cache of unwritten rules of which I'm ignorant. She might have the power—and angst—to deny my purchase which would be a terrible setback. I'm being as accommodating as I'm able and am glad I'm here early enough to grind out a solution. Others waiting to purchase are getting impatient as their fidgeting clearly advertises. Finally, she settles on a hundred-dollar bill and four one-thousand-naira bills. Close enough. I can't believe all that was over math too perplexing to manage "change," but it seems that's all it was. I get my ticket, a two-page document filled with indecipherable coding, and the brother leads me back to the airport terminal where I tip him five hundred naira. He finalizes arrangements with his card-table sister and presses on with my large bags fifty feet east to the baggage check-in counter. I have two large bags to check and, not unexpectedly, note a little apprehension appearing on the faces of the officials weighing them. I'm expecting an onerous levy for my heavy luggage but in the end am assessed only two thousand naira, and upon straightforward payment, their troubled faces resume an apathetic countenance.

CHAPTER 20

EVAPORATING MARGINS

I progress through security and into the adjoining domestic departures hall. It's a big terminal, large enough to accommodate book and magazine shops, food concessions, a dozen boarding gates, and seating for hundreds. I deliberately avoid the skullcap salesman and sit in one of many empty rows of seats to quietly read. I soon realize I can hardly concentrate on the words because I'm so excited to be going home.

Let's see, Frodo was just about to, um, to...

I keep playing all the details and visions through, trying to convince myself everything's on track and going well. I know there are a little more than eighteen hours of flying ahead of me before I touch down in Salt Lake City...

...Oh man, I have to read that last paragraph again. I have no idea what I just read. Gandalf was telling Frodo something really important about Sauron's eye and, um...

...that with boarding and taxi time, I'm going to be sitting in economy class seats for close to twenty-two hours before I smell the air coming across the salt flats west of my hometown airport. I know I'm going to be bent and feel like I'm a hundred years old by the time the parking brake gets set on the plane at the arrival gate.

Gandalf was over two thousand years old. That's what I'm gonna feel like ...CRAP, where's my concentration? Okay, don't look at the orb. Sauron can see you looking...

But I know that only a few minutes' walk will bring me face to face with Marcia, that thirty more minutes will find me in my home without a moment's fear about encountering Boko Haram along the way. There will be a fully stocked refrigerator full of cold beer and fresh, wonderful food, and an expert, loving chef to prepare it.

...and can enslave you for your curiosity's trespassing...

While away, I've been Skyping into rehearsals so I can sing with my choir this coming Sunday morning. The anticipation of it has me terrified. I feel like anything that derails my trip at this point would come close to killing me. I'm more excited than I can ever remember. I give up on one of the most thrilling, epic novels I've ever read, deciding to just let the *tapes* roll on what the next two weeks will bring.

A booming legato female voice cracks over loudspeakers, long ago ruined by excessive volume and age, delivering a litany of distorted sounds containing not a single detectable consonant. I thought I might have heard her mention the number three in her blur-blared announcement which are the only numbers in my flight number, IRS 3333, to Lagos. I begin asking around the hall if anyone has understood the announcement. No one has, and in all likelihood, they haven't understood me either. I ask a uniformed airport official if he knows what was announced, and he assures me he doesn't. But he offers to find out and disappears back into the security section near the ticket counters. I follow him until I run smack into Reid who's just emerging from the X-ray machine. I'm surprised and delighted to see a familiar face. Solo travel in Nigeria is not high on my bucket list. These days, the adventure quotient is too high. Too many supposed enemies of Islam traveling alone find an unfortunate final punch on their bucket list ticket.

The uniformed man returns and tells us that flight 3333 is delayed and isn't expected to land until 3:45. That'll make us at least thirty minutes late, cutting our connection time in Lagos to about three hours and twenty minutes. That's "best case" and seems okay, though a little voice within me seems unconvinced that this is the final obstacle along my passage. Little voices usually know.

Sitting in uncomfortable plastic chairs, Reid relays to me a shocking story of his travel adventure since we had parted less than three hours before. The driver from the Max Air compound did not finish praying at 1:30. It was 2 p.m. before Allah, obviously a patient listener, completed invocations with His servant. This religious driver is particularly good at crashing through horrible traffic and had Reid and Stuart back to the hotel by 2:30. Reid tells me the story…

"I'm so sorry, captain, but I must go now. I cannot take you back to the airport," says the driver, then bowing his head.

"It's okay, sir. I'll find another way. Have a wonderful holiday, and I'll see you in two weeks," Reid says. He packed and decided he didn't have time to shower. In fact, he didn't even really have time to pack.

"I decided to just throw some shaving stuff and some under-wear in my daypack, and my money, and leave the rest. I told the front desk what I was doing and asked if they could have house-keeping bag up my belongings and store them 'til I got back."

Reid asked if there was a driver available to take him back to the airport but there wasn't. A Tahir Palace receptionist arranged a ride for him with a Palace employee. The unfortunate effect of that was that he was now traveling in a regular vehicle with no Max Air emblem or markings. He suddenly became a regular white guy, a no one.

The Independence Day celebrating had begun for those in lofty enough positions to afford intoxicants. That number included machine-gun-toting police officers whose taste for liquor grew as the alcohol's effects settled into their brains.

Rounding one of the rotaries in the thick traffic, a policeman spotted Reid.

"He yelled STOP, but we just kept going. I was sure the cop would let it drop but he didn't. He leveled his AK-47 right at me and yelled louder—STOP! I was afraid I was a goner for a minute," Reid reported.

The cop approached, signaling for Reid to roll down his window. He leaned in, stinking of booze, and told Reid, "My booze is gone and I need more. You will give me money!"

Reid went on. "I was in no position to resist, so I pulled a thousand-naira note out of my pocket. Thank God I threw a few thousand in my pocket. Pulling it from my pack would have been bad. The cop just stood there grimacing. I gave him another. His eyes were bloodshot and blinking a lot, but his mouth was still frowning. He was a mean bugger. I decided to give him one more before I started putting up a stink. He took it and smiled. What a jerk!"

The scoundrel stepped aside and let them go. When they got to the next checkpoint, they were met by a small group of drunk policemen who carelessly waved high-powered rifles around demanding drinking money just like the last guy.

"Super bad day to be traveling without my uniform," Reid said.

The process of extortion was repeated, netting another three thousand naira donated to the depravity of Kano's finest. Life in Nigeria—it's an acquired taste and bitter to swallow.

I walk to a window facing the runway to clear sickening thoughts clouding my head, unable to repel a more gruesome scenario from my thoughts. I watch for our jet. The Fokker F-100 touches down at about 3:50. They announced that the plane will be cleaned and then boarded. We're starting engines and begin taxiing exactly one hour late. Our connection time is down to two hours and fifty minutes. That ought to be plenty. The little voice inside my head is nervous.

Approaching Abuja thirty minutes later, the captain advises us of a large thunderstorm centered over the airport that will necessitate our flight holding for about ten minutes—precious minutes eating away at a margin I have 145,000 frequent flier miles bet against. The captain departs our holding pattern before the storm has moved completely away from the field, and we approach its retreating edge attempting to reduce our tardiness. Skipping the plane cleaning on the ground in Kano would have been a heck of a lot safer means to that end, but nobody asked me.

It's not unusual among Nigerian flying "professionals" to find pilots with underdeveloped instrument flying skills. It is, after all, a very difficult and expensive discipline to master, and some manage to slip through the cracks. A few survive just by learning to operate the autopilot. Heaven help those who draw such a pilot when weather is bad and autopilots fail. We're in a multi-million-dollar Fokker jet descending into ominous clouds that clearly define the outer circumference of a thunderstorm. There are Hawaiian-type volcanic mountain formations welling up on both sides of us, making it clear that a precise, on course trajectory is mandatory to keep air interspersed between mountainsides and the aluminum encasing us. One of my favorite aviation witticisms is, *Always try to fly in the middle of the air. Except for runways, avoid the edges. They're very hazardous to airplanes.* It comes to me right now but seems not in the least bit funny. We begin to heave as we proceed deeper into the cloud, and all reference to the outside world disappears, leaving only instrument interpretation available for guidance and keeping the aircraft upright. I'm in row six and am feeling exaggerated accelerations and decelerations with G loads that are rapidly exceeding my comfort level. I'm beginning to worry these pilots number among the few incompetents populating the country, and we're destined for headline news. I've seen this tragedy too often blazed across newspaper's faces. My heartbeat is accelerating. Reid is in row seventeen where the sensation of any displacement of the rudder is even more exaggerated. Comparing notes later, he tells me he was literally hanging onto his seat's armrests and that he was certain the pilots had lost control. The rudder, he said, seemed to be deflected with far too much force swinging the tail wildly. This was painfully obvious from my seat as well, and we both knew no competent pilot would ever do what this pilot was doing.

Two months and one day after the tragic air disasters on 9/11, American Airlines flight 587, departing from Kennedy's runway 31L, encountered wake turbulence emplaced by a previously departing Japan Airlines Boeing 747. 587's first officer was flying the A-300 Airbus and utilized a technique he'd learned somewhere earlier in his career that called for abruptly displacing the rudder to counter the effects of the roll induced by the Boeing's powerful, tornado-like wake. The American captain asked if he had it under control, and the first officer assured him he did, though he pushed the opposite rudder to counter the wagging tail he'd initiated by his first improper response. In the course of the next few seconds, this confused and poorly trained first officer pushed one rudder pedal after the other all the way to the floor trying to counter the ever-increasing oscillations he himself was inducing but mistaking for the Boeing's wake. On the fifth stroke the tail of the airplane could no longer stand the stresses and parted from the aircraft. Maybe I should stop reading aircraft accident reports, because I'm beginning to imagine I'm about to meet the souls of those two hundred and sixty occupants who died in the crash. Souls who would surely have crawled inside of our pilot's legs to ensure he stop pushing the rudder pedals if only they knew.

The carnival ride has many passengers clutching their seats, and a chorus of panicky screams punctuates the air. It's clear people are fearing for their lives, myself included. I'm watching out the window, praying to see ground before impacting it. After maybe two minutes that seem a lot more like twenty, we break out of the bottom of the storm cloud and proceed to complete an approach and landing on runway 22 at Abuja. The expression "on a wing and a prayer" just became my mantra for the day.

We deplane a score of grateful passengers, many of whom will probably ride bicycles home rather than ever fly again, and emplane an equal number. I catch Reid's eye. I can see he's as shaken as I am, but we're trusting the storm will move away before we take off again. We start engines after a very brief ten minutes or so and proceed back to the runway for takeoff. We're now one hour and fifteen minutes late. We're down to two hours and thirty-five minutes to connect in Lagos.

The thunderstorm has moved well off to the west, leaving swirling eddies of clear, cold air behind. The bumpy ride is no sweat, the flight path, gratefully, clear of clouds. It's a forty-five-minute flight to Lagos. I feel the descent begin accompanied by what seems a premature deceleration to approach speed. For reasons I'll never know, the approach elongates by twenty minutes, extending our forty-five-minute flight to an hour and five minutes.

On the ground taxiing in, I look at my watch—it's 7:15. We're an hour and thirty-five minutes late and still not at the gate. I know it's going to become a tense race with time. My little voice is doing cartwheels; I wish I could offer him Valium.

We deplane after parking at a remote gate and are bused to the terminal. In the bus I'm approached by a man who's very shaken up, asking me if that was a normal flight into Abuja. Because I'm in my uniform, I'm a pillar of authority. I tell him all the riotous G loads were a result of powerful up- and downdrafts in the thunderstorm. He seems unconvinced. Me too. We let it go, happy to be alive, but he eyes me with distrust, thinking I may not have been entirely candid with him. I probably haven't been, but I don't feel like being pulled into some investigation when I'm perched upon a great escape from this country.

Inside I wait for my bags. Reid says, "Dude, we've still gotta take a cab to the international terminal." I had no idea. Airports where wide berths separate terminals always have inter-terminal buses or trains connecting them. Not in Lagos. Getting from the domestic to the international terminal is left to passengers to figure out. This is bad.

My bags come off quickly. People in Nigeria don't seem to check a lot of bags. I gather mine and Reid's, and I head to the street where hordes of peddlers accost us trying to sell taxi rides and a myriad of other services, some unimaginable in the light of day in a profoundly religious country with extremely conservative moral views. I'm shocked. A young man pushes so close I feel his breath on my face, but then he's slammed bodily to the ground by two women who yell obscenities at him. The poor guy's being trampled. This is Darwinian survival of the fittest playing out before our eyes. We're pinned by all these people trying to sell, trying to get money.

Two boys are ripping at my bags trying to take them for me. I tell them no, but they persist until I yell, "NO, I've got 'em!" in a loud, harsh voice. I'm sick of the mobs and the endless tide of outstretched hands. We ask the rough women how much to get to the international terminal. One yells, "Three thousand naira!" There's no time to help the waif on the ground or bargain with the Amazonians. We agree and are rushed through the crowd, like rock stars after a concert, to a car that rends the mob to appear at the curb in front of us. The trunk is reluctant to close on my bags that overfill its interior. Its latch has doubtless been asked too much for too long but is pounded shut by a driver familiar with the idiosyncrasies of his car. We pay the ladies, pimps of transport, and give our driver an extra five hundred naira to entice him to give us his all.

Traffic is bumper-to-bumper. We have to negotiate a roundabout with octopus-like tangents branching in from all directions. It's jam-packed with wildly aggressive drivers who do not mind bending each other's vehicles. They dart forward endlessly, stopping inches from collision. It's like watching a thousand rattlesnakes striking repeatedly for the same prize. We make it around the rotary, but it's taken more than fifteen minutes. A steady stream of bright red brake lights, three and sometimes four abreast, leads all the way to the international terminal more than a mile away. I look at my watch; it's 8:05. We're down to an hour and twenty-five minutes to make our flight. It's another twenty minutes to the terminal. Once close enough to see inside, I'm horrified to find that perhaps all two million pilgrims from Mecca have taken up residence. A security guard in front of the terminal tells us he's never seen such a crowd here. My little internal voice is staggering, nearing collapse.

Luckily for me, there's a Sky Priority line to ticketing and baggage check-in that's very short. "Good luck, Reid," I yell over the riotous throng as we enter the terminal and I join the short line. Reid isn't Sky Priority and must make his way in the long line. Minutes later I'm standing at the ticket counter. It's 8:30, one hour until flight time. Beside me at the adjacent ticket counter is Reid. I'm surprised, but before I can ask how he managed this amazing feat he offers with a smirk, "Someone proposed getting me to the front of the line. It cost me a hundred bucks." We get our tickets simultaneously, mine a positive seat, his standby. Except for his small daypack, Reid has no baggage. His belongings are all back at the hotel. He says, "Frankly, I don't care if it all vanishes down some Nigerian rabbit hole while we're gone. Those people need it more than I do. I'll buy new. I'll just bring a new uniform." Escaping today ranks number one for him. There's no close second.

We separate again as I head to the baggage screening station, all work there performed slowly in a piece-by-piece assembly line. Reid heads to another queue to get through the security. I finish with my bag check in five minutes and plant myself in the security line. I don't realize it's endlessly long. From where I stand it doesn't look that bad, but what I can't see is that it goes all the way to the end of the hall before turning around and meandering back. It's over an hour line—well over an hour. A guy shows up as sharks do, from nowhere. Without prelude he asks if I have any money. I know we're about to negotiate a shortcut. I'm in full airline uniform, so he's expecting a haul. I say yes and he pulls me from the train barging a swath through throngs of people. I say, "I'll give you one thousand naira." He grunts and says, "NO! You must pay me FIVE thousand naira!" I stop and say no. I tell him I've been cleaned out, and a thousand is all I have left. I'm not going to tell him about the US cash in my bag. I empty my pockets to show him I'm broke. I have a single one-thousand naira note and two ten-naira notes. He's frustrated and just stands still, allowing people to flow around us. I back into a corner, firm in my position. He stares at me. I stare back.

Finally he says, "Give me the thousand!" I give it to him, and he leads me to the front of the line where the security guard, seeing me in uniform, unhooks the rope and waves me through. I get the feeling he'd have done this without me paying the extortionist because I'm a pilot in uniform.

I'm directed to a desk that is unattended but is littered with stacks of money-declaration forms long removed from built-in organizing slots. A pen survives the preceding horde lying unguarded on the desk. I use it to fill out the form and walk to a set of side-by-side emigration officers forming a small gauntlet. I hope they don't ask about my money. I've listed only half the real amount. That half is readily available for show 'n tell. The other half is hidden securely, but heaven help me if they get nosy and find it. My mind conjures a racket between them and the Max Air accountant who knows how much I was paid and how much I wired home. I start to sweat and worry they'll notice my tension. They check my passport and barely glance at the declaration. I realize I'd make a really crappy con artist as I walk away from their cursory review. From the corner of my eye, I see Reid approaching.

"Hey buddy,"—his typical mirth is a couple of stations below normal—"how much has it cost you to get this far?" His bearing warns me there's a story coming. I tell him one thousand naira. His frustrated smile registers surprise.

"It's cost me $300."

"What?!" I stammer.

"Yeah, no shit. A hundred to get to the front of the ticketing line and another hundred to get to the front of the security line.

When the security guard saw me pay off my escort, he accused me of bribing someone to get to the front of the line and demanded a ransom. So, I had to give him a hundred too."

"Jesus, Reid, you've been beat up so much today. I'm really sorry, man."

He smiles in resignation. I know the money's important but breaking out of here wins by so much he's not even really pissed. Just exhausted. I glean one clear lesson from Reid's peril today—carry twenty-dollar bills, not hundreds.

We hustle the rest of the way together, finally arriving at our gate with only minutes to spare. Originally, we had just shy of four hours scheduled to connect to this Delta flight. By the time Allah's had His amusement tinkering with our day, we're left with ten minutes. We go through another pat-down and wanding and then I'm led to a special waiting area for Sky Priority passengers. There are only about two dozen of us in here milling among snack tables that are now mostly pilfered of their crackers and cheese, bottled water, and soft drinks. Across a glass partition is a waiting lounge twin to the one in which I'm sitting. Mine has about fifty seats, theirs has at least two hundred. I guess it's live advertising Delta uses to flaunt the regal treatment of their "status" customers. I bet a whole lot of Sky Priority applications get filled out with this shrewd marketing routine. Their side is bursting at the seams. No snacks.

CHAPTER 21

ANY CLASS'LL DO

They begin boarding the flight, and I feel like I'm floating down the jetway on a magic carpet, inches off the floor. Posters line both sides of the skybridge advertising first-class meals being served to smiling couples, people completely stretched out on lay-flat first-class beds sound asleep, and palm tree-festooned beaches in Miami or perhaps Honolulu. Premium comforts go for many extra thousands of dollars. Right now, I'm giddy enough to spend it. Luckily, that opportunity lapsed long ago. As I enter the cabin of this shiny new Boeing 777, operated by smiling, competent professionals, I realize my trusty little inner voice is sound asleep, exhausted and frazzled in some remote corner of my brain.

I ask the chief purser if I may visit the cockpit, and he immediately ushers me forward. Inside, a full double crew will take turns piloting this thirteen-hour voyage across the Atlantic Ocean. They see very few Americans in Lagos, and I'm welcomed broadly with genuine warmth. After some easy small talk and a few laughs, I stroll down the left aisle to my seat, my face plastered with a mixture of joy, relief, and a lot of fatigue. I don't even mind those twelve rows of $10,000 lay-flat first-class seats I pass as I make my way to the Economy Comfort section. My "comfort" seat comes with four extra inches of leg room which is ample for stretching out. I'm on the left aisle seat in a three-across center section. There's a woman in the other aisle seat and no one between us. I feel like kissing the floor it feels so much like America! I've never felt more elation packed into a single moment than when I plop down in my seat. My face has doubtless transitioned into something quite childlike. I hardly know how to arrange it for the ecstasy boiling in my chest. People probably think I'm drunk or maybe crazy. I don't care.

The doors close, and we push back. I'm asleep by the time we're lining up on the runway but awaken at the sound of the engines coming up to takeoff power. I imagine what a US service man or woman must feel after a yearlong deployment in a hostile country when they're airborne heading home. My heart swells. I'm over-whelmed thinking of the sacrifice others have made on my behalf, and my gratitude escapes as tears streaming down my face. I can find no other outlet.

Twelve hours later, we descend and land at Atlanta's Hartsfield International Airport. I'm giddy exiting the plane at 5 a.m. local time. As I approach the customs kiosks, I see Reid making thru-passage and am elated to see he made it onto the flight. In fact, he was awarded a Business Class seat, taking some of the sting out of his harrowing experience during the last twenty hours. I claim my bags and send them on to Salt Lake City after clearing cus-toms. Everyone is so friendly, and not a single person has tried to extort me. I get on the inter-terminal "plane train" and head for the A gates. My phone rings. It's Reid. He's ecstatic to be on US soil as am I. We agree to have a wonderful two-week break and are reluctant to commit to coming back. It seems unimaginable in this moment.

A few hours later my beautiful Marcia and our furry dog, Chaco, meet me at the curb in front of Delta's Salt Lake City terminal on a crystal-clear day where the temperature is sixty degrees and I can see a hundred miles in all directions. The Wasatch Mountains stand a brilliant panorama painted in yellows, reds, and oranges with snow icing the higher elevations. I can't believe the grandeur of where I live or the privilege of my passage through this life. I kiss Marcia deeply and let Chaco lick the African dust from my face.

I reflect for a moment that all those two hundred and fifty million people are still in Nigeria, toiling through another day of survival, often desperate, sometimes failing, some slain, hacked to death by fanatical young men who've found a means to survive by killing others in their new "jobs" as terrorists.

I can't believe so much goodness and beauty can exist next to so much violence and terror on a single planet. I want to understand and bring some sense to the senselessness. I ponder my place in the grand scheme of things and sigh heavily knowing I'll never get it, but resolute never to forget the great fortune of my life.

CHAPTER 22

GOODBYE

It seems nearly impossible that these days have evaporated with such a merciless pace, but there's nothing I can do to delay the calendar's offering of Thursday, October 17th, the day I must return to Nigeria to complete my contract with Max Air. Someone's gotta bring all those pilgrims home from their holy crusade, and my name's on a contract that says I will.

With emotions veiled lest I make our parting even more difficult, I put on a happy face, and Marcia, Chaco, and I climb into our little Subaru to drive to the Salt Lake International airport. There I'll board Delta's flight 1912 to Atlanta, beginning my long sojourn back to Africa.

In front of the same airport terminal that had been the scene of such a joyous reunion thirteen days ago, we now stand to part but thankfully, only for a month this time. Chaco licks my face, and Marcia and I make repeated attempts to find a kiss sweet enough to carry us four weeks separated by an ocean, most of two continents, and living conditions divergent in the extreme from any familiar to us.

Knowing the frustrations and dangers awaiting me in Nigeria adds a measure of gravity to this goodbye that I'd understood so little about the first time out. But providence has brought this financial opportunity, and we both know I have to go.

Before parting, Marcia shares some thoughts that have been weighing on her mind. "I know you know what you're doing and what's over there. Please don't get careless or cocky. I'm not going to ask you to be scared or cower in your room, but I need you to be smart about it. I just want you to come home. I need you. Your dad needs you. A lot of us need you."

I feel like if I say anything, I'll cry as tears begin to well. This is so hard.

"I promise, sweetheart," I manage. "I know what you're saying, and I get it. I'm extremely aware of the dangers. I don't go out. I fly my trips, go to the hotel gym, the hotel restaurant, and my room. I don't flirt with danger. I'll be home in a few weeks. Just about like my old trips with World. It'll be over soon enough, a distant memory. We'll be flush economically, and I can find a new flying job here in the states. I love you so much, baby."

"I love you too," she says. We're both trying to hold back the waterworks. She walks back to the Outback, settles in, and fastens her seatbelt. Chaco vies for her affection, sensing her melancholy, sticking his big wet nose in her face. We have an unannounced contest to see who turns away first. It's a hard connection to cleave. I blow a kiss; she blows one back. I wave; she waves. I turn and walk toward the terminal, heart about knee level. "Goodbye, my love," I sniffle to myself, wiping away tears.

Delta's flight to Atlanta is uneventful. I've recovered my emotions and found my sense of adventure restored. My phone rings as I'm reading a book in the international terminal, and I see the name I've been expecting on the screen. Reid is in the E concourse enjoying last rites in a TGIF before we fly to Lagos. For Reid, beer flows as a precious sacrament while he anticipates a long dry month ahead. My abstinence began after a glass of Merlot last night. We order a greasy, comfort food dinner and then make our way to Gate F-2 to board a Delta A330 Airbus. A persistent unspoken conversation circles between us begging a rhetorical question. *"Are we really gonna do this?"* Reid is flying on a Buddy Pass again with no guarantees about getting on. But when the "Standby" passengers' names are posted on a TV screen in the gate area, there's Reid's, second from the top, with an upgrade to business class again. I'm relieved he's getting on and cheered by his good fortune. He'll sleep lying down most of the way. Such luxury will end abruptly for several weeks in about eleven hours.

Aware that life will be very different beginning in half a day, we steel ourselves for the shock of the Nigerian life we're rejoining. We're under the impression that once we arrive in Lagos, we'll have to proceed to the domestic terminal, engage in uncertain commerce with the IRS Airlines ticketing authorities, and fly on to Kano. It's the part after landing in Lagos where things might get difficult, probably expensive, and maybe even a little perilous. My pockets are stuffed with twenty-dollar bills.

CHAPTER 23
BACK IN AFRICA

Maya blue, like the blue in the core and hottest part of a flame, colors the sky as we approach Lagos in the midafternoon. Touchdown is unusually smooth, hopefully a premonition of things to come. Ten minutes of taxiing brings us to the international arrivals terminal. Reid waits in the jetway as I'm several minutes behind. Scores of passengers separate me from business class.

Passing through customs and immigration is a breeze, completely uncharacteristic of all prior experience arriving or departing. When I answer the question about the nature of my business and how long I'll be staying, the official notices the 3/Nov. stamped on my Visa and restamps is with 30/Nov. It's a relief to have that old headache cleaned up. It gets even better.

As we're exiting baggage claim, we both notice a tall, slim man waving at us. Could it be, I dully wonder? Sure enough, it's Chris from Max Air. We're surprised to see him, believing we would not encounter any company people until arriving in Kano. To our amazement, the company has contemplated the efficient utilization of their pilots and sent Chris to stop us in Lagos because we'll be flying our first few trips from here. This is wonderful news as it eliminates the expense of, and exposure to, the dubious safety offered by IRS Airlines and shortens our day by more than six hours. With Chris's decree, Boko Haram, belligerent drunken police officers, and malaria mosquitoes are wiped from the day's syllabus. We're overjoyed.

Twenty minutes later we're checking in at the Blue Lodge Hotel. Having learned a few things about Nigerian culture, we each slip a thousand naira to Chris, who's handling our check-in as Max Air's representative. We hope this will get us good rooms. The disparity separating tolerable from intolerable rooms far exceeds what I would have ever imagined seven bucks could buy, but experience is a noble trainer, and the lessons here come fast and often. The thousand-naira bribe pays off handsomely for me. I'm assigned a quiet room far from the harshly cacophonous Catholic Church of the Ascension adjacent to the Blue Lodge. Reid, however, is right in their line of fire. He claims the noise won't bother him and makes no fuss about his room's location. By the end of the weekend, he wearily concedes that the church's raucous band and celebrating parishioners wildly exceed anything he'd imagined. Sadly, for Blue Lodge guests, the clergy's discovery of electric amplification has been embraced with exuberant excess.

On Saturday morning, Reid and I decide to see if we can walk to a grocery store if there's one nearby. The front desk clerk we see most often is Idris which means *skillful*. He should be named whatever translates from *cunning pickpocket*. He manages to collect a lot of thousand-naira bills from me. I ask him about the grocery store. He laughs so hard that it takes half a minute to collect himself and then answer.

"You cannot walk outside!"

"Why not?" I ask.

"Because you are WHITE," he bellows with great emphasis on the white part whereupon he begins laughing again. He's not being callous. He's just stating pure fact. This is a dangerous part of Lagos for white people. There are two guards at the front gate carrying AK-47s because white people are common guests here, and the threat against us is serious. Seeing it from his point of view makes me feel ignorant for asking.

He offers to call a friend who can give us a ride into a nearby neighborhood where we might find some fresh fruits and vegetables. A thousand naira later he pulls out his cell phone and makes the call. In twenty minutes, a rusty, smoke-belching 1960s vintage Chevrolet station wagon pulls into the parking lot.

"Ah!" says Idris, "there's your ride."

His friend, Mustapha, walks into the lobby where we're introduced. Mustapha speaks not a word of English. Idris tells him what we want, and Mustapha waves us outside. Reid climbs into the back right seat and I take the front. Mustapha starts the engine which rebels with some shotgun backfire blasts. Reid and I trade nervous glances, but we're too self-conscious to back out now.

The guards give us suspicious looks as we drive out the front gate. Ten minutes later we pass a large dirt field surrounded by a skiff of grass affronting a tall block wall. The gray wall, topped with lazy, disheveled strands of barbed wire that fall down like ivy in some places, is very tall. At least twelve feet I judge, comparing it to the slim young men leaning against it. Two dozen thin young men in their late teens are playing serious soccer. The tall fence defines one edge, the road we're on, the other. Piles of shirts mark goals. They're impressive to watch with sprinters' speed and incredible control of the ball. It might be the most normal thing I've seen in Nigeria and takes some of the edge off our reckless adventuring.

We turn left past the end of the fence into a dilapidated neighborhood whose streets look like they've seen the kind of bombing London used to suffer daily in the 1940s. Mustapha weaves carefully around the craters and presses on into the neighborhood. I don't think the people we see on the sides of the streets are strolling. Their pace is quick, and many are burdened with baskets balanced on their heads. Groceries. I wonder where they got them. Mustapha seems to know.

Just about every person we pass looks in and stares. I think we're getting a taste of what Rosa Parks got in Montgomery, Alabama, in 1955. I'm getting more and more certain I'm not getting out no matter what we find, which turns out not to be a problem. We never find anything that looks like a store. Just a lot of craters and ditches and a ghetto's worth of people that seem resentful of our presence.

We signal Mustapha that we want to go back to the Blue Lodge. We're deposited there twenty minutes later. We each give him a thousand naira and he rumbles off. Inside I'm sure Idris is smirking, but he hides it well. I suspect he had a good idea what we were in for. But we asked for it, and now I'm feeling grateful to be alive. Did this breach my promise to Marcia? If not, it came awful close. Reid says he's going to take a nap, and we agree to meet in the restaurant for dinner at six.

I ask Idris if there's a gym here. He says, "Of course," and points me toward the stairs. I go to the stairway but see no evidence of a door or hall leading to anything that might contain a gym. I go back and ask again. Impatiently, he walks with me back to the stairway and points into the dark cavity under the lowest flight of stairs.

"There," he says.

There are a dozen folding chairs stored in the shadowy confines, but behind them is a treadmill. Idris smiles and walks back to the front desk. I remove all the chairs and then pull the treadmill out far enough to stand on it without bumping my head on the stairs above. I plug it into a nearby outlet and voilà, I'm at the gym. It works perfectly well. I'm probably the only guest that's ever used it. I run a little faster than usual hoping to burn off some of the tension that's built up in me. An hour and nine hundred calories later, if I'm to believe the machine's computer, I cool down and head to my room.

At 6:00, I shuffle downstairs and meet Reid in the cafeteria. It's a plain box-shaped room with seven or eight tables for four. Tables, walls, everything seems particularly bare. We're the only ones in the room. A waiter comes out from the kitchen to seat us. He brings water, which we never drink, and menus. After a few minutes of study we settle on a soup whose name we can't pronounce. I see the waiter peeking around at us so signal him over. He describes the unpronounceable soup as hot, but very good.

The language disconnect precludes learning if he means temperature or spicy.

"What do you think, buddy?" Reid says.

"I think we can't go far wrong. Let's give it a try. Plus, it comes with a basket of bread—if we're lucky, good bread."

We both order the soup. The waiter disappears, only for a moment, then returns with two baskets of bread. It's dark brown, dense, and encased in hard crust. There's nothing left to desire. We've nearly polished it off by the time the soup is served twenty minutes later. Meanwhile, another party of two are seated, and they immediately order the soup. That's a good sign.

One thing's for sure, it's boiling hot. The other hot scale will be revealed in a sip. It smells delicious. Reid goes first. His eyes immediately tear, and sweat beads on his cheeks and above his eyes. He smiles and grabs another piece of bread.

His voice seems far away and high-pitched. "Delicious, dude! You're gonna love it."

He knows I love spicy hot food, but I'm hesitant. His ears have turned red, and he's sniffling—a lot. I take a tiny sip and enjoy all the fire signs perfectly matching Reid. Not only is it super spicy hot, but it's got a taste to die for. It's advertised as vegetarian. I don't have one of those forensic palates that can distill the ingredients. Marcia does. I just know there's stuff in here I've never tasted, and it's off the charts good. Our waiter brings two more baskets of bread. He knows how to get a good tip. We still make food in our rooms, but the soup becomes a biweekly ritual.

Sleep will come easy tonight. Tomorrow we're back on the hajj mission.

CHAPTER 24
RETURNING THE HAJJIS

It's Tuesday, October 22, our first day back in the air. The order of passenger loading is reversed this time with the airplane empty on eastbound legs to Jeddah and full on return trips to Nigeria. Also, we're no longer flying round trips. Steve, Mark, Stuart, and John were all in Kano when we arrived in Lagos and, together with a double crew of flight attendants, they all flew the -400 empty to Jeddah. There, Stuart, John, and one crew of flight attendants deplaned and went to the Ramada, our hotel and dispatch command center in Jeddah. Steve, Mark, and the remaining flight attendants bring a full load back to Lagos.

Our Lagos dispatcher, Mr. Williams, calls to tell us we can expect a wake-up call this evening around midnight. We'll be flying all night so need to execute a sleep strategy that'll have us rested. At 10:30 p.m. my room phone rings. It's Mr. Williams. That time turmoil thing is rearing its ugly Nigerian head again. He anxiously tells me we have to head to the aircraft in fifteen minutes. Unlike firemen, we don't sleep in our uniforms, so it's not going to happen quite that fast. Furthermore, he can't find Reid. I put on my pants and undershirt and go downstairs to assess the rest of the crew's actual state of readiness and to see if I can help find Reid. The lobby is filled with fourteen uniformed flight attendants. *Why did they know about this early departure but we didn't?* I ask myself, fully aware of the futility of the question. Williams is upset, unable to find Reid. The company has given Reid a cell phone, but Mr. Williams doesn't think to call. More likely, no one ever told Williams that Reid has a Nigerian phone or gave him the number. Such a call would have rung through, and Reid would have readily answered.

Almost simultaneously with Mr. Williams's demoralized report about Reid's absence, the front desk clerk informs me he's located him—in the bar. My heart sinks. I run to the bar and find Reid collecting his things, clearly sober. He's taken refuge in the only location available in the hotel where quiet solitude and a good Wi-Fi signal can be found.

Reid goes to his room to shower and change. I share these late revelations with Williams who tells me that it's no problem; he'll take the flight attendants to the airplane and then return for us.

In light, midnight traffic, the Blue Lodge hotel is only ten minutes' driving time from the airport's cargo staging area where all hajj operations take place and where our airplane is parked. Two corrugated steel walls topped with concertina wire protect the airport property. Guarded gates in each must be negotiated to gain access. During nighttime hours they're typically manned by lethargic but well-armed men who readily pass the bus once they see a familiar driver and his charge of uniformed crewmembers. After the second checkpoint, crews are driven directly to a two-story stairway leading steeply up to one of the main cabin entry doors.

Reid and I meet in the now quiet lobby fifteen minutes after the bus departed with our flight attendants. We check out, and I slip Idris another thousand naira telling him how much I enjoyed my room. We're coming back in about thirty hours. We settle on some cushioned benches near the front door to await the bus. Then we wait some more. The twenty- or twenty-five-minute round trip from the hotel to the airplane is now exceeded by double and then some.

In Nigeria, musings of disaster come easily, and we begin to wonder if some terrible fate has befallen our crew and driver.

Reid makes some phone calls to home base. No one answers. We have little choice but to just wait it out. My sleep bank has already been robbed two hours. I wonder how vainly the theft will end up. Nothing's changed since we left two weeks ago. After an hour and a half, the bus pulls into the hotel parking lot.

The delay is classic Max Air. Williams had the bus driver drop him off at the control tower on the way to the airplane. He wanted to file our flight plan in person, an approach utterly extinct in the west, and left no instructions for the bus driver to return to the Blue Lodge to pick up Reid and me. Apparently, the driver and some maintenance engineers he'd picked up at another hotel went out to dinner right after dropping Williams at the tower. Afterward, they returned and picked up Williams, who assumed Reid and I had been delivered to the aircraft during the interlude. After several minutes on the main deck coordinating with the flight attendants, Williams went upstairs and found an empty cockpit. He raced back to the ramp, three stories below, to ask the bus driver where his pilots are. He guessed back at the hotel. And he was right; that's where we were, and Williams barked out orders to go fetch us.

Arriving at the airplane about 12:30 a.m., we discover that it hasn't been catered. Not a crumb of food or a single bottle of water has been boarded. We're also missing critical paperwork, foremost among it weather reports and forecasts for our destination and alternate airports.

Common to aviation regulations worldwide is a mandate to carry certain documents aboard the airplane, and pilots' memories are never a legitimate or legal substitute for them. Weather information must be printed and carried in the cockpit as part of a large package of reference material we must possess to legally fly.

Certainly, and much to Mr. Williams's chagrin, we're not about to embark on a five-hour flight with sixteen people aboard and no drinking water. The airplane has been on the ground for about eight hours, and a dispatcher is responsible to know what is legally required for a flight to take off. Williams is visibly upset that we insist on printed weather reports, stating he has no way of obtaining them. He avoids mentioning the previous eight hours he's had. It's clear that Max Air doesn't expend a great deal of resources on details like properly training dispatchers to do their jobs. I'm sure Mr. Williams is doing the best he can with the skills and training he's had. But it's up to us, the flight crew who are ultimately responsible, to ensure all legal preparations are satisfied before undertaking any flight, so we make it abundantly clear that the aircraft will not move until printed weather reports and bottled water are boarded. Finally, sensing resistance as fierce as Idi Amin's, Williams manages a ride back to the hotel to use their printer and to make arrangements to have plenty of bottled water boarded, netting us full readiness as 2:30 a.m. approaches.

Predictable consistency is vividly on display again. Almost without exception, our wake-up call comes hours before we're told to expect it, a frantic rush is demanded so we can immediately fly away, and none of the key ingredients have been completed to make any of it possible. Our masters give us repeated opportunity to practice poise under stress. I'm determined to go home a better man for it.

After the flight, we navigate Jeddah customs with learned choreography that speeds us through in under an hour. The bus ride to the hotel takes the usual half hour through traffic exactly as bad as I recall. Our hotel, The Ramada, is luxurious. About equal to the Sheraton in Abuja, but the Sheraton wins hands down at the dinner table.

Entering the lobby to check in, we find Shyam, the "king" of Max Air, anxiously waiting to learn from us why we are delayed more than four hours. He has plied his skills of persuasion and doubtless paid some handsome bounties to get departure and arrival slots among those eagerly sought by competing hajj operators, and such a delay undoes much of his maneuvering, hurting his credibility. We explain that we were left sitting in the hotel lobby for over an hour and a half and that upon arriving at the aircraft, we had difficulty persuading Mr. Williams to comply with legal and safety requirements necessary for us to depart. Shyam listens patiently, not necessarily one of his strong suits, and becomes noticeably agitated as our report unfolds. He makes it clear that Mr. Williams will be sorry, intimating that his days of dispatching for Max Air are over.

I feel bad for Mr. Williams, realizing his job is both prestigious and high paying. Given the obvious lack of knowledge he possesses in its execution, it's clear he hasn't invested the time that makes dispatching a lucrative job. It feels crappy to rat him out, but his shoulders are where all the delay faults squarely belong, so it doesn't seem like we have much choice. I hope Shyam's anger recedes before he has a chance to act. In a just world, Williams should either get better training or reassigned a more fitting place in Max Air's enterprise.

Thirty hours after arriving in Jeddah we're back in the sky, on our first pilgrim shuttle back to Lagos, six miles above the dry Sahara. The sky is dark and moonless tonight, but the light radiated by our enraptured charges feels luminous enough to light the night. A gradual descent over the Omo Forest Reserve northeast of the airport leaves only the lights of the city ahead as evidence of earth below. A soft landing on runway 18R gives us a direct and short taxi route to the cargo ramp where our returning hajjis will be bused to a special hajj customs terminal.

Meeting us at the Pilgrim ramp is Mr. Williams, unfazed by the recent history of events. Either Shyam's temper softened or resources available to him in this late stage of the operation limit his actions. If Mr. Williams doesn't do a good job, whose fault is that? Even if his lack of experience and training causes stumbling, the mission still gets accomplished. First-class operations are still a ways off for Max Air, and cooled minds at the helm probably realize that. Mr. Williams stays put.

Idris hands me a key to the same room I'd left two days earlier. He smiles, signaling my matriculation into Nigerian means that keep wheels smoothly turning. He doesn't realize I'd happily pay many times his price for a quiet room.

CHAPTER 25
THE -350

O ne evening, returning from Jeddah, Steve and Mark maneuver routinely to park our two hundred eleven-foot wide
747-400 at Spot #3 on the Lagos cargo ramp. During passenger
disembarkation, a Turkish A330 Airbus with a wingspan of one
hundred ninety-eight feet enters the ramp bound for Spot #4,
immediately to the right of our airplane. According to witnesses,
he seems to taxi carefully and has the requisite wing-walkers below
both left and right wingtips to ensure sufficient parking clearance.
Judging wingtip distances and margins from the cockpit is too
risky given the cramped nature of the parking spots and the great
distances involved with these huge aircraft. Twenty feet short of his
final parking run, his left wingtip nearly slices the winglet off our
right wing. Both aircraft are shaken with tremor-like magnitude,
and several deplaning hajjis stumble and fall in the aisles.

Amazingly, no one except the two airplanes is injured. Both are
grounded until authorities perform investigations and repairs can
be completed. Our winglet is destroyed, but it's a relatively simple
matter to remove it completely. The method of its removal—intentionally designed by Boeing engineers—leaves our green, right-
hand navigation lights intact. Were it otherwise, the airplane would
be illegal to fly at night, effectively taking it out of the rest of this
hajj contract with insufferable financial implications for Max Air.

All aircraft manufacturers write a manual called "The MEL," which stands for Minimum Equipment List. Mated to this document is another called "The CDL," short for Configuration Deviation List. These two large reference manuals tell us what components we can fly without, either because they're broken or missing. If the defect impacts the performance of the aircraft, a very specific tabulation tells us the penalties and additional considerations we need to comply with before flying. If the item can't be found in one of these books, the airplane can't legally fly without it. We can fly without one or both winglets, with an inoperative engine, or even with a fifth engine installed on the wing for the purpose of transporting it to another location. But an ashtray installed on the inside of a lavatory door is nowhere to be found in either book and therefore, if missing, grounds the airplane until replaced.

Our CDL says we must add about five hundred pounds extra fuel to push our slightly less aerodynamic airplane through the sky. If we were flying trips near our maximum range of fifteen hours, we'd need to offload passengers or cargo to allow the extra fuel we'd need. These hajj flights are only five or six hours. Payload stays while profit diminishes minutely.

The investigation and repairs require only two days, and we're back in business. Reid and I are first up to fly the newly configured airplane. All prior versions of Boeing 747s—100, 200, and 300 series models—were built without winglets. Max Air operates four 300 series aircraft and only one -400 model. The flight attendants are giggly as we board, explaining that Max Air no longer operates a 400 series model. Our single winglet airplane, according to them, is re-designated a Boeing 747-350. The name sticks, and it flies out the contract a quirky aberration.

CHAPTER 26
THE END'S IN SIGHT

A week later we return to Abuja rather than Lagos. All the Lagos hajjis have been safely returned, and we're now rotating pilgrims back to Nigeria's capital city. The flight has proceeded easily, but after parking, our five hundred and sixty-five passengers' bodies creak and unfold slowly. An hour and fifteen minutes brings the last ambling hajjis to the single utilized exit door, giving us a green light to deplane.

While customs is streamlined for flight crewmembers, getting there requires drilling a path right through the throngs of Abujans we've just discharged. Weaving a course makes for slow progress when encumbered with bulky luggage. But in a few minutes, we manage to snake our train of sixteen through these tight confines and emerge into bright, hot sunshine where we face hundreds of waiting relatives. There appear to be many waiting family members and friends for each of our passengers, so we're faced with an impenetrable wall of humanity. Kindness registers on all the faces I see in the multitude, its universal language clearly spoken. A corridor spontaneously opens ahead allowing us passage. Through its narrow confines, we're repeatedly thanked, usually in languages foreign to our ears but unmistakable in meaning and sincerity. I'm deeply moved. This is turning into an experience far more gratifying than the mere financial gain for which I'd signed.

Three hours after setting the airplane's parking brake, we arrive at our crew hotel, the Sheraton. Assembling at the check-in counters, we're informed that no reservations have been made for us and there are no rooms available. This becomes a recurring theme during all our Sheraton stays whose root cause is never discovered. Maybe Max Air simply doesn't have a capable reservations taskmaster in Abuja. We repeatedly ask our operations contacts to make sure we have confirmed reservations in this capital city, but despite continued assurances, it's rarely done.

We move to a comfortable, well-appointed waiting area in the hotel's lobby while the chief purser attempts to contact some Max Air authority. Within minutes I'm sleeping soundly in a chair, later recalling a common Nigerian euphemism that states, "show me someone who can't sleep sitting up and I'll show you someone who's not really tired." More than an hour later, I'm gently shaken awake by a flight attendant who offers me a room key. Apparently the "no rooms available" line is routinely delivered to all guests perceived as not having a reservation. The veracity of the edict is not investigated unless some cause later surfaces. All sixteen of us get rooms after someone from management in Kano decides to pay the hotel for our keep.

One of Max Air's pilots has trouble getting into the Saudi Kingdom because of an expired or lost visa. Our airplane is subsequently dispatched to Kano instead of Abuja, so the trouble can be dealt with at headquarters. Not passing perfectly through all the hoops erected by the Saudis regarding entering their Kingdom can be serious trouble. In this case, it requires returning the offender to Kano where headquarters can iron it out. The resulting delay finds our stay at the Abuja Sheraton extended to four days. As the clock ticks past noon each day, our room keys automatically become disabled. Frustratingly, more often than not I find myself on the wrong side of my door after lockdown, in soaking gym clothes, unable to enter. A wait, never less than thirty minutes, ensues, passage of which I while away soaking the nice furniture in the check-in lounge. Eventually, Sheraton's back-office accountant connects with someone at Max Air who sets up payment for another day. So go the rituals of commerce in a society where trust is ensured only with cash or a bank wire.

November 6th, twenty days after arriving in Nigeria, we finally return to Kano. Our exultant Max Air bus driver greets us in the baggage claim area with a toothy smile complemented with warm hugs all around. I'm continually amazed at the depth to which many people in this country invite us into their hearts. My distrust and ill ease about being back in Kano evaporates in the warmth of our welcome, and suddenly, I'm happy to be here.

"Captain," an honorary title universally accorded this kind bus driver, leads us through the throngs of money changers and porters who greet every arriving passenger flight, to our Max Air bus. We're soon bound for the Tahir Palace Hotel. It's about 10:30 p.m., and Captain advises us we should expect to go out about 3:00 a.m.—not the kind of resettlement break I'd hoped for, but our treatment has been so humane we can hardly complain. Three or four hours in a comfortable bed is probably more than most of the nearly eight million inhabitants of Kano will get tonight, so we settle in, sleep fast, and count our blessings.

My room phone rings at exactly 3 a.m. It's Captain calling to advise he's waiting outside, in front of the lobby. I'm surprised at how rested I feel after only three and a half hours of sleep. I'm overflowing with energy and excited to take the flight. Reaching a darkened lobby where I hope to turn in some laundry, I find four employees, all sleeping in uncomfortable positions. One is on a mat on the floor behind the counter, another is on the counter, curled up on his side with only a blanket as padding, and two are sitting in chairs, upper bodies skewed across hard desks. I don't want to disturb them, so I quietly leave my laundry duffel on the counter marked with my room number. This is the second time in recent weeks I've discovered employees sleeping at their workstations, affirming my growing suspicion that this is not an unusual living arrangement. Maybe it's even considered a perk.

We're airborne at 5:40 a.m., getting away without delay. As with most predawn takeoffs, it's quiet, the air's velvet smooth, and the moments seem magical as features below quickly fall into Matchbox scale. With an empty airplane—except for seven hours of fuel and sixteen people—I reduce the thrust available from our powerful engines by twenty-five percent, and still, they lift us heavenward with what seems effortless might.

Reaching 41,000 feet, so little power is required to maintain our most efficient speed it sounds like I've shut off the engines. While Eastern Air Lines coined the term "Whisper Jet" over fifty years ago for their brand-new Boeing 727s, it was a misnomer approaching preposterous, so ear-splitting was their howl. Now, finally, I'm hearing that tag accurately applied. In thirty-five minutes, a few dim, orangish lights appear in the city of Maiduguri below, considered to be the center of Boko Haram's uprising. I shudder for all 750,000 residents and wish them more safety than I fear the terrorists intend. Minutes later we slice the northernmost handle of Cameroon and check in with N'Djamena Control. We won't hear another clear radio broadcast for hours. With the sky quickly blossoming in a bouquet of morning color, Lake Chad slips under our nose telling me we're over Chad. Then we glide across Sudan. The world below is nothing but beige Sahara Desert from Chad to the Red Sea with only the Nile River rending the sand until then. From 41,000 feet, we'll traverse most of the Red Sea's two-hundred-mile width in our descent to Jeddah.

We fly this passengerless trip with growing appreciation for the long adventure we've shared together. The end of this contract is approaching with surprising haste, and we excitedly anticipate the time when we'll return to beloved families and familiar lives.

CHAPTER 27
YOLA AND THE BIG LIE

The following afternoon, Friday, November 8th, we prepare our aircraft, recognizing we're completely full. Our planned destination is Yola, a city of 88,000 inhabitants in Nigeria's far eastern state of Adamawa. Boko Haram has carried out several devastating attacks in this area, and the government has reacted by imposing an emergency curfew from 7:00 p.m. to 6:00 a.m. The curfew has just been extended, adding six months to the half year it's already been in effect.

We learn that customs officials in Yola suspect there are two Boko Haram members aboard our flight returning from the hajj. It seems astonishing to me that such tyrants might feel compelled to participate in something like this and makes me contemplate the bigger story here. I assume people wanting to commune with Allah can't possibly be cut from a cloth that also fabricates terrorists. But a little reflection illuminates plentiful evidence that an extremist faction of Islam not only readily murders people but insists it's a mandate from Allah Himself, that "good" Muslims cleanse the earth of infidels and all enemies of Muhammad. Apparently, the world is more complex than I'd like to allow. Whether I like it or not, some human behavior that seems plainly diabolical and immoral to me is perfectly acceptable in certain circles. Believing the Wizard of Oz story is an easier stretch for me than imagining this to be true, but believe it I must if I'm to open my eyes.

It's clear that we won't land in Yola before the 7:00 p.m. curfew, but our dispatcher assures us that the curfew is being rolled back to accommodate our arrival. Just before closing the boarding doors, Reid hunts down the station manager and asks him to check one last time to assure us we'll have landing permissions in Yola. Again, we're guaranteed Yola airport will remain open for our arrival.

Four hours in unusually smooth skies brings us to the border of Chad and Nigeria in a world painted in darkest hues of purple and gray. Checking in with Nigerian air traffic control nets us a revelation not altogether unexpected. "November Gulf Lima 2190, Yola airport is closed. Please state your intentions."

Reid and I look at each other with raised eyebrows. While kindness seems an almost invariable part of people's demeanor here, honesty isn't always so evident. We ask him to standby while we radio ahead to Kano operations to ask them how they'd like us to proceed. Interestingly, the operations agent who answers is a man. It's always been a woman before. Females in Nigeria are, with few exceptions, not entrusted to positions of authority. In all but the most unusual circumstances, Max Air's radio operations agent's only job is to take radio reports from Max Air pilots who are updating estimated landing times. But tonight, we need to know what the company wants us to do with a multi-million-dollar airplane they own and the six hundred and three souls occupying her seats. In this culture a man is required to make that decision, and one just happens to answer tonight. He seems unsurprised as we convey the report that Yola is closed and without hesitation tells us to proceed directly to Kano. The air traffic controller also responds without pause, granting our requested clearance directly to Kano, which is only half an hour away.

Reid makes an announcement to our flight attendants and passengers, apprising them of our new destination and offering sincere apologies for the inconvenience this will cause. I fear it will be colossal. Upon arriving at Kano, the one thing of which I'm in direct control is the landing, and I'm determined to make it perfect. With great care and a little luck, it's feather soft. Now the clock begins a long slog, ticking a series of nasty surprises for all our guests.

The parking marshaler and crew bus are waiting for us as we exit the runway. It seems this "unplanned" arrival is not very surprising to those supervising the operation, as has seemed evident since the man with unquestioned authority answered our company radio call right after we entered Nigerian airspace.

It's about 9:30 p.m. After two weeks of living under austere conditions in the desert city of Mecca, these hajjis are introduced to ridiculous new levels of suffering that would have been avoidable had Saudi and Max Air officials been honest. What worked best for officialdom is now causing dreadful hardship for our passengers. They were boarded more than two hours before our departure from Jeddah because of a Saudi rule requiring that passengers on hajj flights must have begun boarding before their luggage can be loaded into our cargo holds. In Jeddah, baggage loading takes two to three hours. Why so long will always remain a mystery. At adjacent non-hajj terminals, both domestic and international, loading baggage bays on identical model airplanes takes an hour, an hour and a quarter tops. By the time we land in Kano, our passengers have been in their seats, more densely packed than any other airplane seating configuration I've ever seen, for about seven hours. They'd have to pass through customs before being allowed to move beyond the airport, and there is no provision in place to take care of them in Kano. Customs officials, realizing this and aware of the suspected Boko Haram insurgents aboard, refuse to process them. The sad truth is that these people must spend the night aboard the airplane. Reid and I gather our belongings and exit through aisles crowded with tired and concerned Yolans who are just beginning to realize the depth of their plight.

Yola airport won't reopen until 6:00 a.m.—about eight hours from now. The flight attendants must remain aboard with the passengers until a new crew arrives in the morning to take over their care. I know if I'd spent the last seven hours aboard this airplane believing I would soon be in a hotel room resting, I'd be furious about a sudden change of plan that charges me with caretaking duties for the next seven or eight hours. Our fourteen flight attendants take it as no hardship whatsoever, beaming with good cheer as Reid and I deplane to go to the hotel. I'm painfully reminded of my comfortable passage through life and how differently I view hardship from those with a more intimate experience of it.

All five hundred and eighty-seven passengers and fourteen flight attendants stayed aboard the airplane overnight and were not flown to Yola until dawn the following morning. Adding another measure of duress to their long and tiresome trip, we learn that the customs agents in Yola met the passengers at the aircraft door and assessed every returning resident in search of the suspected Boko Haram terrorists. That stretched the deplaning process into an hours-long event. The last person aboard logged nearly nineteen hours for a four-and-a-half-hour flight.

I've read of a Muslim prophesy that says blessings will be conferred upon any hajji who dies en route, either to or from a hajj pilgrimage. That he or she shall enjoy the highest gifts in Allah's heaven. I'm hopeful that these pilgrims receive some credit toward that status for their torment, but their payout will require still more patience.

CHAPTER 28
ENDINGS AND BEGINNINGS

We spend our last few days awaiting a final flight assignment that never comes. We are finished and have only the tasks of collecting our wages, packing our belongings, saying farewells, and flying home.

The anticipation of going home is overwhelming, and several impromptu room parties spawn. Still, it's incumbent upon us to remain mindful of our whereabouts and respect the widespread abhorrence most Muslims feel about the consumption of alcohol. In the Tahir Palace Hotel, however, westerners and their ways are common and well tolerated, even assisted by staff members anxious for tips. All Tahir team members seem remarkably accepting of our celebrating, and even I succumb to persistent badgering to enjoy some adult beverages with my colleagues. I'd intended my abstinence to last until I got home. It's the easiest self-imposed rule I ever broke.

November 13th arrives with strong rumors suggesting our pay has arrived and is available in the company safe. Supporting the hearsay is a Max Air bus arriving to transport us to headquarters. I sit next to a window as we drive through Kano, still incredulous observing street life which I should be more used to by now. I can't seem to let go of my dismay at the incalculable overcrowding, universal poverty, and pervading filth. What I see collides violently against my personal context of habitation. I'm deeply entranced as we wind through the city, ingesting all that I can, wanting never to forget the almost surreal theatrics that play out on the stage of life here.

We find Max Air officers have everything in order, and we're all paid. In fact, management is so pleased with our group's service and dependability that we're paid an extra week's wages as a bonus—a delightful surprise. Soon we disperse, goodbyes are spoken, long embraces shared, and for some, homebound flights will be boarded—sadly, not mine.

A fine restaurant is a fifteen-minute walk from our hotel. I've been there only twice in all the weeks we've spent here. I still take State Department warnings as dire but risk this walk off campus, believing the risk is an acceptable tradeoff for all the dreariness I've felt coupled with too much isolation. Cilantro Lagos is the one restaurant capable of enticing me into danger's way. Reid and I conspire to enjoy our last night in Nigeria feasting in elated celebration. Half a dozen courses of magnificent Middle Eastern cuisine spill across my tastebuds for ninety delirious minutes. It's not just terrorists with guns and knives that have discouraged my outings to this five-star restaurant. I find the food too enjoyable and can hardly resist appetizers, soup, more than one entrée, and desserts. I've lost seventeen pounds while in Nigeria although I don't tend to have an overly padded frame. Reid's lost twice that. I don't want it back, but I'm not going to miss this final opportunity to break bread with a man who's become so close a friend.

There are seven of us remaining by November 14th. Our flights were booked months ago, and we haven't dared to try and rebook earlier flights so close to departure time. Rocking a steady boat in such otherwise turbulent waters strikes me as a great way to derail my travel plans by days. An extra day here is not something I'd opt for, but it seems by far the safest option.

Morning light comes early, bright, and hot, and I'm eagerly up to greet it. I'm packed and ready to leave hours early. I spend the morning burning off an overabundance of ecstatic energy in a gym that has become a second home to me. Abdul, a new friend I met in the gym only days ago, arrives as promised to say good-bye. With him is his entire brood of children and his male friend, Abraham. There's something vaguely taboo about bringing a wife in certain instances. I guess this might be one of them. There are four beautiful girls and one boy, ranging from two to nine years old. I'm formally introduced and with each, even the toddler, we share mutual bows. It's both comical and touching. Abdul and I have found a common bond in our passion for physical fitness and health in general. We've also engaged in stimulating discussions involving theology, a topical arena usually brimming with land mines. We venture there anyway, without injury.

Getting to spend these few stirring moments with Abdul and his family is quite an honor for me. These people's lives are deeply immersed in religious traditions immeasurably distant from any I've ever seriously pondered. In fact, I've always viewed their world with suspicion and distrust. Yet they've gone out of their way to welcome me to their country and wish me well. I'm embarrassed thinking of the spatial separation I most likely would have maintained with Muslims I discovered exercising in my gym in America.

We part with warm smiles and heartfelt goodbyes, and I know it's time to clean up and make final preparations to leave.

I've rarely felt so sated in my life's journey, yet fear still clings to my thoughts as I anticipate the moments remaining between now and taking off tonight on my Egyptair flight. Too many hours remain in which disaster can strike, and in my anxious mind I continually create dramas that would change my happy ending to one filled with grief. I fight the demons of my imagination with busy preparations accompanied by forced thoughts of a healthier nature.

As I recall the amazing experience this entire venture has been and the new insights that lift my mind and heart, I can't stop thinking of the many Nigerians I've come to know—some by no more than the gracious vibe offered in their body language. There are several guards I've befriended without a single word uttered between us. I've made it a habit to honor them by issuing crisp, military-type salutes whenever I pass their stations. Many have taken to standing at attention when I approach and formally returning my salutes. It's probably as close as we can come to complete communication, but it's heartwarming nonetheless, and I get a clear impression that many of them have little experience being recognized as important people performing valuable duties.

I've managed to collect a pocket full of one-thousand naira bills over the last few weeks specifically for this moment. I can't think of a more affectionate and meaningful gift to impart the warm feelings I carry for so many of these people. Beginning on my own floor in Building G with the chief of the floor and the head cleaner, I furtively offer each a one-thousand-naira bill. They're accepted as most westerners might receive a thousand dollars. They are genuinely awed. For seven dollars, I bring a moment of affluence to each one. It breaks my heart and simultaneously sends it soaring, allowing me a few minutes to enjoy the kind of gratification normally reserved for philanthropists.

I walk the Tahir compound in search of those guards and workers who've become friends through shared smiles and gestures. I give each a one-thousand-naira bill and am repeatedly greeted with dumbstruck gratitude, many bowing deeply, some even approaching tears. I imagine the temporary relief this unexpected moment of good fortune will offer entire families and feel my heart profoundly warmed.

More than any time in my life, I'm wholly aware of the truth presented in the adage that it is better to give than to receive. This is not the first revelation that has found firmer footing within me. It strikes me, maybe for the first time, how easy death would be for me but how dreadful it would be for those I leave behind. I've discovered an acute awareness that I can't take risks with less than a full assessment of the possible consequences. I realize the incumbency of self-preservation upon me not so much for my sake, but for those who count on me such as my wife, my father, my siblings, my son, and my friends. Of course I'll die someday, but I believe I owe whatever remains of my life to those who have so much love invested in me.

CHAPTER 29
A FEW HARD QUESTIONS

There's a good deal I have to reflect upon as a consequence of spending these past months in Nigeria. Some of it isn't very comfortable to ponder. But I think the abundant good nature of so many people around me, who endure hardships almost beyond my comprehension, has gifted me the strength to look a little more deeply and grapple more candidly with the rosy hue through which I often view life.

I remember crying when a distant friend of mine died in a skiing accident when we were young kids. When my mother found me sobbing and learned the source of my grief, she warned me "not to borrow trouble." I understood her point and made an effort to insulate my heart from the troubles of the world, realizing that looking outward very far and embracing the disasters and grief of others could add quite a burden to my life.

But have I gone too far adopting the habits of an ostrich?

Examining my principles under more luminous scrutiny, I find it compelling to ask if I really practice elevated levels of compassion for the downtrodden, and do I incorporate an appropriate response?

The hard answer is, not as much as I could. I realize it mitigates my emotional involvement to think of distressed peoples in large, impersonal groups. It eases my pain to deny them individual accord and value, minimizing heart-jarring consequences of the alternative.

Am I too miserly to give ten percent or even five percent of my income to my church so they can help the needy I claim to care so much about? Even though "No" is usually the answer, sometimes it's true. I contribute, even generously when times are good, but I'm too deeply aware that money can potentially become scarce again and consequently, hoard most of my wealth for me and mine. While considering the wealth of the average Nigerian, I realize my thoughts could benefit from a more honest assessment of what I want, what I need, and the squander separating them.

Am I as good a person as I can be? This essential question needs more frequent introspection. I know I judge too much, especially when I see what looks like patent inconsideration. But are those drivers we encounter on the roads really hateful, self-centered zealots, or are they just self-absorbed for the moment, brains overflowing with thoughts unrelated to driving, but are otherwise kind, loving people? By habit, I plan every action well ahead trying to anticipate every possibility. That's one of my strong points. I have more than my share of weak ones. My reflexive judgment needs taming. I'm done with "good driver" contests.

I sometimes find myself behaving with great impatience, as if personal injury is the intent of those people stopping to greet friends midway through a public entrance, seemingly oblivious to the barrier they impose against the free passage of others. Are they really selfish people with no concern for those around them? They might momentarily lack situational awareness, but I'd be willing to bet that the vast majority are kind, caring, and generous people. Again, I commit to stopping with the "good guys, bad guys" antics.

CHAPTER 30

REVELATION

Nigeria brings me one overwhelming gift—a clearer insight into my own imperfections. Nigeria's population is almost two-thirds of ours in the USA, nearly two hundred million, but their geographic size is only one and one-third times the size of Texas. The overcrowding defies western imaginations, as does the rampant poverty. A hundred times I noticed the looks of distrust and hostility from the indigenous population for my crime of being American, comfortable, and wealthy. But almost without exception, those I met at close range reached out with dramatic sincerity, offering friendship. Reflecting on the prevalence of this kind of human kinship generally across the globe, I realize it's common to all the dozens of countries I've transited.

Is it possible we're all basically "good"? I know it's terribly hard to concede when considering much of the history of humanity with Hitler, Stalin, Genghis Khan, the Khmer Rouge, Rwanda, and all the religious genocides that have taken place. But weren't those aberrations attributable only to a tiny minority of mentally deranged individuals capable of exercising wide influence over others in extraordinary times?

During my last day in Nigeria, while speaking to Abdul, he asks why I have only one child. I explain that I don't want to contribute to the overpopulation of the planet. Although Abdul's religion and culture supply no reference for such a concept, instead of voicing an objection, he explains that this is a new notion to him, and he wants to investigate whatever references I've encountered to support it. I recommend several books that clearly describe the foundations of my beliefs. He leaves me little doubt regarding his genuine intent to gain more familiarity with the issue. He then tells me about a book that explains much of his life's foundation, which I have since purchased. I'm finding in its pages vast areas of unfamiliar philosophy that are thrilling to explore. I'm excited that two people raised in such divergent cultures can freely discuss one another's fundamental beliefs with openness and sincerity, entirely devoid of hostility and suspicion.

What if unfamiliar ideas were so openly considered by everyone? Maybe they are to a larger degree than I've previously conceded. Maybe it's just a small group of humanity that has become so certain of their righteousness that they're unwilling to consider alternative ideas. There are a lot of ways to become entrenched in a singular ideology and develop prejudices against others, but my new experiences suggest there may be greater openness to new frontiers of thought than I'd ever realized.

I used to wonder if the mental agility of most westerners wasn't more advanced than that of the average Third Worlder where education is largely absent or substandard. On the surface it sometimes appears that way, but I think that what I have mistaken for less wit is probably something else. Apparently, the countries we recently considered as developing or third world have been filling our most prestigious learning institutions with superstars. It seems westerners are unable to compete on a par with the musical geniuses coming from Asia. I realize now that the IQ playing field is more level than I once suspected, and I have to surmise that this "field" includes all nations.

CHAPTER 31

RETURN

I carry nothing like the certainty I once felt about all these assertions and questions. My mind is returning to the more questioning nature of youth, and I feel irrevocably changed. My interactions in a country with people I once feared because of their reputed primitive, hostile, and dishonest natures, has left me wide open for new ideas.

I've returned to the folds of my beloved family and friends, my wonderful church choir, and the majestic mountains I grew up in. I'm back in a life practically guaranteed to be safe from ill intent and harm, and from the hunger so much of our planet's population knows intimately. I get clean water at my whim from any of five faucets in my single-family home, as well as from any public drinking fountain.

Without reservation I concede my certainty that I'm blessed beyond the imaginings of most of earth's inhabitants, for being born into such an abundant, fulfilling life. My immersion into the harsh realities of a developing third world country has surprisingly made me feel more alive and whole than ever before. Through an undetectable sleight of hand from some place undisclosed, I've been tricked into a startling awareness that people, no matter where they call home or how strenuous their daily toil, are capable—even naturally inclined—toward kindness and compassion.

In that far away sub-Saharan region of Africa, I learned a good deal more about who I am, an unexpected gift I know will serve me for the rest of my life.

I went to Nigeria in some desperation, hoping to crawl out of an economic hole I was digging for myself and Marcia. While the money I made pulled us from that pit, it paled next to the true wealth I brought home.

CHAPTER 32
THE LAST AIRLINE

During my last week in Nigeria, I got a notice that Southwest Airlines was opening its hiring window. I stayed up all night trying to send the electronic forms that might put me on their radar. The power would go out, and my work would be lost. I'd start over and it would happen again. Ultimately, at 3:30 in the morning, it finally zinged away across thousands of miles of desert, ocean, sea, and mountains to land in the company's headquarters in Dallas, Texas. Two days later I got an email from them saying, "We're delighted to invite you to interview." Two days after arriving home from Africa, I boarded another airplane for Dallas and got the job.

It was indescribably rewarding both in terms of job satisfaction and wealth building, and I'll forever be grateful to the people at Southwest Airlines for taking a chance on hiring a fifty-nine-year-old pilot. I flew until November 16th, 2019, two days before my sixty-fifth birthday—a hard boundary for US pilots to fly for commercial airlines.

On that last day, incomparable miracles nearly equal in magnitude to the birth of my son, JM, or marriage to Marcia happen.

Two days before, during this last trip, I'm scheduled to fly from Chicago to SLC. There I will layover at home. SWA happily flies JM from Atlanta, his home city, to Chicago so he can fly to SLC with me. He and Marcia will fly to Las Vegas two days later to join me on my final flight. That day begins in Austin, Texas, with an ice-covered airplane. Seems apropos to a flight long ago in Alaska. We deice. Then have a flow delay to Houston due to oversaturated airways but still managed to get in only five minutes late. Flight attendants, the ops agent, and even the ground ops people come to the cockpit to shake my hand and genuinely offer best wishes and gratitude for my service. I share the cockpit that day with Chris, a man I've flown with at several other airlines, most notably, Japan Airlines. We were training partners there during first officer upgrade and did much to get one another through. Tighter friendships don't exist after trials like that. Upon our arrival in Las Vegas, my base, the tower tells us to plan a particular runway exit that doesn't really fit the plane we're flying. I know something is up. Sure enough, there are the fire trucks waiting a hundred yards distant, and soon they turn on their powerful streams. We taxi under a huge water arch and into the gate.

Marcia, JM, and several friends are at the gate watching the spectacle. In fact, Marcia took the picture above. When I emerge from the jetway there is thunderous applause and cheering from all the passengers waiting to board as well as from all my friends and family. It's heart-wrenching in the most beautiful way.

After a few minutes, we board my last jet to Salt Lake City. I put Marcia in the captain's seat while I do the preflight. She's never been in an airplane that I'm operating and never ever in the cockpit. It's thrilling for both of us. Another longtime friend, Harry, is on the jumpseat. We flew together at Eastern, America West, Japan Airlines, and World Airways. A lot of history together. The flight is on as blue and pristine a day as I've ever seen. The final controller in SLC calls us "Mr. Walker" rather than our flight number as does Tower. They also tell us to plan a specific exit from 34R, so again, we know there's another surprise waiting. As we pull onto

the parallel taxiway leading back to our gate, we see a "V" formation of Emergency SUVs, lights in full bloom and sirens wailing.
We're told to pull into the formation for an escort to gate F15.

They peel off around two firetrucks, park, jump out, and stand
at attention, crisp salutes all as we taxi under the water arch to the
gate. I'm streaming tears in utter astonishment. All the controllers wish me a happy retirement all the way to the gate. My bio
was circulated to SLC Air Traffic Controllers by one of the Las
Vegas Chief Pilots, advertising that this final flight of mine is landing at the very same airport I'd taken my first flying lesson from
forty-two years, eight months and one day ago. After parking, I
stand and shake hands with all one hundred and forty-three passengers. Then flight attendants and the whole operational support
team come on board offering genuine and hearty congratulations.
Emerging from the jetway brings another full-throated eruption
of cheers and applause as all passengers and even more friends,

some lost to me for twenty-five years, shimmer in waving and clapping hands at the gate.

Tears embarrassingly unstoppable, I finally break away from the gate area and walk, surrounded by a mob of celebrants, to the security exit and there, gathered with party hats, horns, and gigantic signs hung from balconies, is nearly my entire choir, thirty something voices strong, singing a song custom written for the occasion. It's gut-splitting funny. I'm in shock. My brothers and their wives, friends from ice skating, something close to eighty people are here to celebrate this momentous day with me.

It's probably the most thrilling day of my life.

EPILOGUE

I didn't realize how naked I was or how long it takes to dress a *beginner*. I've met *old souls* that seem more advanced in this human experience than I, like it's not their first *visit*. I've felt like a freshman all my life, sometimes even like an impostor for being grown up. Despite my perceived pretender pedigree, I think finishing my career at Southwest is some kind of divine reward for the terrible cycle of job losses I suffered. In forty-three years, I flew at nine airlines, seven of them *career* airlines. Airlines are like spouses—it's best to have only one.

I've been retired for a while now and sometimes dare myself to look back at this long legacy. What crops up most often are the foolish decisions and risks I took. Yes, I have my share of demonstrating great skill and judgment, but those are not the moments that find their way to my wardrobe mirror.

I look back in disbelief that I elected to take off from Sitka into such a potentially dangerous storm. There were other vastly superior choices like spending a night or two in Sitka, which is a wonderful town with a very rich history. I could have flight planned a longer, inland route skirting the weather entirely. I cared so much about the expense that I put our lives at terrible risk, barely beating long-shot odds, for money. Money of which I had plenty, and time we had to spare. But I had a plan and was inflexible. Hundreds of pilots, maybe thousands, have died making that kind of naïve choice.

I was taught early in my flying career that a one-thousand-hour pilot is the most dangerous of all. Just enough time to become cocky but not enough to really have full maturity. The day before our horrifying flight from Sitka to Anchorage, while flying fire patrol in McCall, my total time rolled over the ten-thousand-hour mark. Still, I exercised a whole series of bad decisions. There's simply no magical hour mark that makes one a good enough, smart enough, or careful enough pilot.

They say there are two kinds of "final flights." The ones where the pilot knows it's their last, and the ones where they don't. Phenomenal luck made me a member of the former group.

I live out this gift of life from some mysterious depth I'll never get. Norman Maclean quotes his father in *A River Runs Through It* saying, "...we can love completely without complete understanding." A widened purview gifted from Africa gives me greater insight into the nuance of that profound truth than I've ever had before. With it I will make every effort to live awakened, aware of what good I can contribute to this world in endless thanks to a benevolent Universe.

I will never forget those in the throes of hardship and suffering nor will I forget the ease with which they opened their warm hearts to me—me clothed in skin tones they had every reason to fear and distrust. I owe them so much. It was there, among them, my color began to brighten with new covering. Attire they gifted to me.

There *with* the grace of God *went* I.

ACKNOWLEDGEMENTS

The immensity of gratitude that fills my heart for so many people who helped me with this book is boundless and difficult to articulate. Thank you, David Tippetts, for enlightening me that most bad books simply aren't finished. With your help, I believe we finished this one. To Jeffrey Lowder for revealing that when you think your book is done, it's really just begun. To Sherrie Curtis, Linda Orvis, Rich Casper, and Ericka Prechtel for their expert, generous, and honest help crafting and improving my story. A big shout-out of thanks to my amazing editors, Ann Riza and Ann Suhs. They were delightfully enthusiastic from day one. To Emma Faith Mayo for your exquisite artistic gift that made the book cover such a fun and brilliant reflection of what's inside, and for so patiently crafting my maps.

A lifetime of thanks to my late mother and father, Shirlee and Neef Walker, for all their encouragement in my life's endeavors, the confidence they taught me, and dance of life they inspired me to imitate. To my brothers Wilkes, Tom, and Matt, and my late sister Heidi, for always seeing the good in me and pushing me until I could ski like a maniac. From that bedrock sprang all the majesty, wonder, and awe that has graced my life. To my son JM Walker for his unwavering assurances that my writing would sprint to a great finish, and for the bloom in his heart that helps me know I did something right. To my lovely wife, Marcia, for her endless strength, the tenacity of her encouragement no matter what, and for showing me the way down this breathtaking life path we share. And finally, to Karla M. Jay who has not only become my mentor but my friend. Without her tireless editing, tinkering, and the dogged certainty I had a great story to tell, this work simply wouldn't exist.

Author Page

Andy lives in the mountains east of Salt Lake City with his wife, Marcia. He grew up on a ski slope there, then spent twenty-five years away chasing dreams that netted twenty-two moves before finding his happy place right where he left it, at home. When not writing, he can be found plying the slopes of his beloved Alta, gliding around the ice aspiring to become some modest version of a figure skater, or trying not to break any more bones on his mountain bike.

My life's energy overflows along a passionate circumference, flooding beyond boundaries once constraining. Whether by luck or Providence, my pathway remains wide-open and inviting. In this serene homestretch, I cherish my thorn-infested, sometimes twisty path equally with that which bloomed along the easy trails, for both have led to the here and now—Camelot allied with my dear Guinevere.

You can follow Andy Walker at:
His website: http://www.andywalker.net
Facebook: https://www.facebook.com/AndyWalkerAuthor
Instagram: https://www.instagram.com/altamaniac1

Made in the USA
Middletown, DE
18 May 2022

65871341R00194